THE
EDGE
OF
THE
WEST

Bryan Woolley

THE EDGE OF THE WEST

AND OTHER TEXAS STORIES

by Bryan Woolley

Texas Western Press
The University of Texas at El Paso

Texas Western Press

First Edition
Library of Congress Catalog Card No. 89-051842
ISBN 87404-214-3 (cloth)
ISBN 87404-216-X (paper)

The paper used in this publication meets the minimum requirements of
American National Standard for Information Sciences

♾ — Permanence of Paper for Printed Library Materials, ANSI Z.39.48-1984.

"Remembering Roy" originally was published in *Dallas Life*, the
magazine of *The Dallas Morning News*. The other pieces in this
book originally were published in the *Dallas Times Herald* and
its magazines, *Westward* and *Dallas City*. I am grateful for the
permission of the two newspapers to reprint them here.

I dedicate this book to two brave Texas women
Beatrice Gibson Woolley
my mother
and
Clora DeVolin Gibson
(1892-1984)
my grandmother

BOOKS BY BRYAN WOOLLEY

Nonfiction
The Edge of the West
The Time of My Life
Where Texas Meets the Sea
We Be Here When the Morning Comes

Fiction
Sam Bass
November 22
Time and Place
Some Sweet Day

CONTENTS

Introduction
by Molly Ivins

Reading Bryan Woolley is just pure pleasure. His writing is like sunshine dancing on a Texas river — it makes me happy and it makes me home.

Those of you who know Woolley's writing only through his acclaimed novels are in for a treat — high time his journalism was collected so his fans can savor it again.

During the years Woolley and I worked together at the Dallas *Times Herald* (this was before he finked out and joined The Other Paper just because they made him an offer he couldn't refuse) the Rev. Woolley had a special ceremonial role at our paper, in addition to being the best writer in the building. Don't ask me how Woolley got to be a whiskey-drinkin', poker-playin', lady-likin' newspaperman and also an ordained minister — he just is and it all fits together in Bryan without any strain, even if it is an improbable combination. I suspect that years of writing about the most aberrant and the most entertaining vagaries of humankind has caused Woolley to think a lot about good and evil — at least that's a plausible explanation. Anyway, Woolley was not only in charge of marrying our colleagues who fell in love with each other (we celebrated several such matches at the *Herald*) but also in charge of general ceremonial chores. Appropriate patriotic sentiments at Fourth of July beer bashes, farewell toasts for departing colleagues and the like. No point in having a minister on the staff if you don't use him, we always felt.

Reading these pieces brought back some wonderful memories. The morning after Ernest Tubb died, Woolley and I danced around the newsroom together mournfully singing "Waltz Across Texas" to each other: you need a friend like Woolley the morning after Ernest Tubb dies. Woolley's style appears to be effortless. You could swear there's no art to it, it's so clean and spare and simple. As George Orwell said, like looking at reality through clear glass. Only way you ever know how good he is if you've ever tried to do it yourself. I used to hear young reporters asking, "Where does he *find* these people?" They meant, of course, the people who gave Woolley those great quotes, the quotes so full of Texas that it comes right up off the page:

"I can't stand trees for very long. They get in the way of the sky."

"That's the most rudest bunch of drivers down there I've ever seen in my life."

"When I was just a button. . ."

"The fifth day of February, 19 and 34. . ."

"We have some great visitations. . . ."

"My mom knew Buddy [Holly]. She graduated from high school a year before Buddy did. She never was much of a fan of his. She thought he was just another hippie."

Who but Woolley could get Ross Perot to telling stories about all the bidness tricks he used starting out? Who but Woolley could capture Tex Schramm of the Dallas Cowboys perfectly in one two-sentence anecdote:

"Years and years ago, I said to him, 'Well, you can't win them all,'" his wife says.

"And he looked at me like I had lost my mind and said, 'Why the hell not?'"

What the young reporters don't know is that Bryan Woolley doesn't have a special gift for finding people who know how to say things. Those folks are everywhere, all around us. The difference is that Bryan hears them. He not only has the ear, he has the eye as well, the gift of making us see those West Texas-forever skies, and the towns so sleepy road-runners play on Main Street.

My favorite Bryan Woolley story is about the time Woolley first went off to Harvard Divinity School to study theology. You have to picture him — a long, tall drink of water with shoulder-length red hair, parted in the middle and hangin' down, kind of like Jesus, but unmistakeably West Texas — boots, jeans, belt, shirt, and that accent you can cut with a fork. First rat out of the trap, Woolley runs into some pluperfect Harvard twit who listens to him a few minutes and then says, "My God, man! Where *did* you prep?" Bryan Woolley thinks about it a minute and says, "Fort damn Davis High School in Fort damn Davis, Texas."

It is an honor to know the Rev. Woolley and a pleasure to introduce him to those of you who don't.

—Austin, Texas
March, 1990

At the beginning of 1986, the editors of the Dallas Times Herald decided to publish a special magazine section celebrating the sesqui-centennial of the Republic of Texas. It would be a "day in the life of Texas" sort of thing. A gang of reporters would be sent out, each to a different region of the state, to spend a day and write a piece about what went on there during the course of that day.

As the senior writer on the project, I got to choose first. It took me a millisecond to choose the Trans-Pecos, the place where my soul resides, as the place to go; another millisecond to think of a raft trip through one of the canyons of the Rio Grande as the thing to do.

Whenever I get an assignment like this, I wonder why everybody isn't a journalist.

THE RIVER GRAND

The sky is so clear and the moon so bright that the rocks and bushes and people are casting shadows, and ribbons of light are shining on the water. On the Mexican side of the river, just above the mountaintops, Orion stalks, his belt, sword, shield and faithful dog competing with the moon's brightness. Just below the moon, the high walls of Santa Elena Canyon loom darker than the rest of the night.

The last coals of the fire where Tracy Blashill and Rick Boretti made our supper have died. We've run out of jokes and stories, and the farmer from Illinois has stopped bragging about the way he handles a canoe and the rapids he has run on other rivers. Maybe he senses that we want him to leave. He goes to his wife at his own camp, on the other side of a small mesquite.

Tracy and Rick are professional boatmen. They row the canyons of the Rio Grande in inflated rafts for a Terlingua out-fitter called Far Flung Adventures, showing their customers the grand, hidden places that can be seen only from the water. Today they embarked with five of us on a two-day journey from the village of Lajitas to the mouth of Santa Elena Canyon, eighteen miles downstream. They're young and deceptively slender and smooth-muscled. They've loaded the rafts, rowed eleven miles today to the canyon entrance, unloaded the rafts and cooked our meal, and still show no signs of weariness.

Two of the passengers still standing by the dead coals are Rodney Rodgers and his son, George, both doctors. The father has practiced a long time in Houston. The son will finish his residency at Parkland Hospital in Dallas this summer. They've come to the Big Bend to have each other's company and discuss George's future. "I've always wanted to see this place," Rodney says.

Another passenger is Bryn Moore, a young watercolorist who moved from Denton to the ghost town of Terlingua a year ago, but has never seen the canyon.

Winter is the slow time on the farm, the farmer has said, so he and his wife have driven to the Mexican border with their canoe on top of their car. They intend to be on the river longer than we, from Lajitas to La Linda, about four days below Santa Elena. They're tagging along with us, not really members of our party, but not separate, either. Whenever we've stopped, they've stopped, too, and the farmer has talked of boats and rivers, trying to impress Tracy and Rick with his knowledge.

The young boatmen know the river as well as the farmer knows the path to his barn, and their navigation of it looks easy. But they've hinted to the farmer that maybe it wasn't wise to think of paddling through Santa Elena, a canyon where he has never been, in a canoe alone with his wife and nobody else to help them if they get in trouble. They've mentioned that the farmer's canoe, with its big keel, is designed for flat, quiet water, and isn't a good boat for rapids. But they haven't told the farmer what they're hoping, that he and his wife will paddle into the gorge and see the treacherous Rockslide — a jumble of hundreds of boulders as big as houses and the narrow, swirling channels running among them — and will decide to carry their canoe around the rapids to safer water.

"The Rockslide isn't a good place to swim," Tracy has said. The farmer and his wife might need help, so Tracy and Rick have let them tag along.

The night is still young, but the boatmen and the rest of us have got quiet and are getting cold, so we scatter along the riverbank where the rafts and the farmer's canoe are tied up, and search for soft places in the sand to unroll our beds.

During the night, clouds move across the moon and dew forms on our sleeping bags. Then the moon drops below the mountains, and the wind rises and dries the dew and blows the sand in swirls along the riverbank. The desert is very cold at night, but the myriad stars burn almost as bright as the moon.

It's late morning when we shove out into the stream again, but the sun has been on our side of the mountains for only half an hour. It's just beginning to warm us when our rafts and the farmer's canoe slide into the shadow of the canyon's cliffs and we lose our light and heat again. Our passage flushes a flock of teal from the Texas bank. They fly, honking, into Mexico. The farmer is wearing a straw Mexican sombrero and woolen knickers with long stockings, a strange costume even on the Rio Grande, where almost nothing is considered strange. We raft passengers buckle our life jackets. The river quickens, then enters the narrow gash between the Mesa de Anguila on the north and the Sierra Ponce on the south. It crashes into the northern wall, ricochets, then straightens and calms. Our small craft rush along with it, and suddenly we're inside the Santa Elena.

The canyon walls are only twenty-five feet apart here. They rise more than a thousand feet straight up from the river. Farther downstream, they soar to more than fifteen hundred. The sky is only a blue slash, and for almost the whole seven miles of the gorge, the sun will be lost to us. Every sound — the dip of the oars into the water, the squeaking of them in their locks, the lap of waves against the rafts, the roar of the water over the Rockslide downstream — is amplified in the simultaneous closeness and vastness of our beautiful and threatening world.

We scan the walls, searching out the fossils lodged in them, and the small bushes and cactuses clinging to cracks in the rock hundreds of feet above the water and hundreds of feet below the mesa, and the small caves, high on the wall, where no man has ever been. Tracy points out the brown mud nests of cliff swallows, dozens of them hanging from the undersides of stone ledges. "Last year, I saw two ravens raiding those nests," he says. "One raven would keep the adult swallows distracted while the other raven stole babies from the nests. Then the one that had eaten would distract the adults while the other ate. It was an easy meal."

A blue heron flies along the river, the shadow of its large body and long neck and wings moving beside it along the upper heights of the cliff, where the sun still reaches. Once inside Santa Elena, only the strongest birds can fly out over the walls again. An early writer about the canyon describes a covey of quail trying to fly high enough to escape, only to fail and settle exhausted on one of the lower pinnacles.

A few hundred yards farther into the gorge, the water quickens again, flows around a bend, and there, suddenly, is the Rockslide.

Nobody knows how many thousands or millions of years ago the rocks broke from the cliff on the Mexican side and plummeted into the river. Some are twenty feet in diameter, and heaped in piles of more than two hundred feet. The larger piles are seldom underwater, but enough water has rushed over them during the millenia to round their edges and smooth their surfaces. Their presence splits the river into a dozen narrow streams that rush and fall and jump, dashing into the rocks, dropping into pools and swirls and eddies.

A century ago, this place was called the Labyrinth. In those days of heavy wooden boats it made navigation of the Big Bend of the Rio Grande a painful trip. In 1899, a group of explorers sent a boat over the rapids. It was smashed to splinters on the rocks. The men spent two days carrying their remaining boats and supplies over the boulders to calmer water. They rested on a sandy beach not far below the rapids and named the place Camp Misery. Today's boatmen still call it that.

Over the years, a routine has been developed for running the Rockslide. The boatman beaches his boat above the rocks and climbs a huge boulder called Scout Rock. From that perch he can look down upon all the channels through the seventy-five dangerous yards of the rapids and plot his course, then return to his boat and try it.

Rick beaches his raft and waits, but the farmer and his wife somehow get stalled in an eddy before they reach the beaching spot. They paddle and paddle, but go nowhere at all. "Back paddle!" the farmer screams. His wife tries to do it. "The other side!" he yells. She moves her paddle to the other side of the canoe. They move awkwardly, out of rhythm, at cross purposes. After long minutes of futile thrashing, they finally find the current and move on to the beaching spot.

Flushed and trembling, the farmer climbs out of his boat. "We can't do it," he says bitterly. "If we couldn't handle that little eddy, we'll never make it through the rapids." He glares at his wife.

"I didn't know what you wanted me to do," she says.

"The current is a little crazy here," Rick says.

"Oh, I've got the skill," the farmer says. "But it's obvious that we can't get it together. I'm frustrated. I'm so frustrated I've lost my confidence." He keeps glaring at his wife.

Rick and Tracy and the doctors and the artist are embarrassed to be hearing this. The farmer's wife is embarrassed, too. Tears come. She tries to hide them. Rodney Rodgers says something comforting to her. The farmer, Rick and Tracy climb Scout Rock and study the currents. For almost an hour they perch there, Tracy and Rick patiently describing the dangerous, narrow channels and the boulders just below the water. Rick points to a calmer stream against the north wall. He suggests the farmer and his wife go that way as far as the stream will take them, then carry their canoe over the few remaining rocks to calmer water. The farmer says nothing.

The farmer's wife climbs the rock and lays her arm about her husband's waist. "Are you still freaked out?" she asks.

"I never was freaked out," he says.

Rick runs the rapids first, his arms working the oars in a graceful, controlled frenzy. When his raft is safely beyond the worst of the rocks, he beaches again and climbs a rock to watch for the canoe. "I don't think he'll try it," he says. "He'll go around." On the Mexican bank, Tracy stands holding a line to throw to the farmer and his wife if they tip over.

Manning the bow paddle, the farmer heads straight into the teeth of the rapids, his sombrero bobbing with the fall and rise of the canoe among the rocks, his face hard in concentration. In the stern, his wife's eyes are wide with fear. They paddle frantically through the churning water, seem for a moment to be lost, then the river simply spits them into a calm eddy and out of danger. As they paddle toward the shore, the farmer's wife starts laughing. She laughs and laughs. She's still laughing when they pull their canoe onto the beach beside Rick's raft. She hugs her husband.

"Nice job," Rick says.

"I hesitated for no reason," the farmer says. "It was easy. But I could've done it better alone."

We take it easy for a while, drifting with the current, Rick and Tracy resting on their oars, the farmer reclining in his canoe, his stockings drooped about his ankles, his sombrero tilted over his eyes, the doctors and the artist wet and longing for the sun. We stop for lunch, and the farmer and his wife stop, too, but they don't have much to say. They finish their sandwiches quickly, then shake hands with us all. "We've wasted enough of your time," the farmer says. "We still have a long way to go." They climb into their canoe and paddle away.

The last two miles of Santa Elena are wide, majestic, peaceful and full of sun. Along this stretch of the river, it's easy to believe in the goodness of God or nature or even man. The silver day moon hanging in the pure blue sky in the middle of the door through which the Rio Grande flows back into the wide desert seems an omen of something wonderful. We wish we were continuing on, like the farmer and his wife. We hope theirs will be a happy camp tonight.

[March 1986]

The day this little tribute to Ernest Tubb was in the paper, one of my colleagues — a country boy from North Carolina and a country singer himself — came up to me and said: "Once in a while, the by-God TRUTH gets into a newspaper, and that piece about Ernest is one of those times."

I've never been paid a higher compliment on a piece of work.

A HEART AS BIG AS TEXAS

It was 1941. World War II had been going on for several years already, and America was about to join it. I wasn't quite four years old, and I didn't know anything about Hitler or Tojo or much of anything else yet.

But I was sweating, I remember, so it must have been summer. And I was playing on the living-room floor of a little white frame house on a hill in Hamilton County, Texas. My mother was in the kitchen, and the radio was on. This guy with a voice like a cement mixer was singing a song called "Walking the Floor Over You."

The song created a weird picture in my head. I imagined myself lying on my back under the house and this guy with the voice stomping across the floorboards above my head. Odd. But I never forgot the song or the voice or the sweat that was rolling down my belly when I heard them. It's my earliest memory of music.

Later, of course, I would learn that the man with the cement-mixer voice was Ernest Tubb, that he wasn't walking the floor over the top of somebody, that he was just in love with a woman who had him pacing up and down in a blue funk, that the song was the first hit in a long musical career that would

make it impossible to mention Jimmie Rodgers, Bob Wills, Roy
Acuff, Hank Williams, Red Foley, Patsy Cline, Tex Ritter, or
any other truly great member of Hillbilly Heaven's present and
future choir without bringing up Ernest Tubb's name, too.

Now Ernest has joined the choir. He died Thursday of
emphysema, forty-three years after I first heard him. He was
seventy years old.

I always thought he would die at home in the bus he lived
in. Unlike many of the less sturdy country singers who followed his footsteps to Nashville and the Grand Ole Opry,
Ernest never gave up the road, pleading physical exhaustion,
nervous breakdown, or any of the other excuses that today's
pampered album-and-TV cream puffs use to get out of being in
the presence of their fans. Up to a year or two ago — the last
time I heard anything about Ernest — he was still playing three
hundred one-night gigs a year, routing his itinerary as often as
possible through Nashville, where he was still one of the Grand
Ole Opry's most frequently performing regulars, then hopping
over to his own Ernest Tubb Record Shop, the origination point
of the Ernest Tubb Jamboree, a country disc jockey show that
was as good or better than the live Opry that had preceded it.

There isn't a honky-tonk worthy of the name in the United
States or Canada where honest-to-God, lead-with-your-thighs
two-steppers haven't rubbed bodies to that cement-mixer voice
bellowing "I'll Get Along Somehow" or "When the World Has
Turned You Upside Down" or "Have You Ever Been Lonely?"
into the smoky, sweaty, boozy, musky air.

Lordy, Ernest could get sad. Especially in his younger days
when he still did the blue yodel that he had learned off the old
Jimmie Rodgers records that had made him want to sing in the
first place. And even in his later days, when he would start off
growling a quarter tone flat and get flatter and flatter as more
and more of his misery was unveiled, and he would ask you,
"Have you ever been lonely? Have you ever been blue?" and the
bottom would drop out of your soul. God, yes, you'd been
lonely. Hell, you were bluer than a Panhandle norther at that
very moment. The only answer was to get drunk and dance

close with some willing woman who was just as lonely and blue as you and Ernest, the innards of all three of you wailing like a pedal steel. Oh, it was a sweet misery!

Despite the sequined white suits and the snowy Stetsons that he wore, Ernest never looked phony. All his life he was skinny as a cedar fence post, and his face looked like it had hung out in a lot of weather. And that voice. Everybody knew that any cowboy, truck driver, roughneck or sharecropper would sound like Ernest if he got as gut-lonely as Ernest was and opened his mouth and started bellowing.

Ernest never went trendy on us, either. Oh, he beefed up his band when stereo was invented. But he never took to wearing his shirt unbuttoned and gold chains around his neck and doing little bop movements while he was singing. He would tap his foot every now and then, but that was it for body language. And he never hired a bunch of horn players and syrupy violinists and fresh-faced kiddies to hum in the background like Eddie Arnold and Ray Price did. Nobody could have harmonized with Ernest, anyway.

He started off honky-tonk and stayed honky-tonk, and for more than forty years he kept riding from one honky-tonk to another in that bus. I saw him twice in person — once in El Paso in the mid-1950s and once in Louisville in the early 1970s — and courted a dozen or more girls in various Texas rural hidy-holes to the rough blue voice of Ernest and the whining accompaniment of his Texas Troubadors. It was remarkable how little he changed, and how much we loved him because he didn't.

Maybe it was because he was one of those Texans who were hewn out of the old rock. He grew up in Crisp, a tiny crossroads cotton-gin community in Ellis County, east of Waxahachie, where he became well known at an early age for preferring the guitar to the hoe. "Nobody thought he'd amount to much," said one of his old neighbors the day Ernest died.

But the little community tolerated him, Jimmie Rodgers' widow gave him a stumbling start toward a recording career, and he went all the way to the Country Music Hall of Fame.

And although he lived much of his life in Nashville — the few days a year he wasn't on the road — he remained an unreconstructed and unrepentant Texas chauvinist. "There's a Little Bit of Everything in Texas," he bragged in one of his songs. And he growled to that woman: "I'd Waltz Across Texas With You," which has to be one of the greatest waltzes and certainly one of the greatest love songs ever written. But you somehow know, listening to Ernest sing it, that he loves Texas a lot more than the woman, and if she gets tired of waltzing with him, well, he'll just dance with some other gal.

"He had a heart as big as Texas," said one of Bob Wills' old Texas Playboys the day Ernest died.

That ought to be carved on his tombstone, because there can be no doubt that his heart was about that big. You can know that from his songs. He never holds a grudge against those women who do him wrong. He just feels kind of sorry that they're so rotten, and he's slip-sliding through the blues the best he can. "Let's Say Goodbye Like We Said Hello," he tells one of them. And sometimes, well, "There's Nothing More to Say."

And I guess there isn't. But I wish he'd died in his bus, and not in a Baptist hospital in Nashville. That just isn't Ernest's style.

[September 1984]

I haven't lived there for more than thirty years, but Jeff Davis County always has been my home and always will be. I can't imagine having come from somewhere else and not having the Davis Mountains in my head and heart.

When I learned that Jeff Davis was about to celebrate its centennial as a county — as Jeff Davis County, anyway — I used the occasion as an excuse to visit my mountains and my mother. But I always write about that special place with misgivings. I don't really want the rest of the world to know about it.

IN JEFF DAVIS COUNTY

The first sound you hear is the cowboys whistling, their shrill notes piercing the bright, still air; then the bawling of the herd, querulous and nagging. Then the cowboys, tall on their horses, appear as small silhouettes on the horizon, the herd moving before them like a dark tide across the flat of goldenrod in bloom.

It's the first day of the fall roundup on the o6, the largest ranch in Jeff Davis County, far from most of Texas and the rest of the world. It's a ritual that has been repeated twice a year for more than a century in this high country, in the spring to brand and vaccinate the new calves and castrate the young bulls, and in the fall to choose the beasts that will be shipped to market. Chris Lacey, manager of the o6, says fifteen hundred steers and old cows — about a quarter of the herd — will have been shipped by the end of the monthlong roundup. "This is the only time of year we get paid," he says.

Throughout October and early November, similar roundups are in progress on ranches large and small in Jeff Davis County. Ranching is the only major industry here.

But in the county seat town of Fort Davis, which calls itself "The Best Tiny Town in Texas," a subtle change has been taking place over the past quarter-century. Many of the large ranches that had sustained the town's economy since the 1880s have been sold to non-resident owners who couldn't care less about Fort Davis. Others have been divided among heirs. Parts of some have been subdivided into home sites for a new breed of settler — retired couples from other parts of the country looking for a quiet, safe, pleasant, inexpensive place to grow old.

The nearest airport is more than 150 miles away. There is no railroad. Not even Greyhound rolls through here. But more tourists come to Jeff Davis County every year, looking for rest, solitude, a closeness to nature, an absence of noise and clutter. They leave the barren West Texas interstates at Pecos or Balmorhea and point their campers and RVs southward toward the pale blue mountain range that appears so unexpectedly on the desert horizon. The heart lifts with the altitude. The cool, thin air, moving through the sage and the cottonwoods like a sigh, clears the mind to meditate on a past that seems simpler and more heroic than the hectic present.

Almost every traveler who drifts through here is seeking a piece of the old frontier hope and glory. They believe that if it still lives anywhere, it must be here, in this hidden place, far from the beaten tracks of their personal rat races.

Nineteen-eighty-seven is the centennial year of the founding of Jeff Davis County and the naming of Fort Davis as the county seat. But the founding of this county was no ordinary act of the Texas Legislature. It was an official approval of an act of defiance. It was a legislature full of Confederate veterans shouting a last hurrah for the secessionist spirit. It was the giving back of something that had been lost.

In 1875 the legislature had established the largest county in the United States — twelve thousand almost empty square miles west of the Pecos River — and named it Presidio. Fort Davis, a small village on the fringe of a military post, was named the county seat. But ten years later, the upstart citizens of Marfa, a new town being built along the recently laid tracks of the Texas & New Orleans Railroad twenty-one miles south of Fort Davis, demanded that an election be held to choose a county seat. The seat of Presidio County, the Marfans said, should have up-to-date stuff such as railroads and telegraph service. It shouldn't be some remote mountain hamlet that was still dependent on freight wagons and stagecoaches.

Fort Davis was outraged. It had only recently finished building its courthouse, an adobe structure with a stone dungeon jail under the floor of the sheriff's office, complete with iron rings in the wall for chaining prisoners.

But the election was held. Marfa won, 391 to 302.

Two years later, Fort Davis asked the legislature for permission to secede from the county. So the old Confederates lopped 2,258 square miles off Presidio, created a new county and named it Jeff Davis. But the new county commissioners had to start from scratch. The minutes of their first meeting noted that the victorious Marfans had stripped the Fort Davis courthouse of "all records, books and furniture except five iron cages and a scaffold at the jail."

"We'll have horses and wagons and cavalry," says Texas Bob Reinhardt, who is ramrodding the centennial celebration. The Davis Mountains Brigade, a club of black-powder shooters, will fire their rifles and throw their tomahawks. There will be a barbecue, a dance, a shootout in the street and the hanging of "the meanest man in Jeff Davis County" and, on Sunday, a sunrise church service.

The main event will honor the original reason for the town's existence — the Overland Trail, the road to the California gold fields that Fort Davis was built to protect. "We have the longest stretch of the Overland Trail still existing in a Texas town," says Reinhardt. "There's a mile of it that has never been paved. Eight or ten of the original adobe structures from the 1880s are still there. The Texas Historical Commission is giving a plaque commemorating the trail. We'll dedicate the plaque and have a parade."

"Texas Bob" isn't the name Reinhardt was given at birth, but he considers it his real name now. "I have it on my checks and everything," he says.

He's sitting behind a desk in the jailer's office of the Jeff
Davis County Jail — the "new" jail built along with the "new"
courthouse in 1910. He's dressed like a Western sheriff. He's
wearing a badge. But the jail isn't a jail anymore. It hasn't held
a prisoner for many years. The cells are full of books. It's the
Jeff Davis County Library now. The lettering on Reinhardt's star
reads: "Librarian, Jeff Davis County."

"I grew up in New Jersey," he says. "But I've loved the old
West ever since 1 was a little boy, watching Hopalong Cassidy
on TV."

He came here looking, he says, and stayed.

The first white men known to have seen this place were
Antonio de Espejo and his troop of soldiers, who had been
looking all over West Texas and Eastern New Mexico for two
lost Franciscan friars. When they learned that Indians had
killed the friars, they turned around and headed home to Mexico. On the evening of August 13, 1583, they camped under the
big cottonwoods on the bank of the creek just north of where
Fort Davis now is.

From that day until 1849, when thousands of emigrants
began struggling across West Texas to join the California gold
rush, the American Indians had the place pretty much to themselves. The emigrants and the mail coaches and the few
ranchers who were trying to settle in the region were easy pick-
ings for the Apaches from the western side of the mountains
and the Comanches from the eastern side. So on October 7,
1854, the U.S. Infantry marched up Wild Rose Pass and began
building a fort in a canyon near Espejo's old campground. They
named it after Jefferson Davis, then U.S. secretary of war who
was to become president of the Confederacy. Davis had ordered
its construction "for the protection of travelers, settlers and the
mail." A village of merchants, gamblers, saloon keepers, drifters,
and a few respectable people grew up on the
edge of the post.

When the Civil War broke out, the Union troops marched
out of Fort Davis and Confederate troops marched in. They

stayed a few months, then marched off to the disastrous Battle of Glorieta Pass in New Mexico. The Apaches, in charge once more, burned the empty fort. When the war ended, the federal troops returned. The troopers were black men this time — former slaves, most of them — but the officers were still white. They rebuilt the fort and resumed the Indian-fighting.

For such an isolated outpost in the midst of such a vast wilderness, the fort and the village were fairly lively.

In 1880, for instance, the notorious Jesse Evans and his gang of twenty outlaws drifted into town from New Mexico, where they had been fighting a war with Billy the Kid and breaking out of jails. They terrorized Fort Davis all spring, committing fourteen assaults and robberies in less than two months. The local law officers weren't tough enough to deal with the Evans bunch and were reluctant to try. Finally, the citizens asked the Texas Rangers to come in and clean out the outlaws. They did.

That same summer, the Fort Davis cavalry troopers — the Indians called them "Buffalo soldiers" because their hair resembled the curly hair on a buffalo's hump — chased Chief Victorio and his hostile Apaches all over West Texas, and then to the Rio Grande. The Indians crossed into Mexico, and the Mexican army killed Victorio. His weary followers returned to the Apache reservation at Fort Stanton, New Mexico, ending the Indian wars in the Trans-Pecos.

A few days before Christmas in 1884, a delegation of Comanches headed by Quanah Parker, the last Comanche war chief, registered at the Lempert Hotel. The Indian agent accompanying the Comanches explained that they had come to Fort Davis to seek a certain "herb" that was sacred to the Comanches and, according to tribal tradition, could be found only in the vicinity of Mitre Peak, a few miles east of town. The "herb" they were seeking was peyote. The chief and his companions harvested their "herb" crop and took it back to their reservation in Oklahoma.

In 1891 the Army shut down the fort. The frontier had been tamed. Officially, anyway.

"The last five years, we've had more panthers than we've had at any time in my lifetime," Dude Sproul says. "My little granddaughter found panther tracks not thirty yards from our front door. She and a little friend saw a panther up by the house when they were playing in the creek last summer. In daylight. Panthers killed a sheep in a backyard on the edge of town last year. Two months ago, one killed a deer not twenty feet from our barn."

The land on which Sproul lives, on Limpia Creek north of Fort Davis, was settled in 1886 by his grandfather, one of many men who drove their herds of scrawny longhorn cattle westward from other parts of Texas in the decades after the Civil War. Sprouls have owned and operated the ranch ever since. Dude Sproul, who is seventy-one now, has worked it all his life. In 1986, Texas Agriculture Commissioner Jim Hightower presented a plaque to the family, honoring its history. The Sprouls were the first family in Jeff Davis County to receive such a plaque.

Sproul's father, who was known to everyone in the county as "Mr. Mack," was a great hunter. Ripley's "Believe It or Not" featured him twice — once for the number of bears he killed, and again for the number of panthers he killed.

"There are no bears left here now," Sproul says. "I have two of the feet of the last native bear caught in the Davis Mountains in my deep freeze. They've been there since 1963. I caught him in a trap. There have been a few bears caught here since then, but they were pen-raised bears that had been turned loose to try to re-establish them here. They didn't last long. The ranchers aren't too keen to have bears re-established."

Ranchers in Jeff Davis County face enemies deadlier than the critters sometimes. Sproul is a survivor of the great drought of the 1950s, when almost no rain fell for almost a decade. "Ninety percent of the ponderosa pine in the Davis Mountains died in that drought," he says, "and a lot of the big old juniper trees. I counted over five hundred rings in one of those trees. That tells me that we went through the worst drought this country has had in five hundred years."

Like most ranchers and cowboys, he remembers the dry years and the wet years as vividly as family deaths and births. "In 1959, we had less than five inches of rain all year. We've had a few dry years since that big drought, but never so many in a row. The fall of 1973, gosh, this country got beautiful. It rained and rained. Then one September morning we got up and there wasn't a cloud in the sky, and nobody saw rain drip off a tin roof again for nine months. It got rough. Nineteen-seventy-four was terribly dry until September. That's when a lot of ranchers went broke. Then in September, it rained eleven days that we never saw the sun. And it rained a little bit all winter and snowed a little and kept the ground wet. Cattle that were poor in September were in good shape by spring. That was the first time in my life that our cattle have gained weight through the winter. Nineteen-eighty-five was terrible until August."

Ironically, the fertility and beauty of the Davis Mountains range land are making it more difficult for the old ranching families to keep their ranches intact and impossible for a young cowboy to acquire land of his own. "Over a ten-year period," Sproul says, "you'll make a living and a little bit in the cattle business. But the price of land in this county is just ridiculous now. Range land that sold for four dollars an acre in the late '20s is selling for four hundred dollars an acre now. Think of that."

In Valentine, the only other town in Jeff Davis County, a younger "old-timer" asks that he not be quoted by name "because you have to be careful who you say things to around here." But he's even more bitter about the changes occurring on the land.

"The rich oil men and doctors and lawyers are ruining the cow game for the ordinary good old boys who have been doing it all their lives and depend on cows for their livelihood," he says. "They pay too much for the land, they import these damn exotic breeds that don't fit this country, they hire incompetent help to run their ranches. Anybody can look at the setup and see there ain't no way they can make a profit. But they don't care. They sell their cattle at a loss and depress the market. It's nothing but a tax dodge for them anyway. But they're making it awful hard for folks like me."

The young man is in town to contend in Slim Brown's annual roping at a bunged-up but still serviceable old arena in the middle of Valentine. It's a team event in which two men on horseback work together, one — the "header" — trying to rope a steer's head and the other — the "heeler" — trying to rope his hind feet. The fastest team wins. The roping is listed as one of the events of the Valentine High School homecoming, since the school has no football team. A few cowhands and children are sitting on the hoods of their pickups, drinking beer and soda pop, squinting in the dust that's raised by each swift passage of steers and horses.

The men rope until the steers are tuckered out and the day light is gone. They load their horses into their trailers and go home. Some will clean up and go over to the school for the homecoming barbecue and dance.

"A lot of people will get drunk," the young man says, "and then the knives will come out."

"Valentine, unfortunately, is not growing," says Doris Kelley, the postmaster.

It's an understatement. The sign at the city limits says the population is 328. It lies. Valentine is disappearing, its adobe buildings melting back into the ground.

Like Marfa, Valentine came with the railroad. It was named after the day in 1882 that the construction crew reached this spot on the plain southwest of the mountains. A well that produced plenty of water for the boilers of the steam locomotives and the roundhouse and repair shops that the railroad built at Valentine made it a prosperous little town in its early days. The shops were shut down before World War II, but until a few years ago the trains still stopped in Valentine to change crews.

Valentine High School's last six-man football team graduated in the 1950s. In 1986, only one senior marched down the aisle to receive his diploma. In 1987, there is no fifth grade in the elementary school because there are no fifth-graders.

But every year during the first two weeks of February, thousands of valentines flood into Kelley's small post office to be stamped with the "Valentine, TX" postmark and relayed to beloveds everywhere. Last February, 7,174 cards came from Italy, Australia, Sweden, Canada, Saudi Arabia, the Philippines, Malaysia, Great Britain, the Netherlands, Indonesia, Japan, West Germany, Mexico, Austria, France, Spain, Jamaica, Venezuela, the Virgin Islands, Guam, and every state but North Dakota.

Kelley postmarked them all by hand and sent them on. "It's the big day for Valentine," she says.

Fortune has smiled more sweetly on Fort Davis. The old military post, which for sixty years after its abandonment had been sinking into the ground like Valentine, was purchased by the federal government in the 1960s and is a national historic site now. The National Park Service has restored many of the old buildings and preserved the remains of others. It's said to be the best place in the West to learn what it was like to be a soldier on the frontier.

One of the old barracks, restored and furnished with the kinds of beds, blankets, trunks, uniforms, and weapons that it contained a century ago, is the first memorial anywhere to honor the black soldiers who fought in the Indian wars. "We feel it's a tribute that's long overdue," says Mary Williams, the post historian. Many visitors are surprised to learn that it was black cavalrymen who rode to the rescue of the beleaguered settlers on the Southwestern frontier. "The John Wayne movies don't show it that way," Williams says.

Dude Sproul says the most significant changes in Fort Davis since his childhood are that two of its streets have been paved and wild burros no longer roam the town. But State Highway 17, the main street, is lined now with more shops, hotels and restaurants than some of the larger towns in the area can boast, and the high school football team has grown from six-man to eleven-man. Its field has lights and new bleachers.

Nobody knows for sure what the population is. The citizens have never bothered to incorporate their village. Since there are no city limits, there's no place to stop counting. Ask a resident how many people live there, and the reply will be, "About a thousand." The same question has gotten the same answer for more than fifty years. It's probably accurate, give or take a hundred.

But many of the faces are new. Dr. Paul Jose, an astronomer who used to work at McDonald Observatory outside of town during the 1940s, says he recognizes fewer people on the streets since his retirement. "It doesn't have the easy-going atmosphere it used to," he says.

To others, the changes of the last century are more illusory than real and don't matter at all in the longer scheme of things.

"When I was growing up here, I hated all the gossip and everybody knowing everything I was doing," says Lucy Miller Jacobson, who lived twenty-eight years in Los Angeles before she moved back to Fort Davis. "But when you live in a city and you don't know anybody and there's nobody to gossip about, it's fun to come back here. You can go to a party here, and people will be passing along some bit of new gossip, and in the next breath they'll start talking about some gossip that took place eighty years ago. And it's just as juicy as the current gossip.

"Those people up there in the cemetery are just as much part of this town as anybody else, you know."

It's something she learned while she was still in Los Angeles, she says. "When my daughter died, I couldn't face burying her in Forest Lawn. That was something I just could not do. I was talking to my mother on the phone, and I told her that. And she said, 'Why don't you bury her here?' Suddenly everything was all right. There are five generations of my family out there in that cemetery. I'll be buried there, too. I don't think of myself as a sentimental person, but I love these mountains. I can't imagine being anywhere else. I don't think there's ever been a funeral in that cemetery that they haven't said that psalm, 'I will lift up mine eyes unto the hills. . .'"

At Rockpile, an old Indian camp in the mountains, the angle of the sun on the cholla cactuses makes them seem incandescent. Bees are working amidst the purple wildflowers. From Mount Locke, where the McDonald astronomers shoot laser beams at the moon, one can look all the way into Mexico with naked eyes and scan the horizon of its own blue mountains. In Valentine, the ropers are talking about rain.

"Yeah, we're pretty dry in spots," says one. "We could use a little sprinkle here and there."

"We're drier than hell over on the north side," says another.

In Jeff Davis County, not much changes. Not really. And a hundred years isn't long.

[October 1987]

To Texas boys of a certain age, Doak Walker was the Hero with the capital "H." He was what all of us hoped to be when we became as old as he was. That was when he was in college at Southern Methodist University.

When I met my hero in person, forty years after I had worshipped him, I found him to be a really nice guy, and a really dull interview.

THE DOAKER

On bright autumn afternoons four decades ago, men and boys would desert their work or play and gather around radios in homes, gas stations, and barber shops across Texas to listen to Kern Tipps broadcast the Southwest Conference Game of the Week, sponsored by Humble Oil Company.

Tipps' voice was a lot like autumn — crisp, clear, and golden, about the same color as cottonwood leaves at that time of year, and the football game he was describing was the most exciting thing happening in Texas at that mcment. After the game, the young boys, unwilling to let go of the excitement, would troop to a backyard or a vacant lot, choose sides, and play their own football game, pretending to be the heroes that Kern Tipps had talked about. And the hero that the small boys wanted to be more than any other was Doak Walker of the SMU Mustangs.

"The Doaker," as Tipps often called him, was the complete football player. He ran with the ball, he threw passes, he caught passes. He was the Mustangs' punter and their place kicker. He called the plays. He played offense and defense. In the thirty-five games he played during his four years at SMU, he ran 2,076 yards in 501 plays. He threw 239 passes, completing 138 for 1,786 yards. He caught twenty-nine passes for 479 yards. He averaged 39.6 yards punting. He scored 303 points. He was the first sophomore to win the Maxwell Trophy, given to the nation's most outstanding collegiate football player. He was the first player to be awarded the Heisman Trophy as a junior. He won the Swede Nelson Sportsmanship Award and the Johnny Sprague Memorial Trophy. He was the first player to win All-American honors three times. "The Doaker" was smart, handsome, modest and polite. He went to church and Sunday School. He dated the queen of the campus. His picture was on the cover of *Life* and all the sports magazines. If there was such a creature as "the all-American boy," Doak Walker was it. He went on to become one of the greatest stars in the history of the Detroit Lions, and in January 1986, thirty years after he played his final game, he was voted into the Pro Football Hall of Fame. It was an honor that many of his fans felt was unjustly late in coming, but one that Walker welcomed, anyway. "Now," he said, "I can finally retire."

Hundreds of people will pay $150 each to gather Friday evening for a celebration. The evening's sponsors say the occasion is to celebrate several anniversaries — the Texas Sesquicentennial, the one-hundredth anniversary of the State Fair of Texas, and the seventy-fifth anniversary of SMU. It's also to raise money for the university. But the party is called "A Toast to Honor Doak Walker," and the scheduled speakers — including fellow Hall-of-Famer Bobby Layne, former SMU teammates Robert Folsom and Raleigh Blakely, and sportswriters Blackie Sherrod and Dan Jenkins, who covered Walker for the late *Fort Worth Press* — all have vivid memories of those "golden years" of the game and its hero.

"Doak Walker was the greatest all-around football player who ever lived — anywhere," Jenkins says. "There's absolutely no doubt about that. He did everything. He played almost every minute of every game. And whenever he was on the field, it was magic time. Every time the ball was snapped, anything could happen."

To commemorate the one-hundredth anniversary of collegiate football in 1969, *Sports Illustrated* assigned Jenkins to poll the country's football experts and compile the all time all-star college team. "Doak Walker was the first name I wrote down," he says. "I was going to make sure he wasn't overlooked. He wasn't. He was on everybody else's list, too."

Saturday afternoon, Walker will be the guest of honor at SMU's game against its neighbor and ancient rival, TCU. The game has been moved from Texas Stadium, where the Mustangs play their home games now, to the Cotton Bowl, which used to be called "The House that Doak Built."

"The first couple of years Doak was on the team, SMU still played its games at Ownby Stadium, but he became so popular that people had a really hard time getting tickets," recalls Dallas bookseller Bill Gilliland, who was a Phi Delta Theta fraternity brother of Walker's. "That's why they moved the games to the Cotton Bowl — so more people could see Doak. But Doak was very modest. He was the star of the campus. He was the star of Dallas. But he didn't act like a star."

"I guess you could say that I got my burning desire to play football out of a dark, musty closet at North Dallas High School. It was in this closet that they kept all of the old foot-ball gear, and I got a big boot out of sitting there in the semi-darkness, playing with those old shoulder pads, helmets, hip pads, and pants. And strange as it may seem to you, I liked the smell of that old, beat-up equipment. You know how some people are about the smell of fresh cut hay or the odor of pine in the forest? Well, that is what the smell of that old gear did for me."

So began "Doak Walker's Story," a seven-part autobiography that was published in the *Dallas Times Herald* between December 26, 1949 and January 2, 1950, just after he had finished his last SMU football season and was waiting to graduate. Walker doesn't remember writing his autobiography. He thinks it prob-ably was ghost-written by Louis Cox, a *Times Herald* sports-writer whom he still refers to as "Mr. Cox." "But it's accurate," Walker says. "I can still smell that old leather from the footballs and the uniforms. It's still a pleasant smell, the locker room aroma."

When Ewell Doak Walker, Jr. was born, on New Year's Day 1927, his father, Ewell Doak Walker, Sr., was a teacher and coach at North Dallas High. The closet full of football gear was in his classroom. The child used to accompany his mother to the school in the afternoon to bring his father home. He would play in the closet while his father finished his last class.

"When I was three years old," Walker says, "Dad taught me to drop kick. He had me drop kicking over the clothesline in the backyard. He wouldn't give me a little child's football. He made me kick with a regulation ball. He said if I was going to play, that was the kind of ball I'd be playing with, so I might as well start out with it."

The hero of Walker's early boyhood was Harry Shuford, a great fullback who was playing at SMU, just around the corner from the Walker home in University Park. When Walker was playing elementary school ball, the players had to provide their own uniforms. His father bought him pads, pants, a blue helmet, and shoes that were too big for him, so that he wouldn't outgrow them too fast. "But the best was yet to come," says the autobiography. "One day when I got home, Mother handed me a yellow jersey with the big blue numerals three and seven on it. Hot dog! No. 37. That was Harry Shuford's number at SMU. When I got that outfit on I thought I was the king bee and no mistake."

Walker *was* something of a king bee on the football field, even in his early days. He was captain of his team in the fifth, sixth, seventh, and eighth grades. When he entered Highland Park High School in 1941, he and two other boys were moved from the "B" beam to the varsity about four weeks before the end of the season. His sophomore year, he became the extra-point kicker and fifth man in the Highland Park backfield, substituting for whoever came out of the game. The team's two coaches went into the Navy during the season, and a new coach took over. He was Rusty Russell, who had been hired away from Masonic Home in Fort Worth. He was a tough, hard-driving coach, and the team got to the state quarterfinals before it was beaten, 13-7, by Sunset High.

In 1943, his junior year, Walker became a starter and was elected co-captain. The other co-captain was his good friend, Bobby Layne, who was in his senior year. "Believe me, this is a job that carries plenty of responsibility with it," Walker (or Louis Cox) wrote in the autobiography. "The honor is swell and it means a lot, but if you're a captain you've got to be in there hustling just a little harder than the other guy all the time because you've got to set an example for the other fellows both on and off the field." San Angelo beat Highland Park, 21-20, in the state semifinals that year. Layne graduated and departed for the University of Texas.

Walker was co-captain again in 1944, and led the Highland Park Scotties to the state finals, where they were beaten by Port Arthur, 19-7. Walker made the All-State and All-Southern high school teams, and in normal times would have been looking forward to college. But World War II was still on, and when he graduated from Highland Park in January 1945, his buddy Bobby Layne dropped out of UT, and they joined the Maritime Service. They underwent basic training in St. Petersburg, Florida, then were shipped to Hoffman Island, New York, for a twenty-week radio school. However, when they were ordered to New Orleans to be assigned to a ship, they learned that the Maritime Service had more radio operators than it needed. Their assignment never came, so they decided to return home and enroll in UT together.

As fate would have it, Layne and Walker's high school mentor, Rusty Russell, recently had joined the SMU coaching staff, and the Mustangs were in New Orleans that week for a game against Tulane. The boys went to see the game, and Russell invited them to ride back to Dallas with the team. Layne decided to spend the rest of the weekend in New Orleans, but Walker accepted the invitation.

"I guess today the NCAA would consider it a recruiting violation," Walker says now, "but I rode to Dallas in the team's

railroad car, and Coach Russell talked to me quite a bit along
the way. When we got to Dallas, he gave me a ride home and
spent the whole day with my family. I got a date and left the
house, but when I came back that Sunday night, Rusty was
still there. And my folks said, 'Well, we think it would be a
good idea if you went to SMU.' So by Tuesday, Bobby was back
in town, and he called me to make plans for us to go down to
Austin. And I said, 'Bobby, I'm going to SMU.' And he said,
'OK, I'll see you Saturday.' So I enrolled at SMU that Tuesday,
and Bobby enrolled Wednesday at the university. And on
Saturday, Texas played SMU in Dallas. Bobby started for Texas,
and I started for SMU, and we both played the whole sixty
minutes. Bobby threw a touchdown pass in the last few
seconds, and beat us, 12-7. I still don't believe we did that.
How in the world could anybody do that? That's youth, I
guess."

Walker was named to the All-Southwest Conference team his
freshman year. Then, in Feburary 1946, Uncle Sam drafted him
into the Army. He was shipped to Fort Lewis, Washington,
where he played baseball, then to Fort Sam Houston in San
Antonio, where he played football and basketball until February
1947, when the Army discharged him and he returned to SMU
in time to make the baseball team.

The fall of 1947 began what are still called the "golden years"
at SMU. The Mustangs, coached by Matty Bell and Rusty Russell and sparked by Walker, beat Santa Clara, Missouri, Oklahoma A&M, Rice, UCLA, Texas (led by Layne, now a senior),
Texas A&M, Arkansas, and Baylor and tied TCU, 19-19, to win
the Southwest Conference Championship. Walker celebrated his
twenty-first birthday on January 1, 1948, with another tie,
against Penn State in the Cotton Bowl. He won All-America
honors and the Maxwell Trophy.

When the 1948 season began, he was joined in the backfield
by a young runner named Kyle Rote, and the national sports
press began paying attention to SMU. "This '48 season was the
period in which my picture appeared on numerous magazine

covers," says the autobiography, "and before it was over I think
the team was getting as touchy about it as I was."

The season was almost a duplicate of 1947. Although Missouri beat the Mustangs, 21-14, the Mustangs were conference
champions again and defeated Oregon, 21-13, in the Cotton
Bowl. Walker was a unanimous All-America and won the Heisman Trophy.

"I didn't know the Heisman was important," he says now,
"because I was from the Southwest. We didn't have television,
and the Dallas newspapers had never sent reporters up to New
York to attend the banquet where it was presented. I knew
Davy O'Brien had won it when he was at TCU, but I didn't
really know what it was, and I couldn't spell it, either."

Walker's senior year, which should have been his best, wasn't.
He was plagued most of the season by injuries and an illness
that he couldn't shake. From his normal playing weight of
about 168, he dropped to 150. He missed several games. Rice
beat the Mustangs. So did Baylor and TCU. And, because of
an injury he suffered against Arkansas, he sat out his last collegiate game — against mighty Notre Dame — on the bench and
watched SMU get beat, 27-20.

Despite his troubles, he led the Southwest Conference in scoring for the third straight season and was the fourth-highest
scorer in the nation. When he learned he was being mentioned
for All-America honors again, he did an unheard-of thing. He
wrote a letter to *Collier's* magazine, which supervised the
choosing of one of the most prestigious All-America rosters,
and asked that his name be withdrawn from consideration. "I
believe there are other All-American candidates who have seen
more action and therefore are more deserving of consideration,"
he wrote. *Collier's* withdrew Walker's name but gave him its
sportsmanship award. And he was named to all the other All-
America teams anyway.

He graduated from SMU in June 1950, married his college
sweetheart, Cotton Bowl queen Norma Peterson, not long afterward, and one of his professors, Dorothy Kendall Bracken,

published a book called *Doak Walker — Three-Time All-American.* It was read by small boys across the land.

"Those were glorious years at SMU," Walker says now. "Everything seemed to fit. We were winning, and Dallas was behind us, and we always played to full houses."

Walker was named to a college all-star team that was going to play the Philadelphia Eagles in an exhibition game. The coach of the all-stars was Eddie Anderson of the University of Chicago. All during training camp, he tried to persuade Walker not to go into the pros. "The game is not for you, son," he would say. "You're too little. You're going to get hurt. You really ought to consider going home right now."

"He tried every way in the world to get me to go home," Walker says. "But I ignored him and signed with the Detroit Lions. At the end of my first season, I got a nice note from Dr. Anderson. It said, 'I made a mistake. I apologize.'"

During that first season, 1950, Walker led the National Football League in scoring with 128 points. During his six years on the team, he and the Lions quarterback — Walker's old buddy from Highland Park, Bobby Layne — would lead Detroit to three divisional championships and — in 1952 and '53 — two NFL championships. He gained 1,520 yards rushing and 2,539 receiving passes. He was All-Pro four of his six seasons. In his last game — a 24-19 loss to the New York Giants in 1955 — he scored eleven points on a pass reception, a field goal, and two extra points. He won the NFL scoring title that year, too, with ninety-six points. And at the game's end, his number, 37, became the first ever to be retired by the Lions.

"My life had been sports," he says now. "Games had always come easy for me. That can make things harder later, when things don't come as easy."

Walker moved to Denver after his retirement. His two sons and two daughters grew up. His marriage to Norma Peterson ended. He was in and out of several businesses. In 1967 he became head coach of the Akron Vulcans in the short-lived Continental League. "Our illustrious owner had come from

Chicago, and he made a big splash in Akron," Walker says. "But apparently he owed some money back in Chicago. When we played our first league game, some fellows with dark hats and big holsters under their coats came and took our whole gate receipts. They said they were collecting the money our owner owed them. We couldn't make our payroll. They fired me the next day, and we folded."

And every time he was nominated for the Pro Football Hall of Fame, he was rejected because, the voters said, he hadn't played long enough. "I figured I would never make it because I wasn't qualified," he says.

But life improved. After a one-week courtship in 1969, he married Skeeter Werner, a former Olympic skier. She owns two ski shops in Steamboat Springs, Colorado, and Walker is a vice president of Fishback Corporation, a holding company for a group of construction businesses. He works in his Denver office a lot, travels a lot — including a trip to Dallas about once a month to see his father, who still lives in the University Park house where little Doak learned to drop kick — and joins his wife in the mountains on weekends. It's a good arrangement, he says. "We spend more time together than most people who live together," he says.

And, at last, he has received the only football honor that he had been denied. "It was kind of appropriate that the Hall of Fame's Old Timers Committee nominated me," he says. "When I started, I think $8,500 was about the average salary on the Lions. Most of the guys would play a couple of years and then they'd have to find a way to make a living while they were still young enough. I was paid $24,000 a year until my last year, when I got $35,000. Detroit treated me very, very fair. There was never any squabbles whatsoever. We had a nice relationship. It was an entirely different time. The players liked each other, and we liked our coaches, and the owner was super to us. No one even thought of being traded. Maybe that was unusual. I don't know. There was a lot of loyalty then. You don't see that too often today, I don't think."

Kern Tipps is gone, too. And Humble Oil. And football players who could do everything. "I guess I'm a little old-fashioned," Walker says. "I don't think the game was made for specialists. But that's the way they're playing it now. And that's the way they're paying it. An individual player is just a small piece of the puzzle now."

[September 1986]

Once upon a time. Fort Worth and Dallas were rivals, but Dallas won that little wrestling match years ago. Lately, Fort Worth has been busy trying to keep its identity as a separate city, and not just the tail end of the Dallas-Fort Worth "Metroplex."

It has succeeded by looking westward instead of eastward for its identity. Psychologically, if not really geographically, Fort Worth is still "Where the West Begins."

I wrote this piece as an effort to explain Fort Worth to Dallas. I'm not sure anybody in Dallas gave a damn, but a lot of folks in Fort Worth liked it.

THE EDGE OF THE WEST

Professor of philosophy Gregg Franzwa showed up for his new job at Texas Christian University in 1976, during what he calls "the summer of love at the Cullen Davis mansion."

"Coming from upstate New York, where I had gone to graduate school at the University of Rochester, I was shocked," he says. "There was crime in Rochester, but nothing like this. Not the wealthy classes involved in murder, and it all out on the front page like that. I had never lived in Texas before, and I thought, 'What have I gotten into here?'"

What he had gotten into was Fort Worth. And the crime, of course, was the Byzantine tangle of events that Texans now refer to simply as "The Cullen Davis Case."

No one who wasn't personally or professionally involved with the crime and its long aftermath can hold in his mind all the twists and turns of "The Cullen Davis Case," but many remember the basic facts:

That around midnight on August 2, 1976, a mysterious "man in black" entered the palatial home of oil multimillionaire T. Cullen Davis and his estranged wife, Priscilla, and shot to death Priscilla's twelve-year-old daughter, Andrea Wilborn, and Priscilla's lover, ex-TCU basketball player Stan Farr, and wounded Priscilla's friend, Gus "Bubba" Gavrel, Jr., and Priscilla herself, then fled back into the night, and that Cullen became the richest man ever to be put on trial for murder in the United States.

For the next three years, much of the Texas court system would be tied up with Cullen and Priscilla, their tumultuous marriage, lurid tales of orgiastic sessions of sex, drugs, and rock 'n' roll in the mansion on the hill and the death of the girl.

A Fort Worth judge would declare a mistrial in the murder case; an Amarillo jury would acquit Cullen. A Houston jury would be unable to decide whether Cullen conspired to hire a hit man to murder the judge in charge of his divorce case; a Fort Worth jury would acquit him. Finally Cullen would get his divorce, quickly marry a former Dallas Cowboys cheerleader, and hold a religious revival at his mansion where, before seven hundred witnesses, he would declare himself a born-again Christian. A few months later, he would take a claw hammer to his supposedly priceless jade collection because an evangelist had declared that many of the pieces were carved in the like-nesses of heathen idols and therefore were an abomination before the Lord.

Fort Worth residents were interested in these events, but not alarmed, for they live in a town that's not only unique, but odd — a town in which the image of the Texan as a gigantic hero in a gigantic land takes on a certain quirkiness, an easygoing funk that's foreign to its prim and proper sister to the east.

"Fort Worth and Dallas just go to show you that measuring distances in quantities like miles can be misleading," Franzwa says. "Fort Worth has always been a looser kind of place than Dallas is."

He was a shiny new Ph.D. when he arrived in Fort Worth eleven years ago. If the events that he encountered then were to happen now, he says, he no longer would be amazed. "Texans, by and large, are the most interesting crowd of folks I've ever run into," he says. "The culture in Texas seems to produce more interesting people than any other place I've been. There's just more variety and more craziness, more tolerance for idiosyncrasy, more characters, more old coots and young coots, and they all have opinions about virtually everything. But they're friendly. Fort Worth is the most open place I've ever lived, the most easygoing, relaxed culture I've ever been in. And most people here have very strong moral sensibilities. They're not neurotic. They're not confused about their morality. They're not questioning the meaning of right and wrong. They know what they believe."

On the same day that Franzwa is saying these things, Cullen Davis has been on the witness stand in a courtroom on the fourth floor of the Tarrant County Courthouse. Despite the acquittal ten years ago, Priscilla and her ex-husband-before-Cullen, Fort Worth car dealer Jack Wilborn, are suing him for $16.5 million in damages for the killing of Andrea and the wounding of Priscilla.

The trial is playing to standing-room-only crowds, as Cullen Davis trials always do. The pews on one side of the courtroom are filled with reporters, lawyers who have dropped in to watch their colleagues work, courthouse idlers, and trial groupies. The other side resembles a church. Nearly everyone there is holding Bibles, some clutching them to their breasts like armor, others reading them, pencils in hand, underlining passages, nodding in agreement with whatever the Lord has laid out on the page. This is Cullen's born-again cheering section.

For much of the morning, Cullen has been fencing with Priscilla's lawyer, Bob Gibbins, about the meaning of the term "blind rage." Gibbins wants to know if Cullen was in a "blind rage" that day, a long time before the murders, when he picked up Andrea's little kitten and hurled it to the floor, killing it.

"I wouldn't say I was in a blind rage," Cullen finally replies. "I would say I was real mad."

Fort Worth often is called "the most Texas city" because it seems to embody the characteristics that people think of as

"Texan" — independence, individuality, toughness, stubbornness, brashness, daring, cantankerousness, humor, and a whiff of violence — without much dilution by outside influences. "When the world thinks of Texas," says Mayor Bob Bolen, "it thinks of Fort Worth. Fort Worth is what the world thinks the West is."

Fort Worth, declares the masthead of the *Star-Telegram*, is "Where the West Begins." If the great Texas historian Walter Prescott Webb was correct, the newspaper is wrong. Webb wrote that the West begins at the 98th meridian, beyond which less than thirty inches of rain falls in a year and the dryness requires a different way of living. By his definition, the West begins at Millsap, in Parker County.

"The German and Japanese tourists are always surprised when they see our water and trees," Bolen says. "They come here looking for El Paso, for desert, for those dusty streets they've seen in hundreds of Western movies."

But psychologically and emotionally, the *Star-Telegram* and its late, great publisher, Amon Carter, who made the slogan a permanent part of his newspaper's masthead, were right. The West of the mind and soul begins in "Cowtown."

During the poverty-stricken Reconstruction years after the Civil War, it was through Fort Worth that the cowboys drove their longhorns up the Chisholm Trail — along the route of present-day Interstate 35W, more or less — to the markets in Kansas and became the tallest heroes in the American mythology. It was in Fort Worth that the drovers enjoyed their last whiskey and women and game of cards before crossing the Red River into the Indian nations, and it was in Fort Worth that they found their first entertainment and refreshment on their way back home. It was to Fort Worth and its huge stockyards that Texas ranchers shipped their cattle after the long drives to Kansas were no longer necessary. It was in Fort Worth that the world's first indoor rodeo was held. It was in Fort Worth that the great black cowboy Bill Pickett first exhibited for the public a new rodeo event of his own invention, called bulldogging.

But if a band of six hundred Comanches and Caddos had been as mad as Cullen Davis on a certain summer day in 1850, there would be no FW in D-FW.

On that day, less than a year after the tiny Army post had been established, the Comanches and Caddos ganged up on a much smaller bunch of Tonkawas and were beating up on them just outside the fort. The soldiers watched as several braves on each side got killed. Then, during a lull in the fighting, the Tonkawas sent a messenger to the fort. "Would it be OK if we came inside?" they asked. "Please."

(The other Plains tribes hated the Tonkawas because they were believed to be eaters of human flesh. So the other Indians killed Tonkawas whenever they got the chance. The Tonkawas often asked the whites for protection. On the other hand, when white soldiers went after the Comanches or the Kiowas, it usually was Tonkawa scouts who guided them.)

Maj. Ripley Arnold, Fort Worth's founder and commander, sent some soldiers to escort the Tonkawas to the post. This upset Towash, the chief of the Comanches. He led his warriors — they heavily outnumbered the soldiers — to the fort and declared that if Arnold didn't hand over the Tonkawas immediately, his Comanches and their Caddo buddies would trash the entire establishment. In reply, Arnold ordered a squad of soldiers to carry a large wooden door outside and set it up near the Indians. Then he loaded the fort's only artillery — a howitzer — and fired it at the door. The shell whizzed over the Indians and blew the door to smithereens.

Towash said, "Well, if we can't have the Tonkawas, can we have something to eat?" Arnold gave them three head of cattle and told them to go away.

"Those savages were certainly more hungry than hostile," wrote a witness, "for the next morning there was neither hide, hair, nor hoof of those devoted cattle to be seen. And that was the peaceful outcome of the only (Indian) hostilities Fort Worth ever experienced."

Three years later, the frontier and the Indians had moved a hundred miles westward. Fort Worth now being useless, the Army moved on, too. If the soldiers had bothered to burn down the fort when they left, there might never have been a Stock Show or a Texas Boys Choir or a Miss Texas Pageant or any Fightin' Frogs. But again, indolence prevented Fort Worth from becoming just another wide open space. Settlers moved into the primitive buildings, and newer, more permanent structures were raised beside them as westward pilgrims drifted in and decided to stay.

By 1856, the village was big enough to demand and get a special election to decide whether the Tarrant County seat should be moved there from rival Birdville. Fort Worth boosters stole Birdville's supply of election-day whiskey — giving Fort Worth two barrels of vote-buying power to Birdville's none — and invited friends and relatives who lived in neighboring counties to drop into Fort Worth, have a drink and be guest voters in the election. By a margin of seven votes, it was decided that Tarrant County's version of justice would reside henceforth in Fort Worth.

The courthouse gave the town a reason to survive, and the cowboys, freighters, and hunters — who were slaughtering the vast buffalo herds to the west and hauling the hides to Fort Worth for sale — gave it an economy. They found their pleasure where the Tarrant County Convention Center now stands, in a seething hive of whorehouses, saloons, and gambling parlors called Hell's Half Acre.

Fort Worth became known as a "tolerant" town, and over the years many of the West's notorious desperadoes graced it with their presence. Sam Bass and his gang drank and caroused there. So did George Parker (a.k.a. "Butch Cassidy"), Harry Longabaugh (a.k.a. "the Sundance Kid"), and their associates (a.k.a. "the Hole in the Wall Gang," a.k.a. "the Wild Bunch"). So did Tom "Blackjack" Ketchum, "Deaf Charley" Hanks, and Harvey Logan (a.k.a. "Kid Curry") and hundreds of lesser hardcases. It was in Hell's Half Acre, at the White Elephant Saloon, that gambler Luke Short gunned down "Long Hair Jim" Courtright, a former Fort Worth marshal, in one of the West's notable shootouts.

"There was something popping in Hell's Half Acre every night," says Leonard Sanders, author of the thick historical novel, *Fort Worth*. "There was a night spot called the Red

Light, and over sixty percent of all arrests made in Fort Worth were made there. They had several bars in this huge building, and out back they had the cribs and the women, and it was home-away-from-home for the cowboys."

When the westward-moving construction gangs of the Texas & Pacific Railroad reached Dallas in 1873, the plan was for them to continue building on to Fort Worth. But when the tracks had reached Eagle Ford, a now-disappeared community just west of downtown Dallas, the Panic of 1873 hit, and construction was halted.

"The Panic was worse than the stock market crash of 1929," Sanders says. "B.B. Paddock, who was the newspaper editor here then, used to say that if the railroad had been able to come on to Fort Worth in '73, Fort Worth would have become the metropolis, and Dallas would have been just another nice county seat town like Cleburne or Weatherford. But the railroad didn't reach Fort Worth until 1876, and all the businesses and warehouses and so forth that would have come to Fort Worth had already located in Dallas."

Nevertheless, Fort Worth became the headquarters of the West Texas ranching business. And when, around the turn of the century, Swift and Armour established meatpacking plants on the city's North Side and 184 acres of stockyards were built around them, it was obvious that, like it or not, Fort Worth was going to be "Cowtown."

It also became, says Franzwa, "a border town between Dallas and nothing."

"Drive west from Fort Worth for thirty minutes, and you're out of civilization," he says. "The overwhelming feeling you have is that you're in nature. Aside from a few roads, fences and buildings, you know this is the way the land looked and felt to the people who were here six hundred years ago. But drive east from Fort Worth for thirty minutes and the impression is that you're in an environment entirely created by humans. That feeling keeps growing until you get to Dallas, and you're on the set of that movie, *2001*. Dallas *defines* modernity. Life in Dallas is life in a city that's twenty minutes old. There's no history visible. Going west, you're in nature. Going east, you're not only *not* in nature, you're in future civilization. There's a kind of stockade mentality in Fort Worth when it looks east and sees that vision of the future. It's suspicious of that vision. It's too slick, too modern, and, worst of all, it's too unnatural. When Fort Worth defines itself, it looks west, toward the nothing."

Charlie McCafferty's grandfather and father worked in the Fort Worth Stockyards. In 1945, when he was fourteen years old, Charlie got a job there, too.

"I was so proud of myself I couldn't see straight," he says. "I went down to the Live Stock Exchange building that morning, and I had on new blue Levis and a white shirt. I had me a dollar-and-a-half whip. My boots were polished. I had a new straw hat. I came down here to take my place among my peers.

"I went into the Exchange building and Mr. Fisk — I worked for the Ruskin Fisk Cattle Commission Company — he told me, 'OK, Charlie boy, go over there and stand in the corner until I'm ready for you.' So I go over there, and the cattle buyers and the commission people and the cowboys are all flocking in to the desk to pick up their papers and stuff, and I'm standing there just aglow. And finally, Mr. Fisk says, 'Charlie, come here.' And he very formally put me through this ritual of introducing me to all these men. Now, most of these men had known me since I was just a little old teeny-weeny baby, but they would very solemnly shake my hand, and I would say, 'Glad to meet you, sir.'

"Then Mr. Fisk brought me out here to the yards. God, the cattle were milling and bawling, you know, and the horses were running up and down the alleys, and people were hollering and yelling, and dust was a pall over everything. And Mr. Fisk took me up to one of the commission booths, which were on top of the fences, to introduce me to some more people. I can still see myself standing up there with my hand on the rail, looking out over that sea of cattle, like I owned it all. I could just see myself a cattle baron. Then Mr. Fisk took me over to some pens. And he handed me a broom and a shovel. And I cleaned pens, and I cleaned pens, and I cleaned pens."

After Chicago and Kansas City, the Fort Worth Stockyards were the largest in the country. They would hold fifteen thousand head of livestock. For about fifty-five years, they averaged ten thousand head in the yards per day.

"The cattle culture was a closed society," McCafferty says. "It was a small, tightly knit group of people, and in that society you had social mores and codes of conduct handed down to you. They had been brought from the South by what you call your Scot-Irish people. They called it 'manners' and 'breeding.' You might be as poor as Job's turkey and as ignorant as all get-out, but if you had 'breeding,' you were all right. But if you got out of line, well, they were a violent people, too.

"I was raised up to take my hat off when I talked to a lady, and never to look a lady in the eye. If she offered me her hand, which was very, very seldom, I was to take hold of the tips of her little pink fingers for just a second — never grasp a lady by the palm of the hand — and then take a step back. You said, 'Yes, ma'am,' and 'No, ma'am.' You stood up when a woman walked into the room. If twenty women walked up twenty times, you stood up twenty times. You never said anything untoward to a woman — or to a child, for that matter. If you were drunk or rowdy, you never acknowledged that you had even looked toward a lady. You cocked your hat down over your eyes and walked a wide swath around her.

"It's well and good to talk about gallantry, but there has to be a certain amount of either self-discipline or community discipline to enforce it. At the least, you could be socially ostracized if you got out of line. And if you violated the code to a real bad degree, or maybe three or four times, then some man or group of men would take you to task, and you could get seriously hurt. I don't say those men were any better or any worse than men today, but we knew how to act, because there was that underlying violent retribution that could happen. You never knew when it was coming. You might be standing up at the bar and some guy would come up and lay one on you for

some action that you'd done six months ago. There's something
lacking in society today because of the lack of manners."

As McCafferty talks, the chant of the auctioneer rattles over
the public-address system in the sale ring. A couple of dozen
men in new summer straw hats and polished going-to-town
boots lounge in theater seats in the almost empty building, eye-
ing the cattle, listening to the salesman's song. They are the
buyers — representing feedlots and packing companies — and
the sellers — ranchers from Argyle, Aledo, Lewisville, Weatherford. The auctioneer knows them all, and calls them by name.

Outside, a few hundred head of cattle mill about a few pens,
awaiting their turn to be driven into the ring. But many of the
acres of pens were torn down long ago, and the rest are rotting.
Armour closed its packing plant in 1962, and Swift shut down
in 1971. Billy Bob's Texas, the world's largest honky-tonk, now
stands where many pens used to be. Others are filled with tall
weeds and small trees, sprung from seeds that cattle brought
here years ago. Except for these vestiges and the restored beauty
of the Live Stock Exchange building and the Cowtown
Coliseum, where rodeos still play every summer Friday night,
and the Stockyards Hotel, where the ranchers and cowboys
used to stay and Bonnie and Clyde once hid from the law, the
glory that once was Cowtown is gone.

Entrepreneurs and civic groups are struggling mightily to save
a remnant of the Stockyards and renovate the buildings around
the intersection of North Main Street and Exchange Avenue —
the heart of the old cattle district — to attract businesses and
tourists and pass on a piece of the past to the future. Sue
McCafferty, Charlie's wife and the president of the North Fort
Worth Historical Society, is a zealot of the preservation effort.
She knows the tourists are necessary, but she's ambivalent
about them.

"The last few years," she says, "the freeways have become
more crowded, the drivers have become more rude, tempers
have become shorter, we've become victims of hustle and bus-
tle. It's been only in the past year that I emotionally have been
able to accept it. There are still times when I feel like running

out in the middle of Exchange Avenue and screaming at the top of my lungs: 'Everybody go home! Get out of our Stockyards! Leave us our peace and quiet!' But we've worked very hard on tourism. And it's fun to see people come and enjoy the place. Some tourists are disappointed. They're expecting a sort of cowboy Six Flags. But a cow or a horse is the biggest tourist attraction we have."

"You'd come down here in the morning," Charlie says, "and you'd hear those thousands of cows bawling, the pigs squealing, the sheep bleating, the horses neighing, the mules braying, the trains coming and blowing the steam and the whistles, the people going to work and everybody cussing and hollering, and it was one helluva thing. To me, that was all I ever wanted to do, was work in the Fort Worth Stockyards. There was nothing in the world better than that. I was talking to my friend Tommy Ryan the other day — Tommy and I grew up together and went to the same school; his daddy was a commission man — and I said, 'Tommy, in your wildest imagination, could you ever have dreamed that these immense yards would ever disappear?' And he said, 'No, I thought this thing would be here like the pyramids.'"

When Dallas was selected as the site of the official Texas Centennial celebration in 1936, Amon Carter was hopping mad. He goaded Fort Worth into staging a countercelebration of its own, featuring such attractions as fan-dancer Sally Rand and Billy Rose's orchestra. It's said that he had billboards reading "Dallas for Culture, Fort Worth for Fun" erected along the state's highways. "During that time, they just suspended the liquor laws," Leonard Sanders says. "It became known that people could do pretty much what they wanted to in Fort Worth."

But about twenty-five years ago, culture began earning a little respect Where the West Begins. The Texas Boys Choir, which had been founded in Denton, moved to Fort Worth because so many Fort Worth boys were in it and so many Fort Worth people supported it. It's now considered equal to the ancient Vienna Boys Choir. The Van Cliburn International

Piano Competition, from a standing start in the early 1960s, has become one of the world's great classical music contests, and the great pianist recently bought a Fort Worth mansion and declared the city his home.

"I remember when the Amon Carter Museum of Western Art opened in 1961," Sanders says. "*Time* magazine just lampooned the hell out of it. The headline said something like, 'Museum of Yippy-Ti-Yi-Yay.'" Since then, the name of the place has been shortened to simply the Amon Carter Museum and the scope of its collection has been broadened far beyond Carter's beloved Russells and Remingtons to include works by Winslow Homer, Georgia O'Keeffe, William Michael Hartnett and most other major American painters and sculptors of the past two centuries. "Now museums in the East borrow things from the Amon Carter to exhibit in New York and Washington," Sanders says. "And when the government did one of its first cultural exchanges with Russia in 1973, they came to Fort Worth and asked the Amon Carter to put on an exhibition there."

In the early 1970s, the Kimbell Art Museum opened next door to the Amon Carter and immediately was acclaimed as one of the architectural gems of the country. It housed the collection of its donor, Kay Kimbell, a wealthy wholesale grocer. Some of the paintings were great and some were marginal. But Richard Fargo Brown, who was hired from the Los Angeles County Museum of Art to be the Kimbell's director, came to Fort Worth with a grand concept: to acquire a priceless, representative piece of art from each major art period throughout history. The Kimbell has become one of the nation's great museums.

The Carter and the Kimbell, together with the Fort Worth Art Museum, the Fort Worth Museum of Science and History, Will Rogers Coliseum, and the Casa Manana Theater now officially make up the Fort Worth Cultural District, and the word "culture" is on the lips of every Fort Worth booster.

Another phrase on Fort Worth lips these days is "the Basses." It refers to Sid and Bob Bass, the very wealthy, very bright and very sophisticated nephews and heirs of Sid Richardson, one of the legendary Texas wildcatters. During the past decade, the Basses have been making downtown Fort Worth over in their own image, building skyscrapers and hotels and renovating several blocks of turn-of-the-century buildings into Sundance Square. Named for the Sundance Kid, the co-chieftain of the Wild Bunch, it's a complex of restaurants, shops and the Sid Richardson Collection of Western Art, the wildcatter's own collection of Russells and Remingtons. Sid's wife, Anne, until Sid left her for another woman, spent several years and hundreds of thousands of dollars trying to bring the Fort Worth Ballet up to New York standards. And, according to one local social critic, the Basses even gave Fort Worth its first "yuppies."

"Until the Bass brothers set up here," the critic says, "there was nothing like an upwardly mobile yuppie bunch — you know, like bankers and lawyers and all that Dallas stuff," he says. "The Basses created them during the late '70s. Upward mobility is a whole new idea in Fort Worth. In recent years, I think the Basses have created a sort of snotty sense of elitism, just by being concerned about what the world thinks about Fort Worth. But the so-called 'high society' bunch here is tiny. Basically, nobody in Fort Worth gives a damn what other people think."

The critic, who asked — "out of fear," he claimed — not to be identified by name, has lived in Fort Worth, off and on, since childhood. He's about to leave again. "This is a very peculiar town," he says. "It's private. It's a town that simply does not accept public values. People don't go out. That's why you have a lot of good country clubs and no good restaurants. That's why you have great art collections — because those old guys wanted to take the pictures home and look at them in their blue jeans — but opera and other performing arts are almost negligible. When I was growing up here, I think there was more middle-class peculiarity, middle-class drugs, middle-class sexual deviation, middle-class bizarre behavior here than in Dallas or in West Texas — maybe with the possible exception of Amarillo. Amarillo's pretty damn bizarre."

The real culture of Fort Worth, he says, has nothing to do with the Basses or the yuppies. "The art produced by people who grew up here is mostly pretty weird," he says. "Weird writers like Gary Cartwright, Dan Jenkins — *Semi-Tough* is probably the best book about Fort Worth — and Bud Shrake, who all grew up on Fort Worth's South Side. . . . There was Candy Clark, a fine actress. She was in *The Man Who Fell to Earth*, and she was the blonde in *American Graffiti*. She's real nice, but she was always embarrassed because she went to Texas Tech. The best thing about Fort Worth culture is Delbert McClinton. He comes back here about every three years and stays long enough to get crazy, and then he goes off to L.A. or Nashville again."

The critic's own claim to fame, he says, is that he was in the third grade in Fort Worth with Lee Harvey Oswald. "All I can remember about him is that his mother made him wear them dumb Billy the Kid jeans to school," he says. "That was the worst thing a guy's mother could do to you was get you them dumb jeans with little horseshoes on the hip pockets and make you wear them to school instead of real Levis. And Lee Harvey's mother would send him out there, and we would all make fun of him. Maybe that's why he turned out the way he did."

From time to time, someone starts a movement to change the image of Fort Worth, to forget the cowboy past and turn the city's eyes from the West to the East — toward Dallas and New York. One such campaign suggested that the nickname of Fort Worth be changed from "Cowtown" to "Now Town." It — and all others like it — failed.

"A lot of people who started in business here at the Stock-yards as cattle dealers or horse dealers made a lot of money," Charlie McCafferty says. "But their children and grandchildren try to downplay the rural aspects of their past. They don't want to think about pig manure or bawling cattle. So they set up in their black ties and tuxes and say, 'Well, I have culture.' Hell, they don't have culture. They've just got a patina of culture. And it just burns me up when they say 'Culture District' in Fort

Worth, like that's the only place in town where you can get cultured. To be cultured, you have to know and appreciate your own heritage, your own tradition. A people without a tradition, without a heritage which is their culture, they're a bastard people."

Although Mayor Bolen's livelihood comes from his ownership of a chain of greeting-card shops, he also owns several pairs of boots and several cowboy hats. "Sometimes I wear them," he says, "and sometimes I wear a three-piece suit. It depends on who I'm trying to impress. When conventions are in town, I almost always wear my boots and hat. They expect it. They want it. It's one of the reasons they came to Fort Worth. And I've learned that when I travel to Europe or Japan, I've got to take my cowboy hat and boots. I just hate to do it, but no matter where I am, that's what they want me to wear. And once they see my hat, they won't let me take the damn thing off."

Eight of the jurors in Priscilla's civil case against him believe Cullen Davis was "the man in black" who killed Andrea Wilborn. Four jurors believe he wasn't. After four days of deliberation, the score never changes. Once again, the judge declares a mistrial. The born-again half of the courtroom crowd bursts into applause and shouts "Amen!"

"I give credit to the Lord Jesus Christ for the outcome," Cullen tells the reporters.

"That's good," Priscilla replies, "because that's who he's going to have to answer to."

The other big story on Page One is about culture. The Kimbell Art Museum has purchased a painting by Andrea Mantegna, one of the masters of the Italian Renaissance. It's called "Holy Family with Saint Elizabeth and Saint John the Baptist." Its price is believed to be between $5 million and $6 million.

"Fort Worth's not cosmopolitan," Lee Harvey Oswald's old classmate says, "it's just weird."

[July 1987]

I love a good joint. By "joint" I mean a drinking — and eating — establishment where, whatever else is for sale, the main merchandise is beer. And where the bartender is the owner or his son or a guy who has worked there so long that it's impossible to imagine the place without him. And the waitress calls all customers of both sexes either "Hon" or Darlin'." Pool and shuffleboard are desirable options, but not essential. Absolutely essential, however, is a good jukebox loaded with genuine country music.

Adair's is such a place.

BURGERS, BEER, AND PATSY CLINE

One neon sign in front says it's Adair's Saloon. Another says it's Adair's Bar & Grill. The T-shirt on the waitress says it's Adair's Beer Joint. The regulars just call it Adair's, and if you're a Dallas-dweller of a certain type, Adair's is heaven.

Looking at some of the customers at lunchtime, you know what has happened. These guys have walked out of some glass office tower, out of some meeting with a boss or a banker, the heat on the street has hit them like a ton of lighted charcoal, their suit coats have begun to fit like straitjackets, and they can't stand the thought of one more person telling them to have a nice day.

And somebody has said, "Hey, this is an Adair's kind of day!" And they've crawled into a car and driven over to that long, narrow, shady room at 2624 Commerce Street in Deep Ellum. They've probably told themselves that they're going to have a quick burger and get back to the office, but they've probably lied.

Ordering lunch is easy at Adair's. You get a hamburger, or you get a cheeseburger. Lettuce, tomato, pickle, and onion. Choice of mustard, catsup, or mayonnaise. The bread is a hamburger bun just like the ones your mother used to buy at the grocery store. The meat is gray and greasy and weighs half a pound. The cheese on the cheeseburger is American. The whole thing is topped with a jalapeno and held together with a toothpick and served in a plastic basket.

It's the kind of burger you used to buy a long time ago in places called Joe's and Louie's and Pancho's, where the burgers were built by Joe or Louie or Pancho in person. Joe's or Louie's or Pancho's might have offered you a few alternatives — ham-and-cheese, say, or egg salad — but Adair's doesn't. If you don't want a burger, you don't eat at Adair's.

On the side, you can get plain potato chips or barbecue potato chips or potato chips with those little grooves in them or Fritos. The side dishes cost extra and come in sacks. To drink, there are your basic American soft drinks and your basic American beers, served with the cans still on them. You can get a drink of the hard stuff, too, if you don't order anything fancy.

For those who liked Joe's or Louie's or Pancho's, Adair's provides the best lunch available in the vicinity of downtown Dallas. But the best thing about Adair's isn't the lunch. It's the place you get to eat it in.

If you grew up in Fort Stockton or Round Rock or Durant or Odessa or some other place that had a real beer joint and you sometimes get homesick, entering Adair's will bring a tear to your eye. The long room is dark and cool, lighted only by the sun through the front plate-glass window and the half-dozen neon beer signs on the walls and cooled by a big air conditioner that hangs from the ceiling and by ceiling fans.

Also on the ceiling are hundreds of gimme caps that somebody nailed up there and hundreds of paper napkins that customers have wadded up, soaked in beer, and thrown up there to stick during the bar's two and one-half years on Commerce Street, where it moved after twenty years on Cedar Springs Road.

The walls, adorned with Texas, Confederate, and American flags and portraits of Bob Wills, John Wayne, and Hondo Crouch, also are full of words. Some are rules and information posted by Adair's management:

You Daince With Who Brung You Or No Damn Daincing.

Dress Code Enforced: Clean Clothes.

Yes! We Serve Crabs. Have A Seat.

Bob Wills Lives.

Public Notice: As A Public Service Announcement, This Establishment Will Notify The Next Of Kin Of Any Person Who Dares Drop A Puck On This Damn New Table.

This reference is to the shuffleboard table, which stands along the wall between the two pool tables at the front of the room and the pinball machines farther back, near the patched, vinyl-covered booths and wobbly tables.

There are other signs that used to stand beside Texas highways, identifying or directing motorists to Hondo Creek, Tarpley, Bandera, Orangefield, and, of course, Camp Adair. But most of the words on the walls were written by customers.

The Adair's graffiti collection must be the largest in Dallas, and it covers the entire spectrum of the graffitist's art: classic restroom poetry, insults of all known ethnic groups, praise and abuse of various universities and fraternities, individual brags and lies signed with names or initials, comments on Texas foreign policy *(The Border Patrol is on the wrong river)*, and bits of personal philosophy *(As I look back the only thing I would of saved for my old age is the years between twenty and thirty)*. Some very tall customers, including the Secret Service agents who guarded Vice President George Bush during the Republican National Convention in 1984, wrote their remarks on the ceiling.

But the soul of Adair's, the thing that makes Adair's *Adair's*, is the music. "We have some who come in for lunch and stay all afternoon listening to the jukebox," says Charline Johnston, who hefts the burgers from the cook's window to the tables.

The Adair's jukebox is simply the best country jukebox in Dallas, probably the best in Texas. So in the very shadows of downtown's towers, within earshot of Central Expressway's roar, the good old grown-up country boys take off their suit coats, loosen their neckties, nurse a cool one and sing along with Hank Williams on "Cold, Cold Heart," Hank Thompson on "The Wild Side of Life," Bob Wills on "Faded Love," Webb Pierce on "There Stands the Glass," Patsy Cline on "I Fall to Pieces," Ernest Tubb on "Walking the Floor Over You." Some even try to imitate Jimmie Rodgers' blue yodel on "Muleskinner Blues," accompanied by the click of pool balls, the ping of pinball, and many fractures of the *No Profanity* rule.

Eyes glaze and minds slide easily into memories of two-stepping thigh to thigh with some long-ago sweetie in some faraway high school gym, of sweaty adolescent grapplings in the backseats of '53 Fords under the bright Southwestern moon, of the first beer drunk — illegally, probably — in a joint much like this.

In Adair's, on such a hot afternoon, it's hard to remember you're really a lawyer or a judge or a cop or a computer programmer or a truck driver or an auto parts salesman who still has work to do. It's even harder to care.

[July 1985]

I first met Ralph Yarborough during the torrid, dry summer of 1956, when I was an eighteen-year-old reporter for The El Paso Times *and he was running for governor of Texas against Price Daniel. He didn't have time for a sit-down interview, but he let me ride in the car with him while he roamed El Paso County, looking for votes. The driver was a fellow named Gootch, I remember, and he sped Yarborough and me to cotton gins, shopping centers, anywhere there were hands to be shaken. At a barbeque and political rally in Ysleta, Yarborough made the best stump speech I've ever heard. And between stops, while Gootch was burning up the highways and byways of the county, Yarborough talked to me, and I listened.*

More than thirty years, dozens of political campaigns, and hundreds of interviews later, that remains one of my most memorable days as a reporter.

I didn't see Yarborough again until 1983, when I interviewed him for this profile. He had changed hardly at all.

NOTHING BUT PEOPLE

On election night in 1957, when Ralph Yarborough was elected to the U.S. Senate, an Austin lobbyist dropped by his campaign headquarters, where a victory celebration was in progress. "It was amazing," he told reporters later. "There wasn't a big shot down there — nothing but people."

A framed enlargement of the newspaper story chronicling the lobbyist's astonishment still hangs on the wall of Yarborough's Spartan law office in downtown Austin. It's surrounded by dozens of autographed pictures of presidents and astronauts and Indian chiefs and plaques and certificates of appreciation and stacks and heaps and piles and mounds of books and documents relating to the long life of Ralph Webster Yarborough and his adventures among the political giants and trolls of Texas and Washington.

It has been a life spent battling "big shots," and losing more often than winning. Of his nine statewide political races between 1938 and 1972, Yarborough won only three. And during the thirteen years in the Senate that those victories gave him, he dedicated himself with a rare energy and eloquence to "nothing but people," a stance that ended his Washington career when his influence was at its peak and still makes his name an anathema in the board rooms and fat cat clubs of Dallas and Houston and Austin.

In 1970, the Texas business and political establishment spent $6 million — an astronomical sum at the time — to unseat its state's senior U.S. senator and give the Democratic nomination to Lloyd Bentsen, a rich man from the Rio Grande Valley. Some of Bentsen's TV commercials during the campaign featured the riots at the 1968 Democratic National Convention in Chicago. They hinted that Yarborough — a declared opponent of the Vietnam war — was somehow responsible for them. The Texas Democratic electorate apparently believed it.

Such things had happened to Yarborough before — in 1952, 1954, and 1956 — so regularly, in fact, that Yarborough's years in the Senate were for a long time regarded by weary and embittered Texas liberals as an aberration, a freakish outbreak of grassroots democracy in a state ruled openly, with only the faintest lip service to The People, by The Establishment and its Big Money.

"Lyndon Johnson had all the money he needed for any kind of operation he wanted to run," Yarborough says. "I had practically none. I could raise a little and borrow some to run, but the minute the campaign was over, I couldn't raise money to pay the debts off. I was in debt all the time. I had no resources. My older brother, who was practicing law in Dallas, urged me not to run for political office. He already saw that Dallas syndrome. 'You can't beat that money,' he said. 'They'll buy it every time.'"

Ralph Yarborough is about to turn eighty. He looks maybe sixty. He's still trim for a man of his stocky build and walks quickly, with a spring in his step. His brown hair has aged silver-gray, but his dark eyes are clear. They still flash when he's riled. A movie casting director searching for someone to play a Southern senior senator or elder statesman could do no better. His mind is still an encyclopedia of law and Texan and American history and statistics and political anecdotes. They fill his conversation, and when his talk turns to the preoccupation of his life — the eternal battles between The People and Big Money and between expedience and integrity in politics and government — his rich East Texas voice still rises to the fiery hyperbole that distinguished his hot Texas summer campaigns of the 1950s — a time when running for office meant making speeches from flatbed trucks and shaking the hands of the electorate in hundreds of courthouse squares, before the professional TV image-makers decreed that anger and emotion are political liabilities, before a candidate for public office became simply another brand of soap to be sold. "He will not hire high-pressure hucksters to direct a campaign," says a Yarborough campaign biography written for his 1957 Senate race. "He does not belittle their effect; he knows what they can do, and he has the scars to prove it. But patently their job is to corrupt the judgment of the electorate; and that, he sees, is evil."

"Evil" is a word that has almost disappeared from the American vocabulary. It's an old-fashioned "hot" word that doesn't fit into the bland, "cool" political vernacular that TV has created. But Yarborough's hellfire-and-brimstone denunciations of those he considers evil and his belief in some kind of cosmic justice seem refreshingly strong and deep in a time when slickness and shallowness have replaced courage and ideals in so many public figures.

"This James Watt wants to detribalize the Indians and take their reservations," he says. "He calls them socialists. Hell, they've got minerals, and Watt wants the fat cat Republicans to have them. He's the most vicious son of a bitch, next to Reagan, who has ever held a high office in our government."

"We're fixing to build an Army base in Honduras," he says, "to operate against Nicaragua. It's going to be Vietnam all over again, except those countries are so small and close by that we probably can kill them off."

"I'm not super-religious," he says, "but I believe if you abuse people long enough, you're going to pay the penalty for it. I believe there are forces of retribution in nature."

Such thoughts are direct descendants of the Baptist sermons and Populist-influenced Democratic stump speeches he heard in his youth in his home village of Chandler, in Henderson County, on the edge of the Piney Woods. He was born there in 1903 to Charles Richard Yarborough, the local justice of the peace, and his wife, Nannie Jane. He was the seventh of their eleven children. Both his grandfathers were Confederate veterans, and the talk around the family supper table was of Texan and Confederate history. It was there that Yarborough began his hero-worship of Sam Houston, who, like Yarborough, always was a fighter against long odds. Under the sycamore tree in the yard, Yarborough and his brothers and sisters played with Ray and Opal Warren, the children of the Chandler school principal, who lived next door. Yarborough went to school in Chandler, then graduated from Tyler High School, twelve miles away, in 1919. Congressman Jim Young appointed him to the U.S. Military Academy, but after a year there, Yarborough decided against a military life.

He was only seventeen when he came home to become a school-teacher at Delta, and then at Martin Springs, tiny one-room schools where some of the pupils were twenty-five years old. "There was no state aid to schools then," he says, "and each community had to tax its own resources for schools. The railroad went through Chandler, so we could tax the railroad and have seven months of school a year. But those kids six miles away from the railroad had only three months of school a year, because those tenant farmers didn't have much to tax. I taught all grades from first through eighth, all in one room. One year I had the ninth grade, too."

When school wasn't in session, Yarborough took courses at Sam Houston State College in Huntsville, but never got his degree. "Then he got the tickle-foot," his old campaign biography says. "Sometimes it is a way of young men that they must put a passel of miles behind them in a great search before finally they find what they are looking for — that is, find themselves." He was one of that American generation that wandered the earth after World War I, obeying the same impulses that took F. Scott Fitzgerald and Ernest Hemingway to Europe. He worked his way from New Orleans to France on a French cattle boat, hoping to attend the Sorbonne, which rejected him. So he wandered on to Berlin, attended the Stendahl academy for a year and worked for the American Chamber of Commerce. He laughs at the memory now. "People don't usually think of me as a Chamber of Commerce man," he says, "but I once was."

By 1923 he wanted to come home, but the European docks were crowded with young Americans trying to get maritime jobs that would get them across the Atlantic. He worked his way across the English Channel, and in Britain had better luck. As he was standing on a dock with a crowd of job-seeking Americans one day, a ship's agent called out, "Anybody know about handling horses?" and Yarborough sang out, "I'm from Texas!" He got the job, nursing a shipment of horses across the sea. Then he joined a wheat threshing crew in its migration though Oklahoma and Kansas, saved his wages, got engaged to his childhood playmate, Opal Warren, and in the fall went to Austin, where he got a job in a boarding house and enrolled in the University of Texas School of Law. In the summers, he worked — building oil tanks at Borger during the wild boom of 1926, as a librarian and quiz master at the university. He graduated in 1927 with highest honors and intended to go back home and run for county attorney.

"I had been engaged to Opal for three years," he says. "Back in those days, you didn't get married and then start to college. You went to college first. And I was in debt and desperately looking for a job. The easy, preferred way for a young lawyer to get started in those days was to be county attorney. Then you either became district attorney or went out and started practicing. But it so happened that of the fifty-three of us who graduated from the law school that year, three of us were from Henderson County. The other two were from Athens, the county seat, and I was from a little town twenty-five miles away in the northeast corner of the county. They both decided to run for county attorney, so it was foolish of me to think of running against them with no money and in debt when they were where the votes were."

There was another reason he didn't launch his political career immediately. When he announced to his fiancee that he might run, Opal said, "If you run, the wedding is off. I won't marry a man in politics." He dropped the whole subject for ten years, found a law job at the other end of the state, in El Paso, that paid $150 a month, came back to East Texas in 1928, married Opal and moved her west. Fifty-five years later, they're still happily married. In 1931 their only child, Richard — now a Washington lawyer — was born.

Yarborough became an expert in land law and was assisting one of his firm's senior attorneys in a case involving the boundary between Texas and New Mexico. For about twenty miles, the Rio Grande is the border between the two states, and the river had changed course, leaving some formerly New Mexican land on the Texas side. New Mexico sued. When the senior lawyer suffered a heart attack, his young assistant had to argue the complicated case through the courts, then before a committee of the Texas Legislature, then before Texas Attorney General James Allred. Allred was so impressed with Yarborough's argument that he not only ruled in his favor, but offered him a job as an assistant attorney general. Yarborough accepted. And later, when Allred was elected governor — "the last progressive governor that Texas has had," Yarborough calls him — he appointed Yarborough to fill a vacant seat as a Travis County district judge, a post to which he was later elected in his own right. Opal changed her mind about politics, and he took a brief leave from the bench to run for attorney general in 1938. He lost to SMU's All-American quarterback, Gerald Mann.

When the Japanese attacked Pearl Harbor, Yarborough joined the army and was commissioned as a captain. "I was too old

for the draft," he says, "but I had attended West Point for a
year, and I decided I had a duty to go." He fought in Europe
with the 97th Division under Patton and Eisenhower, then went
to the Pacific and served under MacArthur. By now a lieutenant colonel, he ruled the central Honshu Province — one-
seventh of Japan's land and people — under MacArthur's military government. By the time he got home, he had decided to
try politics again. Politics in Texas in those days meant
Democratic politics, since the Republicans had no more chance
of being elected than the Prohibitionists or the Vegetarians. The
Democratic Primary in July, not the General Election in
November, put candidates into state offices. And, in those days,
the terms of those offices were only two years. An election was
barely over before candidates began gearing up for the next
one.

"I was planning to run for attorney general in 1952," Yarborough says. "John Ben Shepperd was secretary of state, and
he was going to run for attorney general, too. So I was walking
down a corridor in the Capitol one day, and Gov. Allan Shivers
stopped me and said, in a very friendly way, 'Ralph, I understand you're thinking about running for attorney general. I
don't think it's advisable. They've already decided who the next
attorney general is going to be.' By 'they,' he meant The Establishment. He wasn't saying, 'You don't run.' He wasn't bombastic
at all. He was trying to put on his best friendly manner. Well,
he didn't convince me not to run. But I started getting calls
from people in East Texas, saying, 'Listen, Ralph, Shivers is
unpopular. He would be easier to beat than John Ben Shepperd.'"

So Yarborough announced as a Democratic candidate for
governor and became the lifelong enemy of The Establishment.
He called upon the voters to save themselves from Shivers'
"money-centered political machine bent on treachery to The
People." He accused Shivers of disloyalty to the Democratic
Party. (Shivers later supported Eisenhower in the 1952 presidential campaign.) He accused the Shivers administration of doing
nothing to help the small farmers and ranchers who were being

driven into foreclosure by the terrible drought of the 1950s. And he accused the Shivers administration of corruption. "They were selling insurance company charters," he says. "If you wanted an insurance charter, you paid the administration's bag man. They had different prices, depending on the size company you wanted. A lot of crooked insurance companies were cropping up in Texas. But I couldn't stir up the press. All the city newspapers were against me. Newspapers are big business, too, of course. They're part of The Establishment."

In a bitterly fought campaign, Yarborough got 36 percent of the vote. Shivers was re-elected. But by 1954, discontent with his administration was getting heavier. Two more years of drought had wiped out hundreds of small farmers and ranchers. "And the corruption didn't end," Yarborough says. "It was getting worse, and it was seeping out around the cracks. After they thought they had me polished off, they got more brazen. Dallas had twice as many insurance companies as any other city in the United States, and Dallas wasn't a very big city in those days. They were fly-by-night companies. A lot of them were going broke and trimming their policyholders." Yarborough called for a "complete investigation of the insurance mess" and accused the governor of allowing "fixers and influence peddlers to operate in Austin."

He had pulled together the old Democratic coalition of union labor, small farmers, ranchers, businessmen, and minorities and had carried the fight to a Democratic Establishment that was beginning to look more and more like Joe McCarthy's brand of Republicans. He ran a close second in the primary "but they pulled it out in the runoff," Yarborough says, "with 'The Port Arthur Story.'"

"The Port Arthur Story" has to rank as one of the dirtiest tricks in the history of even Texas politics. In November 1953, 430 CIO Port Arthur retail workers had gone on strike against their stores, demanding recognition of their union. During the primary, Shivers had railed against the unions as "Communist-dominated." "While I know my opponent is not a Communist," he said of Yarborough, "I feel that he is a captive of certain people who do not approve of being tough on Communists." During the runoff, a TV film called "The Port Arthur Story," produced by Shivers' staff, accused the CIO of "personally supervising the death of a city" and portrayed the deserted streets of Port Arthur — an apparent ghost town. Shivers charged in his broadcasts that what had happened in Port Arthur could happen anywhere in Texas if Yarborough became governor. A network of Red unions was being erected all along the Gulf Coast, he claimed; "the pushing of a single button in Moscow" would paralyze Texas, and Yarborough was sympathetic to the unions. Later, a member of Shivers' staff admitted that the film of the deserted streets was shot at 5 a.m.

"It was a terror campaign," Yarborough says. "It scared the thunder out of people, scared the hell out of them. The few country editors who supported me had the windows broken out of their buildings."

Shivers won again, but Yarborough's strong showing against him and the continuing corruption in his administration damaged him badly. The insurance scandal was joined by another, this one involving crooked land deals by the state Veteran Land Board. Two of the three members of the board were Shivers and Attorney General Shepperd. And the drought was worse than ever. "Shivers was planning to run again in 1956," Yarborough says, "and I knew in my bones that I could beat him this time. But The Establishment pulled him out and brought Price Daniel home from the U.S. Senate to run against me. He had two years to go on his Senate term, so he was safe. If he lost the governorship, he'd still be a senator and would have two more years to prepare for another campaign."

By 1956 school desegregation had become a red-flag issue throughout the South, and two rabid racists, Panhandle rancher and author J. Evetts Haley and former governor "Pappy" Lee O'Daniel, also threw their hats into the ring. Haley promised to send the Texas Rangers to shut down any public school system that tried to desegregate. O'Daniel called the U.S. Supreme Court's decision in Brown vs. Board of Education "Communist-inspired" and ranted about "blood running in the streets." Price

Daniel's speeches sounded as if his opponents were the NAACP and "Walter Reuther of the CIO." Liberal Texans sponsored racially integrated political rallies in a few cities, but Yarborough was the only gubernatorial candidate who would speak to them.

It was a blistering, drought-ridden summer, and he stumped the state from El Paso to Orange, from Dalhart to Brownsville, preaching to the sweating crowds about justice for The People and reform in Austin. "I loved those hot summer campaigns, when the primary was in July," Yarborough says. "Campaigning wasn't as much fun after they moved the primary up to May." In the runoff, Price Daniel beat him by fewer than five thousand votes. Yarborough still talks of stolen boxes and burned ballots, but The Establishment had won again.

However, Daniel's Senate seat was vacant now, and a special election had to be held to choose a successor to complete his term. According to Texas election law, there would be no runoff. Anyone of any party could enter, and the man polling the most votes would win, whether he had a majority or not. Yarborough promptly announced his candidacy and — to the embarrassment of The Establishment — quickly became the favorite against Congressman Martin Dies, the Red-baiting former chairman of the House Un-American Activities Committee, and Thad Hutcheson, a young Republican. The Establishment, led by Senate Majority Leader Lyndon Johnson and Governor Daniel, urged the Texas Legislature to change the election law in the middle of the campaign, so that a runoff would be required. The purpose of the scheme was to prevent the election of a liberal. The "Gut Yarborough Bill," as it came to be called, easily passed in the House, but failed in the Senate by two votes.

"On the night before the election," Yarborough says, "it started raining. After seven years, the drought had broken. I thought, 'Good Lord, now they're going to beat me with the rain.'" But Dies and Hutcheson split the conservative vote, and Yarborough was elected with 38 percent. It was his first statewide victory in five tries. And the following year, 1958, he won his second, easily trouncing The Establishment's candidate, "Dollar Bill" Blakley, a Dallas magnate in insurance, banking, ranching, oil, gas — the whole spectrum of Texas wealth — for a full Senate term.

It's with reluctance that Yarborough discusses the injuries inflicted upon him during those campaigns. He doesn't want to be remembered simply as a stubborn champion of lost causes, a valiant loser. "To me," he says, "the bottom line of my career is not all those campaigns. The bottom line is, 'What did you do while you were there?' When I was elected to the Senate, I had certain objectives I wanted to work toward. During the years I was running for governor, Texas was forty-sixth out of forty-eight states in the Union in public health and old-age pensions. We were thirty-eighth in education. We were about forty-sixth in aid to dependent children. Now that there are fifty states, we're forty-ninth. We're the richest state in the Union, and we're near the bottom of the ladder in all social programs. We're forty-eighth out of fifty in the acreage per capita that we have in state parks. Texas is over thirty times as large as little New Jersey, and New Jersey has three times the acreage in state parks that we have. Everything in Texas has been for money. We turn the land over to those who will destroy it to make a dollar. I had a list of about eighteen things in which Texas was behind. And I thought, 'Well, here's my chance to do something about this. It won't raise Texas in the context of what the nation is doing, but it will raise Texas along with all the other states.' But I never introduced a big bill to try to do everything in one piece of legislation. I followed Abraham Lincoln's advice to 'whittle them to death by littles.'"

Yarborough quickly established his independence in the Senate by refusing to sign the Southern Manifesto — a sort of blood oath among the senators of the old Confederate states to fight civil rights with all the strength and vigor at their command. "I wouldn't fight integration," he says, "and that made them mad." Later, he would be the only Southern senator to vote for the Civil Rights Act of 1964 and the Voting Rights Act of 1965. "I've never let anybody tell me how to vote," he says. "I don't care whether he was the president or anybody else. After all, I was older than Lyndon Johnson and John F. Kennedy and Hubert Humphrey. I didn't need any advice on how to vote. I had a fellow call me the other day. He was writing a biography of Hubert Humphrey. He wanted to know if Humphrey had influenced me to vote for civil rights. I said, 'Hell, no. I was for civil rights before I ever heard of Hubert Humphrey.'"

Yarborough had barely learned his way to his Senate desk before he began whittling on a whole forest of projects aimed at improving the lot of The People. When he arrived in 1957, he was appointed to the Labor and Public Welfare Committee, the Education Subcommittee, and the Health Subcommittee — all dealing with issues dear to him — and he remained on all of them throughout his career. He discusses his Senate work with a great deal more relish than his old battles against the Texas Establishment.

"I think my major influence in the Senate and on the country was in higher education," he says. "When I went on the Education Subcommittee, only three million people were in college in this country. The reason was, nobody else had the money to go, and the facilities weren't there, anyway. There was no way a student could get federal money directly in his pockets to go to school. But within seven or eight years, we passed five different bills to put money straight into the pockets of students. The first big breakthrough bill was the National Defense Education Act in 1958. The Russians had put up 'Sputnik I' in October of '57, and the country got scared that Russia was ahead of us in science and engineering. The bill did many different things. We had grants — scholarships — in there for the students, but Lyndon Johnson opposed that, and it was changed to loans on the floor of the Senate. We passed a bill giving grants to families so impoverished that they couldn't repay a loan. We passed government-guaranteed loans for students from middle-income families. Then there was my Cold War G.I. Bill to let the veterans go to college. The Pentagon fought that. The Defense Department thought servicemen wouldn't reenlist if they got a chance to go to college. What a horrible attitude for the Pentagon to take! I said, 'You send those men to get their feet blown off by land mines, to get hooked on dangerous drugs, to contract tropical diseases — yet you won't let them go to school.' And we won."

Through the years, Yarborough introduced history's first bill in the Senate to provide federal funds for the education of children with learning disabilities. He wrote and cosponsored bills to provide schooling for the blind and the physically handicapped, Operation Headstart for disadvantaged children, adult education, bilingual education. He promoted federal funding for high school science and language laboratories, for libraries in public schools, universities, and medical schools.

"We were pushing education on every front," he says. "Our aim was to double college enrollment in ten years, from three to six million. But in 1968, we had eight million in college. I think it's twelve now. And I had more to do with that than any other one senator. Ten years after passage of the National Defense Education Act, the president of *Encyclopaedia Britannica* was testifying at an evaluation hearing on how the program was working. He called it 'the greatest education explosion in the history of the world.'"

Senator Wayne Morse, a maverick himself, dubbed Yarborough "Mr. Education of the Senate," an appellation that still pleases him. "I was very honored by that, because Morse was not a senator to praise people lightly," he says. "Most of us bragged a lot about other senators. Wayne Morse seldom did. But there's no political gain in that kind of legislation. The school kids weren't voting, and they didn't know about it, anyway. When one of my major bills became law, the Texas papers wouldn't mention that I had anything to do with it. It didn't even pay to put out news releases on those bills because their opponents were saying we were trying to turn our schools over to the federal government. That's the trick the big corporations of Texas always use to get people scared of federal money: 'They're trying to take over!' 'They' — that indefinable thing. Later, I would make speeches at high schools and mention where they got the money for their laboratories and libraries, and the people were completely surprised. The school boards hadn't told their people that they had been built with federal funds. They had suppressed that information."

Yarborough also supported legislation to provide FHA-type loans for people who wanted to build homes in the country, and money to build public water systems for little towns and villages. In 1969 he launched a federal War on Cancer. In 1970, as a lame duck senator, he passed the Occupational Health and Safety Act over President Nixon's veto. "After that," he says, "Nixon tried to kill it through maladministration." And in conservation, Yarborough was instrumental in creating in Texas the Padre Island National Seashore, the Guadalupe Mountains National Park, the Fort Davis National Historic Site, and the Big Thicket National Preserve.

During his thirteen years in Washington, Yarborough passed more national legislation than any Texas senator in history, including his hero, Sam Houston. But for the first half of his career, he wasn't assisted much by the fact that the majority leader was his fellow Democrat from Texas, Lyndon Johnson. "Johnson tried to kill my Padre Island bill," he says, "but I got it passed. It took me five years. Then I started on the Guadalupe Mountains. That wasn't so tough. Johnson didn't try to kill that because some of his friends out in West Texas wanted it. But he tried to get somebody in the House to pass it first so I wouldn't get credit for it."

Getting credit for what he accomplished is a preoccupation with Yarborough now, for the Texas press didn't give him much when he was in office, while it gave Johnson credit for many deeds that were done by others. And, Yarborough feels, LBJ is still grabbing unjustified glory from beyond the grave. "People who fought me on a lot of these things are now trying to get credit for them," he says. "They're trying to steal these things from me. Over at the Johnson Library, they're saying he was an education president, claiming he passed all those education bills. But Johnson and I weren't the bitter enemies painted up by the press. He just wanted credit for everything I did."

Yarborough was riding in the car behind President John F. Kennedy on November 22, 1963, when the shots rang out in Dealey Plaza. He was at Parkland Memorial Hospital when Kennedy died. "Excalibur has sunk beneath the waves," he told the press.

Later, reporters and historians wrote that the purpose of Kennedy's Texas tour had been to mend a rift in the state's Democratic Party, between Yarborough and Gov. John Connally, both of whom would be running for reelection in 1964 — as Kennedy also planned to do. Yarborough strongly denies that was the reason for the fatal journey. "I never heard that a single time until after Kennedy was assassinated," he says. "I challenge anyone to find any reference previous to the trip to any such thing being the cause of his coming to Texas. Kennedy was a sharp politician. The idea that he would come here for three days and roam over Texas to patch up a quarrel between Connally and me is just ridiculous. Connally and I were both trying to get closer to Kennedy, and it wouldn't hurt Kennedy if Connally and I were quarreling, so long as we both were on *his* side. Kennedy's purpose in coming to Texas was to get ready for the campaign of 1964. He came here to raise money."

Whether mending a rift was the purpose of the trip, there's no denying that such a rift existed. Lyndon Johnson was unopposed for the Democratic presidential nomination in 1964, and his longtime friend, Connally, wanted to get an Establishment man back in the Senate. He was promoting Congressman Joe Kilgore from the Rio Grande Valley to oppose Yarborough in the primary.

A popular legend is that Johnson called him off and presented the nomination to his old foe as a gift. Some say he did it because he wanted a Texas vote in the Senate for the Civil Rights Bill. But Yarborough denies that, too. "Johnson, under cover, was doing everything he could to beat me in that race," he says. "But he was running for the presidency, and he didn't want it to be known publicly that he was trying to beat a senator of his own party. Johnson called me to the White House and told me, 'It's not true that I kept Joe Kilgore from

running against you.' And I believe that was one time he was
telling the truth. If he had kept Kilgore from running, he would
have demanded something from me, because if Johnson gave
you a match for your cigarette, he wanted a ranch in return.
He told me that Kilgore gathered his financial backers into a
room and hooked up the phone so everybody in the room
could hear. Then he called Johnson and asked if he should run
against Yarborough, expecting him to say yes. But Johnson
thought he was having a private conversation with Kilgore. He
didn't know the others were there. He said, 'No, I don't think
you ought to run against Ralph Yarborough.' Kilgore said, 'Well,
I could beat him.' And Johnson said, 'I'm not sure of that.' So
Kilgore's money men got discouraged. And when Johnson called
me to the White House and told me that, he was mad that Kilgore had exposed him before all that crowd. He was irritated as
the mischief about that."

Yarborough's only opponent for the nomination was Gordon
McLendon, a wealthy Dallas broadcast executive, whom he
beat handily. In the General Election, he defeated Republican
George Bush by an even larger margin than Johnson beat Barry
Goldwater in Texas.

Now that Johnson was president in his own right, Yarborough's Senate bills looked more attractive to him. "The truth
of the matter is, a lot of Johnson's Great Society legislation was
mine," Yarborough says. "I introduced a lot of those bills before
he got to be president, and he didn't support them then. Go
back and look at Johnson's record in the Senate. You won't find
him introducing any of those education bills and the bills for
progress that I did. The Kennedys, Wayne Morse, Paul
Douglas, and I were the progressives of that period. We had
been pushing those bills for years. But Lyndon swooped them
up and called them 'my Great Society.' He wanted to be a great
president, and he knew that to be a great president, you can't
be opposed to progress. Whenever I would pass one of my
bills, he would sign it and turn around with a great big grin
and say, 'Ralph, this is part of my Great Society.' He jumped on
the bandwagon. And I'm glad of it, because if we had had

some reactionary in the White House, he could have caused us untold trouble."

One issue on which the two Texans never agreed, however, was the Vietnam war. Yarborough early aligned himself with Robert and Edward Kennedy, Eugene McCarthy, and other Senate "doves" and spoke out against its expansion. "I kept voting for the appropriations for it, though," he says. "I wasn't about to send our boys over there and then not send them the supplies to protect their own lives. It wasn't their fault that they were there. And I knew what the military was trying to get Lyndon to do. The military wanted him to drop the atomic bomb. And there was a lot of support for that. During the latter years of the war, I had people holding degrees from the University of Texas stop me on the streets of Austin and say, 'Ralph, what's the matter with you and old Lyndon? Lost your nerve? You've got to dig them commies out just like rats. You've got the weapon. Why don't you *use* it?' But to Lyndon's credit — his *eternal* credit — he wouldn't drop the atomic bomb. He refused to start the atomic war."

And in 1968, when Robert Kennedy and Eugene McCarthy — two of Yarborough's closest Senate allies — announced that they would oppose Johnson for a second term, Yarborough was caught in a bind. His reluctance to endorse Johnson enthusiastically didn't sit well with many Texas politicians who hoped to ride Johnson's coattails again. By the time that chaotic Democratic National Convention convened in Chicago — a convention to which he wasn't a delegate — Yarborough had supported three different candidates for the presidential nomination.

"I preferred Kennedy over Johnson," he says, "but I thought to try to change horses in the middle of the stream would bring defeat to the Democratic Party. And I thought Johnson was a better alternative than any Republican would have been, although I disagreed with him on so many things. So when Lyndon announced that he wasn't going to run — and that *astounded* me — I came out for Kennedy. Then he got assassinated. That left me with a choice between McCarthy and

Humphrey. I chose McCarthy. But if I had waited thirty days, I wouldn't have. He had been doing the right things and picking up steam, but after I announced for him, he immediately started doing stupid things. When the Russians invaded Czechoslovakia and every other politician of both parties denounced them for it, McCarthy wouldn't. He said the Russians were just doing what we did in Vietnam. Then he announced who his cabinet would be, and they were all millionaires and Republicans. There wasn't a Democratic politician in his cabinet. Then he said he would withdraw from the race if Ted Kennedy would run. McCarthy didn't believe he could win. I wish I had just stayed home and stayed out of it. I supported three different people before it was over and finally wound up not supporting anybody."

The debacle of 1968 weakened Yarborough's political strength in Texas, and when he sought nomination to another term in 1970, The Establishment was ready. Lloyd Bentsen and his six million dollars drove him out of office. In 1972 Yarborough tried again to return to Washington — this time to sit in Republican John Tower's seat. But Barefoot Sanders — now a federal district judge in Dallas — defeated him for the Democratic nomination, and Tower beat Sanders.

For the next ten years, the liberal wing of the Texas Democratic Party — it prefers to call itself the "progressive" wing now — appeared to be dead. Since Yarborough's last defeat, both Tower and Bentsen have been re-elected. Ronald Reagan is in the White House. Texas even elected its first Republican governor since Reconstruction. Yarborough has spent those years in Austin, quietly practicing civil law, quietly living in the unpretentious house that he and Opal bought years ago, which now is filled with their collection of antiques and the rare books and documents about the Texan and American history that Yarborough loves with the fervor of a scholar. And he fears for The People and the federal programs that he and the Kennedys and even Lyndon Johnson had erected on their behalf.

An amateur is thrilled to meet a champion, and as a poker player of the newsroom sort, I was thrilled to meet Bill Smith. He had just won the World Series of Poker in Las Vegas. But meeting him wasn't easy.

It took me the better part of a week to find out his unlisted phone number, which somebody in Las Vegas finally told me by mistake. And when I called him — it was about noon — I woke him. He had been up all night playing poker, he was irritated, and not interested in being interviewed.

When I challenged him to a game, though, he couldn't resist.

JUST A FRIENDLY GAME

By the end of the third day of the World Series of Poker, the field of 140 players had been whittled to six. Bill Smith of Dallas held $404,000 in chips. Scott Mayfield of Grants Pass, Oregon, held $280,000. Berry Johnston of Oklahoma City held $277,000. T.J. Cloutier of Dallas held $259,000. Jesse Alto of Houston held $106,000. Hamid Dastmalchi of Spokane held $74,000.

Sometime the next day, the last hand would be played and one of the six would sit alone with $1.4 million stacked on the green felt in front of him. He would be the new champion. He would be hailed as the best poker player in the world. He would keep $700,000 — the richest prize in World Series history. The remaining $700,000 would be divided among the eight best players he had conquered.

On the first day of the tournament, the bookies' odds on Smith were 40-1. On the second day, he was 20-1. On the third, he was 10-1. On the final day, he would be even money. "I went to bed at two o'clock in the morning," he says. "At 4:30

my eyes came awake. There was no way I could go back to sleep. So I got up, decided to take a shower and shave and go down to the bar and drink a beer. The tournament wouldn't start till one o'clock in the afternoon. That's a long time to wait. And while I was shaving, I was thinking: 'You've got $400,000. This tournament is about to end. All you've got to win today is a million dollars.'"

The rules of Texas Hold 'Em — the only game played in the Las Vegas tournament — are simple: After the ante, each player is dealt two cards face down; a round of betting is done; three cards are dealt face up in the middle of the table; a round of betting is done; a fourth card is dealt face up; another round of betting is done; a fifth card is dealt face up; the last round of betting is done. The face-up cards are called the "flop." The player with the best five-card hand — using as many of the "flop" cards as he needs — wins the hand.

By 3 P.M. of the last day, Alto and Dastmalchi had lost their last chips. By 4:10 P.M., Mayfield and Johnston were broke. Only the two Dallas men remained. Meanwhile, Cloutier, who over the years has sat at many a poker table with Smith, had jumped into the lead with $952,000. Smith held $448,000. But on the tenth hand of their head-to-head contest, Smith's two pairs — aces and kings — beat Cloutier's two pairs — aces and nines — and Smith pulled in $1,222,000 in cash and chips. It's said to be the largest poker pot in Las Vegas history. A few hands later, Cloutier recovered $500,000 with a flush, and the game lapsed into a war of attrition. For the next twenty-six hands, Smith and Cloutier swapped small pots of $40,000 to $50,000 each.

Then, on the thirty-sixth hand of the day, Cloutier looked at his face-down cards — an ace and a three — and made his move. He shoved his entire remaining bankroll — $319,000 — to the middle of the table. Smith immediately matched the bet. Since Cloutier could make no more bets, the dealer turned up all five cards of the "flop" at once. Three fives, a nine, and a king. A tiny smile flickered at Smith's lips. He flipped over his hole cards. A pair of threes. Three fives plus two threes. A full house.

"I won it in four hours," Smith says. "The last day usually takes twice that long."

Ron "Cold Eye" Calhoun, Steve "Oklahoma Slim" Knickmeyer, and Ron "Sleeve Card" Smith are crowded into the backseat. Ray "El Gordo" Herndon is driving. I'm riding beside him.

"He's made his living playing poker since 1958," Sleeve Card says. "And he's only fifty-one."

"He puts on his pants one leg at a time," I reply.

"Right," Cold Eye grunts.

We are the elite of our Thursday night poker crowd. No one has yet won $700,000 in our game. I hold our record — $118 in a single night. But we consider ourselves pretty good. I had informed Bill Smith of that when I called him to issue the challenge.

He started telling me his troubles. "I was supposed to have a free suite at the Golden Nugget for two weeks," he said, "but I had to get out of Vegas the day after I won. There were a lot of kooks out there. They kept calling me . . ."

"I'm not a kook," I said. "This is serious."

Smith said nothing.

"We think we're pretty good," I said.

"Well, maybe we can work something out," he said.

"When?" I asked.

"I can't today," he said. "I've got a poker game."

Something in the way he said "poker game" ruffled me. What did he think I was proposing? Old Maid? I stifled a smart retort. "Then when?" I asked.

"Tomorrow," he said. "Since I'm playing today, I'll be sleeping late, so we'd better make it in the afternoon. Two o'clock."

"Where?" I asked.

"You name it."

"Your house?"

"Fine. But don't tell anybody where I live. The kooks. . . ."

Tension is building in the car. It could be sliced with a knife. "It's like playing tennis with John McEnroe," I say.

"Or boxing Larry Holmes," Oklahoma Slim says.

Cold Eye giggles.

"Hey, it's a game of chance," I say. "He could be unlucky."

The Smith house is the one with the For Sale sign in front. I punch the doorbell. Smith lets us in. "Professional gambler" is written all over him. Skinny. Dark hair. Pencil mustache. Silk shirt with pictures of lions on it. A gold king of hearts hanging from a gold chain around his neck. A pretty blonde wife named Cie. He's smoking an unfiltered Camel in a holder. Drinking a Bud. I introduce my companions. They bow and scrape like Smith is the Pope or something.

Smith offers us a beer. We accept. We sit down at a round glass table in the kitchen. We chew the fat, getting acquainted. The table is littered with books about poker. Maybe Smith has been studying up for us. "How did you do in your game yesterday?" I ask.

"I won," he says.

"How much?"

"Twelve hundred dollars."

I look around for a poker table. I don't see one. Smith starts talking about kooks again.

"They thought I had that whole $1,400,000 in my pocket," he says. "I was getting a lot of bad calls. I told this partner of mine, 'Let's hire ourselves a jet and get out of here.' We went to the cage and got $487,000 in cash and put it in paper sacks, like grocery bags. And I told Jack Binion, the owner of the Horseshoe, where the tournament was, I said, 'I want two of the biggest, meanest security guards you've got.' And he said, 'You've got 'em.' They drove us out to the airport in a limousine and put us and our sacks on a Learjet, and we took off for Lubbock to visit some friends. When we landed, my wife said, 'Boy, it's sure nice to be back in Texas.' And the pilot said, 'It sounds like you guys didn't do very good in Las Vegas.' And I said, 'We sure didn't.'"

My companions laugh nervously. I mention something about getting the game under way.

"Oh, we're not actually going to *play*," Smith says. "I never gamble in my own house. I'm just going to give you a demonstration."

"Look," I say. "We're loaded. We've each got a hundred dollars of company money in our pockets. We came here to make it grow."

Smith regards me with cool respect. "I don't even keep a deck of cards in the house," he says.

El Gordo has brought a couple of decks of his own, and a rack of chips. He gets them from the car. Smith glances at Cie. She shrugs. We clear the kitchen table. Cie covers it with a gold table cloth. We count out the chips. Smith deals the first hand of Hold 'Em. It's 2:30 P.M.

"If you think of it as money. . .," he says. "Well, when it got down to me and T.J., we were anteing a car. The first bet was a small house. The next bet was a big house. You just can't think of it that way. I had that money stacked in front of me in cash, in $25,000 boodles. There was a million dollars in cash on the table, and $400,000 in chips. I said to myself, 'Now, you can't think of this as money. If you do, you're gone.' You've got to think of it as just a way of keeping score."

"Sure, fella," I'm thinking to myself. "You think your way, and I'll think mine. To me, this is money."

The first two hands don't amount to much. I fold them both. On the third hand, Lady Luck smiles. The "flop" gives me a queen-high flush. I bet big. El Gordo raises. I raise back. He calls. I flip my hole cards and reach toward the pot.

"Wait," El Gordo says. He flips his hole cards. He has a flush, too. Ace-high. I count my remaining chips. Already, I'm down eighty-eight dollars.

On the fourth hand, the Lady smiles again. I wind up with two pairs — aces and nines. I reach for the pot. "Wait," Cold Eye says. He holds aces and nines, too. We divide the pot between us. It's a small one. Too small. Then I remember that

T.J. Cloutier lost that $1,222,000 pot with aces and nines, so I'm a lot luckier than he was.

On the fifth hand, I have to fold early. I still have ten dollars of the company's money. Just enough to see the first "flop" of the next hand. It looks promising. I've got a good shot at a straight. I use seven dollars of my own money to stay in. But I've stopped thinking of it has money. I think of it as two cheeseburgers. The second and third "flops" fail me. I fold.

"In 1958," Smith says, "I was working for Humble Oil Company as a draftsman for the whole sum of $330 a month. I had a new home and three kids. This was in Roswell, New Mexico. And at the Elks Club there they played poker every afternoon, starting at two o'clock. There was a very wealthy attorney who played every day, and he lost every day. But I didn't get off work till 4:30, and when I would get over to the game, there wouldn't be a seat open till that attorney left at six every evening. And when he left, well, the game wasn't any good. So I said, 'I can't handle this. I've got to quit my job and be over there at two o'clock every day.' So I quit my job, and I was there every day at two o'clock. I had me a seat when they started. And I made more money than I did with the oil company. So I never did find another job. I just kept playing."

I have enough money to ante the seventh hand. I look at my hole cards. A pair of kings. I pull out my wallet and bet four dollars. I would like to bet more, but I have to conserve my now-meager private reserve. The first "flop" gives me a pair of fives. I bet five dollars, and everybody folds. I win, but it's a tiny victory.

I fold the eighth hand quickly. So do Sleeve Card, Oklahoma Slim, and Cold Eye. El Gordo stays. Smith turns over the first "flop" and bets $100. El Gordo blinks and folds. I smile. The fool. Who does he think he's playing against?

My hole cards for the ninth hand are an eight and a ten. I call the bet, but can't afford to raise. The first "flop" gives me another eight, but I just call again. The second "flop" is another eight. This is my hand. I can taste it. I bet all I can afford. A couple of cheeseburgers. Everybody folds but Smith. This is my

chance. I'm, finally going to get to the champ. He bets. I raise.
He calls. "Three eights," I announce.

"Three eights what?" he asks.

"Three eights ten," I announce.

"Three eights jack," he says.

Depression is setting in. My hole cards for the tenth hand are
a pair of eights, but I no longer trust eights. The stack of chips
in front of me is very small. I call the bet, but no more. The
"flop" gives me a pair of kings. I win, but the pot is pathetic.

"The longest game I ever played was four days and four
nights," Smith says. "It was in Roswell, more than twenty-five
years ago. We were sitting in folding steel chairs in an upstairs
room. The old man I was playing with was losing, and he
didn't want to quit. Finally, after four days and four nights, I
said, 'Look. Let's go sleep for eighteen hours, and then I'll play
you some more. He finally agreed to it. I had to grab the rail
with both hands to go down the stairs. I got home and went to
bed, and I was so tired I couldn't go to sleep. I can't play that
long now. If I play all night now, I'm just give out. I try not to
play over eight hours a day, because I lose my concentration
after that."

I sneak a peek at my watch. We've played less than an hour,
and I'm on the ropes. I fold the eleventh hand early. And the
twelfth. And the thirteenth.

On the fourteenth hand, I have three eights again. I win, but
since I had so little to bet, the pot is another small one. On the
fifteenth, I fold, and Smith beats El Gordo with a better pair.
The sixteenth gives me a pair of eights.

Eights again. Maybe eights are my lucky hand today. I go for
it. El Gordo and Sleeve Card have a pair of queens each. They
split the pot.

My palms are clammy. It's do-or-die time. My hole cards for
the seventeenth hand are two clubs. Not great, but possible. I
call the bet and stay in. The first "flop" makes my heart sing. A
heart and two clubs. One more club needed for a flush, and
two cards still to come. How can I possibly lose? I raise the
bettor. The second flop. It's black. My heart jumps. I lean for a

better look. It's a spade. But I've got it. I know it in my gut. I raise the bettor. Smith turns the third and last "flop." It's the nine of diamonds.

"That card is called the Curse of Scotland," Smith says. "A long time ago, the king of England was playing cards, and he was losing. He was in a bad mood. And a messenger came to him and said, 'Your majesty, the Scots are in rebellion.' Well, the king was holding the nine of diamonds in his hand, and he took it and wrote a message on it: 'Kill 10,000 Scots.' He gave it to the messenger, and the English army went out and killed 10,000 Scots. If the king had been winning, maybe he would have had only 5,000 Scots killed. Anyway, ever since then, the nine of diamonds has been called the Curse of Scotland."

I understand the King of England completely. "I'm finished," I say through clenched teeth. "I'm down to stay."

Sleeve Card gives me a smirk. "How deep were you into your own money?" he asks.

"Forty dollars," I confess.

El Gordo looks at Oklahoma Slim and snickers.

Smith lays two $20 bills in front of me. "Here," he says. "I don't want anybody losing their own money at my house."

"Nothing doing," I say gallantly. "I challenged you to a real poker game, and I meant it."

"You take it," he says. "I won't have anybody losing his own money in my house. It wouldn't be good."

I pick up the two bills and meekly stick them in my pocket. Smith asks Cie for another beer. He's notorious for that, drinking while he plays. Most professionals won't drink at the table. "For the World Series, they work out, eat wheat germ, do all kinds of stuff to get in shape," Smith says. "Me, I go to the bar." He promised Cie he wouldn't drink bourbon during the tournament this year. So for four solid days, while he was playing his way toward $700,000, he had a glass of Budweiser beside him.

I call for another beer, too, and try to relax. The game quickly gets dull without me. In a few minutes, Oklahoma Slim's pair of kings loses to El Gordo's flush. "I'm gone," Oklahoma Slim says. "I'm broke." He gives me a sheepish smile.

The new hand is dealt. Smith looks at his hole cards. "I'm going to tell you what I've got," he says. "It's a Kokomo Slim. If you know what a Kokomo Slim is, you know what I'm holding."

A Kokomo Slim is a king and an eight, it turns out. A deuce and a three are Nits and Lice. A five and a ten are a Woolworth's. A deuce and a six are an Aynesworth. A three and a six are a Blocky. All the pros know these things.

Suddenly, Sleeve Card gets green around the gills. His two pairs — eights and threes — are beat by El Gordo's flush. He's down to stay. Only El Gordo, Cold Eye and Smith are left in the game. El Gordo and Smith have huge piles of cash and chips in front of them.

"I gotta tell you guys something," Smith says. "I gotta start playing poker now."

It's 4:20 p.m. The game is only an hour and fifty minutes old. Smith deals. Cold Eye folds. Smith bets a hundred dollars. El Gordo folds. El Gordo deals. Cold Eye checks. Smith bets twenty dollars. The others fold. On the next three hands, they fold on Smith's twenty-five dollar bet, on Smith's six dollar raise of Cold Eye's five dollars bet, and on Smith's $100 bet. On the next hand, Cold Eye makes his move. After El Gordo folds, Cold Eye calls Smith's hundred dollar bet. Smith turns up an ace-high diamond flush. Cold Eye is finished.

"How do your children feel about you playing poker for a living instead of working?" El Gordo asks.

Smith gives him a sharp stare. "Who says playing poker isn't work?" he says. "A psychiatrist told me a poker player burns up more calories than a ditch digger. Because of the tension and the long hours."

Smith doesn't seem tense. On the second hand of his head-to-head contest with El Gordo, he starts betting twenty dollars on the hole cards and twenty-five dollars after the first "flop." Then a hundred dollars on the hole cards. El Gordo folds ten consecutive hands. His pile of cash is dwindling. Then he calls Smith's twenty dollar bet and wins a small pot. Suddenly he seems to be adjusting to the new pace. He wins a few more.

Then he calls Smith's hundred-dollar bet on the first "flop," and Smith's bet of two hundred on the second "flop." And El Gordo wins with two pairs.

"I've seen softer things than you in a blacksmith shop," Smith says. El Gordo looks at me and grins. He thinks he's hot stuff. On the next hand, Smith bets twenty on the hole cards. El Gordo calls. Smith bets a hundred on the first "flop." El Gordo calls. Smith bets four hundred on the second flop. El Gordo folds. The grin disappears.

His opening bet on the next hand is a modest five dollars. Smith raises a hundred. El Gordo calls. Then Smith bets a hundred on the first "flop." El Gordo calls. After the second "flop," a pair of tens and a pair of fours are lying face up on the table. Smith bets four hundred. El Gordo folds. His cash pile is disappearing fast.

The first two bets of the twenty-first head-to-head hand are modest. Then El Gordo bets a hundred on the second flop. Smith sizes him up. "How much money have you got in front of you?" he asks.

El Gordo counts it. "A hundred and ninety dollars," he replies.

"Well, that's what I bet," Smith says. He lays a stack of bills in the center of the table.

El Gordo gets red in the face, hesitates, then shoves the rest of his money into the pot and shows his hole cards. He holds a five-high straight. Smith flips his hole cards. He has a six-high straight.

The game is over. It's 5:30 P.M. In exactly three hours, Smith has picked us clean. I suspect that he could have done the same job in fifteen minutes.

"Bill," I say, "what's your advice to somebody who wants to play poker for a living?"

"Don't do it," he says.

During the long ride home, we glow. Sure, we lost. How else could it have ended? But the magnificence of the thing we have done fills us with joy. For three glorious hours, we have sat at the same table with the greatest poker player in the world.

Fondly, we replay in our minds the hands we won and those we almost won. We will never forget those hours. And so long as one of us has the strength to deal a hand and tell a story, our wives, children, grandchildren, and poker buddies won't forget them, either. We won't let them.

"Did you hear what he called me?" El Gordo says. "He called me an iron man."

"Shut up and drive," I reply.

[June 1985]

A divorced father has to find ways to be close to his children. For several years when they were children, my boys and I found a special kind of closeness at a cabin on Lake Whitney, Texas. My friend Donald Eastland, the owner of the cabin, would give me the key, and Ted and Pat and I would just be together there during the boys' spring break from school.

This piece moved on the Los Angeles Times-Washington Post *wire and appeared in an amazing number of newspapers in the United States and Canada. I got letters from fathers all over the continent, saying they liked what I had written, and one from a woman who called me a "blockhead."*

THE FISHING TRIP

Throughout the recorded millenia and surely for countless years before history began, women have bludgeoned, black-mailed, sweet-talked, and seduced their way toward the domestication of the male and the civilization of society.

It isn't from their fathers and uncles and brothers that boys learn to bathe, shave, hold jobs, mow lawns, hang wallpaper, build churches, and not make rude noises at the dinner table. Boys are born to be dirty and lazy and irreverent.

Girls, on the other hand, are made to supervise the creation of a better world. They're born knowing it. And very early they learn that the *raison d'etre* of their beauty is to lure the male into the irresistible web of softness and sweetness, remodel him into something that doesn't cause a stench, and harness him for the construction of a more comfortable nest and a gentler culture. "Otherwise," generations of mothers warn generations of daughters, "you and I shall wind up scraping buffalo hides again."

Thus we've been brought from the Stone Age to the Computer Age.

The men have been remarkably agreeable to it all. Oh, in stag company we look back upon our days of youth and singleness with dewy eyes. We exhume from our romanticized and exaggerated memories the raunchy exploits and adventures of our unfettered barbarism, before the hand and voice of some woman — or perhaps several women — brought us to heel. We smile. We sigh. But, when pressed, only the terminally immature claim to want to return to those days and that life.

Maybe it's because our brags are lies or only half-truths. Maybe we remember — but won't admit — that behind our old wildness was a loneliness, an incompleteness too desperate to mention. Or maybe it's because we're really as lazy as women think we are and just can't muster the will to resist domestication. Or maybe, despite our strutting and bragging, we secretly *like* candlelight dinners better than gnawing bones around the campfire, secretly *prefer* an everyday job and its steady paycheck to the hazardous thrills of the wild.

In even the most domesticated male soul, however, vestiges of the old instincts remain. And it's important that their sons should know it. They ought to have the opportunity from time to time to see their sires stripped of the trappings of domesticity, of civilization, of duty, of responsibility. It's healthy for sons to know that behind the facade of fatherness still resides a savage boy who is capable of running away from the settlements in search of adventure and socially unacceptable behavior. It reassures them somehow about their own growing up and their inevitable capitulation to the rules made by women.

My sons spend a lot of time around women. They live in another state with their mother, my ex. Some of their teachers are women. They spend parts of their vacations with their grandmother and great-grandmother and parts with my wife and me. The women make most of the rules in all their houses, and they aren't tyrants. They love my sons, and my sons love them and enjoy their company. But there's one time a year that we reserve for ourselves, a time for maleness in all its gross excesses. We call it The Fishing Trip. It occurs in the spring at Lake Whitney, Texas, at a cabin owned by a generous friend, and no women are invited. Our annual trip there is hardly a return to the cave or the bedouin tent. The cabin has three bedrooms, two baths, a kitchen, a phone, a comfortable living room with a TV, stereo, fireplace, and well-stocked library. There's a sun deck, a basketball hoop, some bicycles, a couple of porch swings, some lawn chairs, and lots of trees with bird feeders hanging in them. But while we're there, the rules by which we live the rest of our lives are suspended, and we arrive with a howl of primitive glee. It's hard to explain exactly what goes on there. We fish, of course, but the boys' spring break comes in March, when Texas weather can be cold, rainy, windy, or perfect, so our luck is never predictable. We sit on Soldier's Bluff and murder dozens of minnows, lose two or three lures each to entanglements, and endure or enjoy whatever the weather is. Sometimes we catch something. Sometimes we get bored with fishing and fly a kite. Sometimes we go back to the cabin and shoot baskets.

We go to one of the little stores along the highway and buy supplies that aren't nutritious. Beer, pop, chips, hot dogs, doughnuts, baloney, Wonder Bread, marshmallows. When we feel the need of a "real" meal, we heat a can of chili or scramble some eggs. If the evening is cool, we build a fire in the fireplace, play penny-ante poker into the wee hours, watch a trashy movie on TV. Nobody says, "It's time to go to bed." Each stumbles off whenever he's ready. And we get up the next day whenever we want to. We wipe our noses on our sleeves and our hands on our jeans. We walk through mud in our sneakers. We wear the same socks and underwear as long as they feel comfortable. We belch and break wind without apologizing.

I suppose The Fishing Trip would be the perfect time to pass on fatherly advice and wisdom to my sons. Every year, I think that's one of the purposes of our journey. But I've never come up with a piece of advice or wisdom that I've felt I could volunteer without sounding silly, and the boys have never asked me a question that required a particularly deep answer. Our conversation is about ordinary things. Sometimes we don't say anything at all for hours. I've found no opportunities to lecture.

This year, since both boys have become tall and are growing hair on their legs, I thought I might tell them about girls and the domesticating influences that females are going to bring to bear upon them before long. Their days as barbarians are numbered, I intended to tell them, and there's really nothing to be done about it. They won't even *want* to do anything about it. It's the way the whole human arrangement works.

But after they're domesticated, I intended to say, they should reserve a little time for a beer with the boys, a night at the poker table, a trip to the lake. They should always have a time to stink and a time to howl, a time to brag and a time to strut, outside the presence of women. A little barbarism is the pepper in the soup of civilization, I intended to say. I didn't say it, of course, and we caught no fish. We didn't even get a nibble.

A few days later, when the boys called to tell me their plane had arrived safely in their own city, I told them I was sorry that the fishing was so bad this year.

"That's not the important thing," one of them said.

Maybe they already know.

[April 1984]

At this writing, in 1989, Federal District Judge Barefoot Sanders is one of only a handful of Kennedy-Johnson Democrats still holding positions of power in Texas. He's the only one in Dallas.

Unlike most who have made a career of politics and government, he's quiet and self-effacing. He blushes when people say nice things about him. He refuses to talk about any case that's pending in his court. He has been a frustration for reporters, especially those assigned to cover the Dallas Independent School District and its unending battle in his court over desegregation.

So when I called his office and asked for an extensive interview about his life and career, I was surprised that he agreed to it.

We spent several hours together in his office, quietly discussing a great number of things. I remember that afternoon with pleasure, and of the many profiles I've written over the years of people famous, people infamous, and people obscure, this remains one of my favorites.

It's simply the story of a decent public man.

THE JUDGE

Fifty years ago, while Texas was celebrating its centennial at its new Fair Park, Harold Barefoot Sanders, Jr., first came to the attention of the public.

"They held the contest on Kids' Day," he says. "Kids could get into the fair for a nickel on Kids' Day, which was every Tuesday, and it cost just three cents to ride the streetcar out there. The competition was based on the number of freckles. They put this magnifying glass around on your face. I remember they said they saw 1,300 freckles in one of my ears and 414 on my nose. How they figured that out, I don't know. I ended up with 5,000-and-something freckles."

That was enough to win the boys' competition, but the judges found that one of the girls had even more freckles than

Sanders. She was named the Texas State Fair Freckle Queen.
"One of my prizes was an all-day date with the Freckle Queen,"
Sanders says. "We got to go to all the interesting places on the
midway, and we had lunch with the midgets, and we got our
picture in the paper. I remember I was really embarrassed
about that for some reason. I don't know why. I was eleven
years old."

Sanders has spent a lot of time in the public spotlight since
then, as a state legislator, a hard-campaigning but unlucky candidate for higher public office, a high-ranking attorney in the
Justice Department, and a White House aide. Since 1979, when
President Jimmy Carter named him to the federal district bench
in Dallas, he has been in the news even more frequently than
he was before, usually for threatening, cajoling, leading, and
driving the Dallas Independent School District one slow step
after another toward a legally desegregated school system.

The first DISD desegregation suit — called *Bell v. Rippy* —
was filed in federal court in 1955, less than a year after the U.S
Supreme Court handed down its historic *Brown v. Board of
Education* decision declaring racially segregated public schools
to be unconstitutional. Also in 1955, the Supreme Court
ordered segregated school systems to desegregate "with all
deliberate speed."

"Since then, in most places," Sanders says, "the emphasis has
been on deliberation, and not speed." Dallas has been one of
those places. Three more suits have been filed against the
school district since 1955, all claiming racial segregation still
exists in the Dallas schools, and so far the courts have agreed.

The current case — a class action suit filed in 1970 by Sam
Tasby, a father of schoolchildren — had dragged on for eleven
years already when U.S. District Judge William Taylor, who
had presided over it since its beginning, unexpectedly withdrew.
The names of the five remaining Dallas federal judges were
placed in a hat, Barefoot Sanders' name was drawn out, and
*Eddie Mitchell Tasby et al v. Dr. Nolan Estes, general superin-
tendent of the Dallas Independent School District et el.* was
transferred to his court. Suddenly Sanders had the power and

the responsibility to place the education of hundreds of thousands of children under the protection of the Constitution.

"I was very nervous," he says. "I was scared. I hadn't had anything to do with school desegregation before. So I just closed the doors and tried to figure out what was going on. That involved a lot of reading. There's a huge body of case law now involving school desegregation. I read hundreds of cases. But it all boils down to about a dozen Supreme Court decisions. They establish the principles, and the main principle is that every school district has to achieve the maximum desegregation that's practical. That's what a unanimous Supreme Court says the Constitution says, so it's the law. A lot of people have a hell of a time accepting that, but there it is."

Forcing the DISD to comply with the law has been no easier for Sanders than it was for Taylor, and his patience sometimes wears thin in the courtroom. His rebukes for what he considers delays and lackadaisical compliance with his orders sometimes have been caustic. Once, in attempting to cite a case to compare with the molasses pace of *Tasby v. Estes*, Sanders reached outside the law into literature, likening it to the case of *Jarndyce and Jarndyce* in Charles' Dickens' blistering anti-lawyer novel, *Bleak House:* "Innumerable children have been born into the cause; innumerable young people have married into it: innumerable old people have died out of it. Scores of persons have deliriously found themselves made parties in *Jarndyce and Jarndyce* without knowing how or why." And last month, his voice trembling with anger, Sanders fined the DISD ten thousand dollars for missing two deadlines he had set for hiring the teachers for three new education centers in West Dallas. "This plan is not going to work unless I have the school district's attention," he said, shaking a finger at present DISD Supt. Linus Wright, "and I don't think I have the school district's attention."

He then suspended the fine, provided that DISD meet all court-ordered deadlines for the next six months.

The education centers — sometimes called "super schools" — are remedial education centers offering smaller classes, extended school days, special tutorial and after-school programs for

children in their own neighborhoods. Three have opened so far
in South Dallas and three are authorized to open in West
Dallas. Eventually, there probably will be nine of the centers in
the two areas. The idea for them arose from discussions among
the plaintiffs, the school administrators, and the judge. They're
the latest attempt to provide quality education in a school system where population is now 78 percent minority and busing is
losing its effectiveness as a desegregation tool.

Although some black parents claim the "super schools" are
part of an effort to "resegregate" a school district that has never
been desegregated, Sanders believes they provide the best
chance now available to comply with the Supreme Court's
demands. "It is pointless," he has said, "to bus minority students
from the minority neighborhoods in West Dallas to attend
predominantly minority schools in North Dallas. And I think
the willingness to establish the centers is a credit to the community."

There's nothing fancy or obtuse about Sanders' rulings, either
orally in his courtroom or in his written decisions. They are
frank, forthright, and unvarnished. And there's still something
of the freckle-faced kid about him, something in the way he
runs his fingers through his graying red hair or in the slants
and angles of his lanky body as he listens to arguments in his
courtroom that creates an impression of Tom Sawyer grown up
to be a judge. As he sits behind his big desk in his chambers in
the late afternoon, drinking decaffeinated coffee from a
Styrofoam cup, smoking a cigar, unwinding from his day on
the bench, talking softly — almost shyly — about his life, the
name Barefoot and the rustic image it calls to mind somehow
seem to fit him. But the image is misleading. He isn't a simple
country boy now, and he never has been.

The first Harold Barefoot Sanders — the judge's father —
was a well-known Dallas lawyer. He called himself Harold and
passed his whole name on to his eldest son, who didn't know
what to do with it. "Barefoot is an old Anglo-Saxon name,"
Sanders says. "It was my grandmother's maiden name. But
when I was growing up, I tried to keep it a secret. I was known

through high school by my initials, H.B. Every now and then, somebody would find out about my middle name and poke fun at it. I was very embarrassed about it."

Although hardly rural, Dallas was a smaller place in those days. Barefoot, his parents, and his younger brother and sister lived five blocks from North Dallas High School, which is an inner-city school now, but wasn't many miles from the edge of the city then. "Dallas ended around Southwestern Boulevard," Sanders says. "I had a .22 rifle, and my dad would take me out to that area, and it was countryside, and we could target practice. The streetcar line ended at Daniel and Hillcrest, near SMU. I used to ride the streetcar out there, because I took piano lessons from a lady in that area. Those were good days to be growing up. In some ways they were the best times. My mother and father had come from backgrounds which required them to work their way up through the world. They were strong Democrats. They had a great sense of fairness and were strong for the underdog."

A close friend and political ally of the Sanders family in those days was a lawyer named Sarah T. Hughes, who many years later would become the first woman to administer the oath of office to a U.S. president. She also would administer the oath of office to Barefoot Sanders when he joined her on the federal bench — a result, perhaps, of a decision Sanders made in 1942, when he graduated from North Dallas High.

"I was about to enroll in the University of Texas," he says, "and the university was a big place. It was hard for anybody to be noticed there. So I decided Barefoot would be a good name to go by, after all. It would set me apart. It would give people something to remember about me."

He was right. He immediately was elected cheerleader. But there was a war on, so after only a year at UT, he joined the Navy. He served on a destroyer in the Caribbean and the Pacific for three years, earned credit for some college courses while he was aboard, got discharged in 1946, returned to UT, ran for cheerleader again and got elected again. Then he got ambitious. "In 1948, I decided to run for president of the

Student Association," he says. "And I thought maybe I could really use my name to my advantage. So I made some stencils in the shape of bare feet and got some buckets of whitewash, and real early in the morning before the election, my friends and I scattered over the campus and painted bare feet on all the sidewalks leading to the polls. Nobody could walk anywhere that day without being reminded of Barefoot. And I won."

The presidency of the UT Student Association has been the springboard for many a political career in Texas, and so it was for Sanders. He graduated from the UT law school in 1950 and spent a couple of years establishing a practice in Dallas. In 1952 he married Jan Scurlock — a Dallas native whom he had dated at UT — and announced his candidacy for the Texas House of Representatives. He declared himself against a state sales tax or a state income tax and in favor of a tax cut, an economical and businesslike government, higher educational standards, a pay raise for teachers, and an investigation into the need for reforms in the penal and juvenile detention systems — all pretty standard Texas political stuff in 1952, as it still is in 1986.

But 1952 was no ordinary political year in Texas. For more than twenty years, the federal government had been fighting with the state over the ownership of the oil-rich tidelands off the Texas Gulf coast. The federal government claimed that they belonged to the United States, as the tidelands of the other coastal states did. Texas argued that they belonged to Texas, since the Treaty of Annexation, under which Texas joined the Union, stated that Texas — unlike the other states — would retain ownership of all its public lands. President Harry Truman had vetoed a bill that would have settled the dispute in Texas' favor, and in the presidential election of 1952, the tidelands were a hot issue in the state. When Adlai Stevenson declared himself in agreement with Truman, and Dwight Eisenhower declared himself in agreement with Texas, the state's popular Democratic governor, Allan Shivers, declared himself in favor of Eisenhower for the presidency.

The tiny Texas Republican Party was jubilant. "They were cross-filing," Sanders says. "They would put a Democratic candidate on the ballot as the Republican candidate, too, if he would say he was going to vote for Eisenhower. Nearly everybody did that. Nearly everybody ran on the general election ballot as both a Democrat and a Republican. But I didn't. I said I was going to vote the Democratic ticket. Adlai Stevenson didn't help me any, though. He came in here and told everybody why he was against Texas having the tidelands."

Texas went for Eisenhower, and in 1953 he kept his promise and signed a bill acknowledging Texas as the owner of its tidelands. Since then, the law has meant hundreds of millions of dollars in offshore oil revenue for the state government. After Ike's victory, being Republican suddenly became respectable in Texas — especially in Dallas, where Bruce Alger was elected to Congress on Eisenhower's coattails to become the first GOP congressman from Texas since Reconstruction. Sanders survived the Eisenhower landslide and went to the Legislature. He proved popular enough to be reelected in '54 and '56, and decided to try for a bigger prize — Alger's House seat — in '58.

Dallas County was a single congressional district in those days. In population it was one of the largest districts in the nation. "Henry Wade had lost to Alger in 1956, a presidential election year, and I figured that the popularity of Eisenhower had hurt Wade," Sanders says. "I figured that without Eisenhower on the ticket, Dallas County would return to the Democratic fold and I could beat Alger."

Sanders' opponent in the Democratic primary was Joe Pool, a conservative running on a blatantly segregationist platform. He called Sanders "a loyal supporter of the integration movement" and claimed that in eleven votes on six segregation bills during his years in the legislature, Sanders had voted for integration nine times and against only twice. Sanders' response was as liberal as a Southern candidate could get and still hope to win: "I support the Dallas Independent School District and all other local authorities in their efforts to work out in a peaceful, lawful, and orderly manner the very difficult problems created by the U.S. Supreme Court decision on segregation. I oppose the use of force as well as violence."

He beat Pool in the primary, and he and his wife conducted one of the most exhaustive — and exhausting — general election campaigns in Dallas County history. For months, the couple spent more than twenty hours a day shaking hands, handing out leaflets, meeting with groups of voters, and making radio and TV speeches. "Alger was very ideological," Sanders says. "He was running against the federal government. He hated the federal government. That was his big issue. Federal money was evil, and he didn't want any coming into Dallas. He didn't want it for school lunch programs, or for urban redevelopment, or even to build a new federal courthouse. And he was running against Sam Rayburn to a considerable extent. That wouldn't have been a very popular stand anywhere but Dallas. Considering what Mr. Rayburn had done to help Dallas over the years, I thought it was singularly ungrateful. So I tried to make the issue being an effective congressman for Dallas County.

"But I had misread the tea leaves. Dallas had become *very* conservative. *Very* conservative. Alger was the prevailing wind here at the time. It was a very hard race physically, and it was a fairly close race. But Alger had a lot of money and I didn't, and he outdid me. And once you've run a political race and done everything you can to win, there's no use looking back and thinking, 'There's something else I could have done.' There's *nothing* I could have done that would have changed that race. That's just the way Dallas was then."

Dallas hadn't changed much two years later, when Sanders signed on as Dallas County cochairman — with Sarah Hughes — of the Kennedy-Johnson presidential campaign. Right-wing emotion ran so high in that one that a claque of Alger's screaming female supporters spat on Lyndon and Lady Bird Johnson in the Adolphus Hotel lobby.

Nor had it changed much three years after that. On November 22, 1963, Sanders was the U.S. attorney in Dallas and Sarah Hughes was a federal district judge. They had been appointed by President Kennedy on Vice President Johnson's

recommendation. "I wasn't in favor of the visit," Sanders says,
"but nobody asked me. I think President Kennedy was determined to come down here. A lot of us were apprehensive
because of what had happened to Stevenson the month before."
(Adlai Stevenson, the U.S. ambassador to the United Nations,
had been hit in the head by a picket sign, swung by an anti-
U.N. demonstrator in Dallas.) "We were afraid some kind of
unseemly demonstration might happen. But I haven't run into a
person yet who expected there would be a shot fired."

A haze of pain clouds Sanders' face as he recalls the events of
that day. "I was on the welcoming committee at Love Field, and
I rode into town on the White House bus," he says. "And we
were right down in front of the old county jail, and we
stopped, and I couldn't see around the corner. We were stopped
for two or three minutes, and then we rounded the corner and
got on the freeway, and I could see the convertible ahead of us,
and it was going at quite a clip, but I had no idea what had
happened. We got out at the Trade Mart, where the luncheon
was to be, and they wouldn't let us in. The whole Trade Mart
was closed. But I knew one of the policemen, and he let me in.
And when I got inside, I started picking up the rumors. So I
then asked a policeman to flag a car, and I came back down to
my office. The plane — Air Force One — called me and told
me to contact Judge Hughes. I tried to reach her at her office,
but she wasn't there. I called her at home and told her where
the plane was, and she headed out. She knew what had happened. She had been at the Trade Mart with my wife. But she
didn't have an oath of office to administer to Johnson. She told
me to have the oath for her when she got to the plane and she
would call. I was looking for the oath, and in Washington the
Justice Department was looking for it, and finally a fellow up
there said, 'Why not look in the Constitution?' And that's where
we found it. Judge Hughes never called me, though. Somebody
had called her from Washington.

"All the pressure in my office that day was on who did it and
how to find them. We were drafting various forms of com-
plaints that we could use to hold people who might be arrested.

We didn't know anything at the time. There were some false alarms. There was a man arrested down at the site, and he was brought in, and people were really getting after him, but he had nothing to do with it. He was just picked out of the crowd. And there was another fellow picked up who was just going to Fort Worth. There were three or four incidents like that. Then the police picked up on that Tippit thing (Dallas Police Office J.D. Tippit had been shot to death in Oak Cliff by Lee Harvey Oswald), and that turned out to be the hard lead. As it turned out, the state had jurisdiction in the case, but I wanted to make sure of that, too. So I stayed at my office all that night."

In 1965, after Johnson had been elected to the White House in his own right, his attorney general, Ramsey Clark, called Sanders to Washington and made him an assistant deputy attorney general. He was promoted to assistant attorney general a year later and put in charge of the civil division of the Justice Department. Then, in 1967, Johnson named him the legislative counsel on the White House staff. His job was to try to get Johnson's legislative program — especially civil rights legislation — through Congress.

"I had known Johnson reasonably well — I won't say closely — since my days in the Legislature," Sanders says. "I was with him some during the 1956 campaign when he came back to Texas to campaign for the Democratic ticket, and he made a speech in Dallas in 1958. I was around him quite a bit in 1960 during the campaign. And he was the one who got me my appointment as U.S. attorney. I had been down to the ranch a few times for social affairs. I won't claim I was a close friend, but I was a good friend. I was loyal to him at that time, and I still am. He was a very demanding fellow to work for, particularly in the legislative field, because he knew the business better than anybody. He was always interested in everything I was doing, but there wasn't anything I could do that was new to him, so I couldn't impress him. And he didn't hesitate to call at any hour of the day or night about something. He often did. But he drove himself as hard as he drove others. My experiences with him really brought home to me the need to be pragmatic about things. I already felt deeply about civil rights, and Johnson's attitude was 'Instead of just talking about it, let's find some way to do it.' He also taught me the need for loyalty in politics. Working with him, you ended up knowing that if you were really *his* friend, he was really *your* friend.

"I think he has been treated very unkindly by history. He did an awful lot of things that a lot of other people just talked about. I hope that will change someday, but it always depends on who's writing the books. He enacted the Democratic plat-form into law, and the Democrats have had trouble ever since, trying to figure out what to run on."

In the last days of the Johnson administration, the president appointed Sanders to be a judge on the District of Columbia Circuit Court, but Everett Dirksen and other Republicans in the Senate refused to confirm him and several other last-minute Johnson appointments, leaving their posts open for the incom-ing President Richard Nixon to fill. Sanders returned to Dallas and reentered his law practice, but it wasn't long before the political bug bit again. In November 1971 he announced his candidacy in the '72 Democratic primary for the U.S. Senate seat held by John Tower, the first Republican elected to statewide office since Reconstruction. A few weeks later, former U.S. Senator Ralph Yarborough, who had been unhorsed in 1970 by Lloyd Bentsen, announced that he, too, wanted Tower's job. So did three lesser candidates, who won enough votes to require a runoff between Sanders and Yarborough. Yarborough had outpolled Sanders in the first primary, but Sanders won the runoff. Not that it mattered that year.

Sanders says, "Nineteen seventy-two was the worst year in memory to be a Democrat. That was the McGovern year. It only took about two days out in the country to discover that if you were tied up with McGovern you were out of it. Besides that, I didn't agree with McGovern on a lot of the issues. At all. He was simply out of step with people in this part of the country at that time. In the Rio Grande Valley, for instance, he sent anti-defense literature down there, never reckoning with

the fact that the children of a lot of the Hispanic families down
there were making their careers in the armed forces. McGovern
was unrealistic. So I tried to keep my distance from him and
run my own race. I kept saying, 'It's me running for the Senate,
not McGovern.' I was always having to be on the defensive
about him. Tower had a lot of fun with that. McGovern got
only 33 percent of the vote in Texas. I think he got 21 percent
in Dallas. I ran fourteen percentage points ahead of McGovern
— 1.5 million to 1.8 million — which was close enough to be
respectable, but not close enough to say, 'Gee, if I'd had
another week, I would have made it.'

"I believe in the two-party system," he says, "and I believe
that when you're on the ticket, you vote the ticket. That's basic.
You vote for every Democrat on the ticket. But that doesn't
mean you campaign for all of them."

A Democratic candidate whom he supported with much more
enthusiasm was Jimmy Carter. And when Congress enlarged the
federal judiciary in 1979, Carter — on Senator Bentsen's recommendation — named Sanders to the new spot on the Dallas
federal bench. On the day she administered the oath to him,
Judge Hughes said, "I do not have a son. I never had a child. If
I had a son, he would be the same age as Barefoot. I would
hope that my son would be just like Barefoot."

Since the late Judge Hughes' retirement a few years ago,
Sanders has been generally considered the "liberal" federal judge
in "conservative" Dallas. It's a reputation that he doesn't mind,
but he doesn't consider it important.

"I think your political background and where you came from
plays a part in the way you approach a case," he says. "The
way you were raised and your economic background plays a
part in it, too. But with most judges on the trial bench —
which is where I live — none of that plays much of a part in
getting to a result. I would say that in the vast majority of
cases — 90 or 95 percent — every judge here would decide the
same way. I'm not going to say we would all come out the
same way in the school case. I don't know that. I've never

asked anyone about that. And one thing we're good at around here, we don't give each other advice about our lawsuits."

Sanders won't discuss the specifics of any of the about six hundred civil and criminal cases pending in his court, but he will predict the outcome of one: When he hands down his final ruling in *Tasby v. Estes*, the Dallas public schools will be as desegregated as his court and thirty years of water under the bridge can make them. "Theoretically speaking, if the DISD had desegregated after *Brown v. Board of Education*, it wouldn't be in my court now. If it had desegregated before the current suit was filed in 1970, it wouldn't be in court now. The schools which acceded to desegregation early on are the school districts that have bade the federal courts goodbye. But for the DISD, that's speaking in terms of what might have been."

During the years the Dallas Independent School District has been in court, Sanders' own four children have grown up. His daughter Janet is a lawyer in Boston; his daughter Honey is vice president of a computer company in Dallas; his daughter Mary is involved in movie and video production in Dallas; and his son, Harold Barefoot III, who calls himself "Biff," is on the West Coast, trying to break into the music world as a producer and performer. The judge and his wife are about to become grandparents for the fourth time.

Ten years ago, Judge William Taylor handed down an order that required about eighteen thousand Dallas children to be bused for desegregation. During the five years Sanders has been in charge of the case, that number has decreased to fewer than six thousand, mainly because white students are a shrinking minority in the DISD, and busing is no longer an effective tool for desegregation. Sanders' bet now for getting the school district out of his court is the new "super schools" in South Dallas and West Dallas. "I think they'll work," he says.

"This case is on the downhill road, I sure hope," Sanders says. "I think the two sides are making progress. They have an excellent set of lawyers to give them legal advice, and we have a good working relationship. I think there's finally a constructive approach on everybody's part."

He relights his cigar and takes a long drag. "Ordinarily, you expect to get more conservative in your outlook as you get older," he says. "I guess in some ways I have, although in other ways I haven't. I want to do what I think will work. And I've probably gotten more impatient as I've grown older. And I think I've gotten a little less certain of my own righteousness. I'm not always sure I'm right.

"But I *decide*," he says. "That's what I'm paid to do. And there *will* be a time when I can say, 'OK, the Dallas Independent School District is desegregated,' and there won't be any more cases. I can't tell you when, but that time will come."

[June 1986]

It's a terrible thing for a young person to die, and it's a terrible thing for that person not to be remembered. It happens all the time. Most young people who die are remembered by only a few, because not many people knew them.

WHERE BUDDY LIVED

Someone has brought a wreath of silk flowers and a note: "After thirty years your short life still touches ours." Somebody has brought a sand dollar from a distant beach and broken it into pieces and laid the pieces on the gravestone. Someone named Ron S. has left some guitar picks.

Jay Brownlee and Tim Summit have brought a small bouquet with a card tied to it: "Thanks, Buddy. We remember."

They don't really remember. They're students at Texas Tech University. Buddy Holly had been in his grave in Lubbock City Cemetery for a decade already when they were born. But they love his music, so they brought the flowers.

And the tokens that they and the others left on the grave were just about the only remembrance that Lubbock's most famous native son got in his hometown on the thirtieth anniversary of his death.

Year after year, rock fans come to Lubbock from around the world, seeking some contact with a life that has been important to them, but they don't find much to make the pilgrimage worthwhile.

There's the grave, of course, the simple slab with Holly's name and dates and the Fender Stratocaster guitar etched into the granite. There's the Buddy Holly Recreation Area, a bleak park built over an old landfill in a rundown and — some say — dangerous part of town. The park is surrounded by small, decaying houses, steel companies, sheet-metal yards, welding supply companies, a giant cotton warehouse complex, and the Holly Park Mobile Home Sales, advertising "Luxury Living." There's nothing of Holly at the park but his name on the sign at the entrance. There's the Buddy Holly Suite at the Day's Inn in downtown Lubbock, but it's under renovation. And there's the statue of Holly, eight and a half feet tall, erected with funds raised by a few of his friends. It stands between the Civic Center and a huge monument to the victims of the 1970 tornado.

And that's it. Fans who have been to Graceland find it puzzling, especially since Lubbock isn't overflowing with tourist attractions.

Summit, trying to explain, says: "My mom knew Buddy. She grew up here. She graduated from high school a year before Buddy did. She never was much of a fan of his. She just kind of knew him as a local guy. She thought he was just another hippie. She never realized how famous he was."

Brownlee says: "My dad was here in '58. He went to Tech. He says most everybody here thought Buddy was strange. You know, kind of weird. For some reason, he was never really accepted here."

Summit says: "It's the kind of country town Lubbock is. They all thought he was a rebel or something."

In downtown Lubbock, Shawn Fair, who grew up in Lovington, New Mexico, is the only person gazing up into the face of Buddy Holly's statue.

It's a strangely passive-looking statue to portray someone with the energy that Holly had. His legs are bent slightly, and he's picking his guitar, but his mouth is shut. He's not singing, and you can't see those big, famous teeth.

"The first time I saw *The Buddy Holly Story*, when I was just a kid, I was inspired by him," Fair says. "I fell in love with his music." Fair's lips are trembling as he speaks. The temperature is close to zero. "I went to his grave just awhile ago, and just stood there and wondered what it would be like if he was still alive."

Fair works for a courier service. He drives from Lubbock to Midland and back every day, and he has just finished his run. "All the stations have been playing Buddy today," he says, "and I've just been sitting back and listening to him."

The wind is hurting his face. He has to get out of it, he says. He walks toward his truck. "I lived in California last summer," he says. "People there were always asking me: 'Who's famous in Lubbock, Texas?' And I said: 'Buddy Holly.'"

This is the thirtieth anniversary of the plane crash in the cornfield. The three young musicians — Holly, Ritchie Valens, and J.P. "The Big Bopper" Richardson — became rock 'n' roll's first casualties of the road, the new music's first martyrs.

"Lubbock takes a lot of criticism for not making a big deal out of Buddy Holly, like Memphis did with Elvis," says a Lubbock insurance man who asked not to be identified. "But Buddy Holly wasn't Elvis. He didn't live long enough."

It's true. Holly was just getting started, and then he died.

"Buddy had only three albums out when he died," says Ralph DeWitt, owner of Ralph's Records and Tapes, across the street from Texas Tech. "He had been recording only about two years. To people here, he was just a kid who had a band and played at the skating rink and at high school dances. They didn't realize how good he was, and how famous he had become all over the world. Of course, the legend wasn't born until years after he died. He hadn't had time to build up to superstar status. But then in '78, People started coming here — big people from Hollywood — and they started making that movie and looking around for Buddy Holly stuff. So all of a sudden we had a park named after him, and after the movie came out, they put up the statue."

When fans have complained that Lubbock provides no opportunities for people to gather and commemorate the anniversaries of Holly's death, the official Lubbock reply has been: "We prefer to celebrate his life, not his death."

And for several years, there was a Buddy Holly Music Festival in Lubbock on the weekend nearest September 7, his birthday. But in 1987, Holly's widow, Maria Elena, who thought

Lubbock was doing a shoddy job of preserving her husband's memory, persuaded the Texas Legislature to pass the "Buddy Holly Law." It prohibits the use of a dead celebrity's name for commercial purposes in Texas without the permission of the celebrity's family. The city changed the name of its celebration to the Lubbock Music Festival, and the die-hard Holly fans moved their observance about a hundred miles west to Clovis, New Mexico, where Holly made his first recordings, and where the "Buddy Holly Law" can't reach.

"The Lubbock festival has been really going downhill," says Damon Greer, one of Ralph's employees. "Every year it gets smaller and smaller, both in the number of activities they have going on and the number of people who come. There's really not much to do. You just go down and look at the statue, go to the grave, and go home."

But one of the local TV stations is offering Holly fans a special treat on this thirtieth anniversary. It's airing *The Buddy Holly Story*. "Buddy Holly is a legend," the station's radio promotions intone. "He knew how to rock 'n' roll. And he knew how to rock the boat. . . . *The Buddy Holly Story*. Lubbock's legend lives on . . . Coming February third."

"People from all over the world come in here looking for Buddy Holly's music," DeWitt says. "But very few local people."

He shrugs. "It's not that Lubbock's that bad," he says. "It's just pretty apathetic about everything."

[February 1989]

It has always offended me that politicians don't care how country people vote — not enough to go out and ask for their votes, anyway. So during the primary campaigns of the presidential election year 1988, I decided to do what no presidential candidate had ever done — go to the most sparsely populated county in Texas and find out what the voters were thinking.

As it turned out, as Loving County went, so went the nation.

MILES BETWEEN HANDSHAKES

At 2:30 in the afternoon, a roadrunner emerges from the brush beside Keen's Place and trots to the middle of State Highway 302, the main street of Mentone, Texas. He stops near the center stripe and glances to the southwest, toward the Pecos River, and then to the northeast, where the cities of Kermit and Notrees lie beyond the flat horizon.

The highway is empty as far as the roadrunner or any creature can see, which is a long, long way in Mentone.

The bird stands there for four, maybe five minutes, motionless except for the sharp-beaked head and its blinking yellow eyes, searching first one way and then the other up and down the endless stretch of asphalt.

Nothing's coming. No car, pickup, or semi. No dog, cat, or horny toad. Nothing's moving at Keen's Place, the four-table cafe whose sign, halfway through January, still wishes a Happy New Year. Nothing moves at the post office or the Exxon station across the road or the Loving County Courthouse. Nothing moves in the sage and mesquite that line the highway. Nothing's moving in all of Mentone.

The roadrunner trots on across the highway and under a barbed-wire fence and disappears into the scrub. The silence is so intense that you would swear you heard his toenails scratching the pavement as he departed.

That's the way it is during this presidential campaign year in Loving County. Quiet. It's the way presidential campaigns always are here. "No presidential candidate has ever campaigned here," says Mary Belle Jones, the county Democratic chairman.

"Not even Lyndon Johnson?" she's asked.

"Not even Lyndon Johnson," she says. "The most important candidate ever to come to Loving County was that little fellow who used to be in the Senate."

"John Tower?"

"Yes. John Tower."

The miles between handshakes are many in Loving County, and the votes to be won are few. So candidates for national office who willingly slog through every cranny of such minor-league states as New Hampshire and Iowa and the big cities of Texas and the South on the way to "Super Tuesday" just pretend that Loving County isn't here.

It barely is. Jones says Loving is the most sparsely populated county in the United States. It's certainly the most sparsely populated in Texas. In 1980 the census-takers counted ninety-one highly individual persons scattered about its 671 dusty square miles. Jones thinks the population has grown since then. "Right now we have four babies in diapers," she says.

Fifteen or sixteen of the people (estimates vary) reside in Mentone, which was named by a lonely land surveyor for his faraway hometown of Menton, France. Nobody knows why the "e" was added to the name.

Mentone is the only town in the county. Besides the homes of its few residents and the courthouse, the gas station, the post office, and Keen's Place, the only structures are a school building that's no longer a school (the county's eight students are bused thirty-one miles to Wink) and the tiny white frame Mentone Community Church, which was moved to its present

site in 1930 after a Pecos River flood wiped out a town called
Porterville. Built in 1910, it's the oldest building in the county.

It took two tries just to get Loving County organized. The
first attempt, in 1893, failed when the promoters of a crooked
canal and irrigation project absconded with the money raised
from taxes and the sale of public lands and the Legislature
determined that many of the signatures on the petition requesting creation of the county were phony. The Legislature took
away Loving's county status, making it the only county in
Texas ever to be officially disorganized.

For a while, settlers attempted to establish farms along the
arid banks of the Pecos, irrigating their fields from the river.
Lloyd Goodrich, whose family has lived in Loving County since
1908, remembers when three thousand acres of the desert were
under cultivation, but his eighteen acres of alfalfa are the only
irrigated land in the county now. "If you think you've got trouble," he says, "wait till you try to irrigate with Pecos River
water. It's got salt, and it's got Republicans and Democrats and
New Mexicans and Texans and federal judges and a whole slew
of lawyers in it, all fighting over water rights."

There's no good well water in Loving County, either. It's full
of chlorides and magnesium salts and arsenic. The residents
drill shallow wells for water to flush their toilets and wash their
clothes, but drinking water must be hauled in from outside the
county or caught from the rain. Goodrich drinks the rain, and
his supply is getting low. "The Republicans can't bring rain, and
the Democrats can't bring rain," he says. "Only God can bring
rain, and he doesn't seem to want to."

Instead of water, God gave Loving County oil. The West
Texas oil boom of the 1920s brought people back to this empty
corner of the Permian Basin, and in 1931 Loving became a
county again. Since then, the fortunes — or misfortunes — of
the county and its citizens have been tied to oil.

In 1980 Mary Belle Jones, who also is the county's tax
appraiser, placed a value of $500 million on the taxable prop-
erty in the county. Today that has shrunk to $267 million. The
382 oil and gas leases in the county account for $224 million of

that. "The land itself is worth very little," she says. "It sells for about fifteen dollars an acre. Nearly all of the shrinkage in value is because of the situation in the oil business. In 1980 one of our taxpayers' drilling rigs was appraised at six million dollars. Now they're appraised at five hundred thousand dollars. Over the same period, we've had to increase our tax rate from ten cents per one hundred dollars evaluation to thirty cents."

So there's an issue in Loving County, even if there are no candidates. "The only thing that's important right now is the price of oil," Goodrich says.

On the day he's speaking, the price of oil is $16.56 a barrel, so low that it's hardly worthwhile to switch on the pumpjacks and suck the stuff out of the earth.

"It's probably smart of those candidates not to come to Loving County," Goodrich says. "You can do yourself more damage than you can do good here by showing up. You may talk to the wrong person or say the wrong thing, and that can ruin your chances."

Of the approximately eighty voters in Loving County, only three admit to being Republicans, but party affiliations have more to do with tradition than with ideology. Ronald Reagan outpolled Walter Mondale fifty-seven to sixteen in 1980. Republican Phil Gramm whipped Democrat Lloyd Doggett fifty-five to fifteen in their race for the U.S. Senate.

"The Republicans don't hold a primary here, so if you want to vote on your local officials you've got to vote in the Democratic primary," says Goodrich, who's the assistant Republican chairman. "Your Republicans don't come out of the woodwork until the general election."

Goodrich says he switched parties in 1978, when Texas elected its first Republican governor in more than a hundred years. "When that happened," he says, "I discovered that Loving County didn't have anybody to talk to in Austin, so I said, 'Well, I'll be a Republican.' So now, whoever the governor is, we've got somebody to talk to him."

"Who do the Republicans in Loving County like this year?" he's asked.

"You'll have to ask them," Goodrich says. "There are probably three different opinions on that."

"Who do you like?"

"I'm going to vote for George Bush."

"Any particular reason?"

"Yeah. I promised him four years ago I was going to vote for him."

"I'm going to vote for Gary Hart," says a woman who refuses to be identified. "I like an adulterer."

Goodrich collapses with laughter.

"Not really," the woman says. "And don't you dare say I said that. What is Gary Hart, anyway? Is he a Republican or a Democrat?"

"He's a Democrat," Goodrich says. "The Republicans don't have no adulterers. Thieves we've got. Adulterers, no."

Over at the Exxon station, Mattie Thorpe says she likes Bush, too. "I think he's the best," she says. "I just think he's smarter than the others. He has worked for President Reagan, and President Reagan is smart."

"Aren't you a Democratic precinct chairman?" she's asked.

"Yes," she says, "I belong to the Democrat Party, but I don't vote for the party. I vote for the man."

Almost everybody you talk to in Loving County says that: "I vote for the man." They also say: "I'm a conservative." County Judge Donald Creager, who's also a rancher and an independent oilman, says those things. "I am a Democrat," he says. "I'll say that I'm a Democrat, but I may not vote that way. I'm not a liberal. We're very conservative out here. We were raised up that way."

He also says he's bitter. He believes that the conservatives whom Loving County voters have helped put into office have let them down.

"Vice President Bush used to live in Texas, and he used to be in the oil business," he says. "I felt that when we got him in there, we might have a little help. But we haven't had any help from this administration. The price of oil is being manipulated more by the stock exchange up there in New York than by

OPEC. There are guys up there making billions of dollars off of our misfortunes, and the government is allowing it to happen. Boy, it's pitiful. I don't mind paying my share of taxes, and I don't mind tightening my belt when the economy is down. But when people start making money off of our misfortune, it's terrible. And it's even more terrible that the government allows it. I'll bet it's costing the taxpayers $250 dollars a barrel to bring that oil from the Middle East right now, with all the military personnel we have over there. And the people up north have tunnel vision. They see the price at the gas pumps, and that's all. The candidate who stands up and sounds the best on that issue is the one that this county and the state of Texas will go with."

"Who do you think that will be?" he's asked.

He shakes his head. "I don't know," he says. "Nobody's saying anything."

Outside, an orange-and-white cat is walking down State Highway 302, headed toward the river. It's so quiet you would swear you heard his toenails scratching on the pavement.

[January 1988]

I enjoy watching a football or baseball game, but I'm not a serious fan. I skim the sports pages every day, but I don't make a study of either game or its players. If a favorite team of mine begins to show signs that it might make it to the Super Bowl or the World Series, or whatever, my interest in it perks up, but if it doesn't survive the playoffs, my life isn't ruined for more than an hour or two.

As television has made most professional athletes into wealthy whiners and egomaniacs, even my interest in winners has waned quite a bit.

It's a privilege to know a person with a passion, though, and Tex Schramm had one — the Dallas Cowboys. I've never seen a man suffer so exquisitely over a game.

THE MAN WHO INVENTED THE COWBOYS

Yes, the sportswriters have quoted him accurately, he says. No, they haven't exaggerated. Last Sunday — December 6, 1987 — was the lowest point of his thirty-eight years in the National Football League.

In ten years as an executive with the Los Angeles Rams and twenty-eight years as the only general manager the Dallas Cowboys have ever had, he has never felt so embarrassed, so frustrated, so. . .

Over the phone, Tex Schramm sounds as if he's in exquisite pain, as if he's speaking from an eighth circle of hell created and reserved especially for him, so horrible that Dante left it out of his book.

"I've never been with a team that reached so low," he says. "Without question, this season has taken more of an emotional toll on me than any other."

A day earlier, the Atlanta Falcons — almost universally considered to be the worst team in the NFL — had thrashed the home team 21-10 before the smallest crowd ever assembled in Texas Stadium to watch the Cowboys. Indeed, it was the tiniest gathering of the faithful since medieval times — December 11, 1966 — when the players wore black shoes and played on real grass in the Cotton Bowl.

And for the organization that only a few years ago was adored and envied as "America's Team," it was a day of catastrophic significance — a sort of gridiron Waterloo or Gettysburg or even — some are saying — Hiroshima. The loss virtually guarantees that for the second time in two years the Cowboys won't make the playoffs. It virtually guarantees that for the second time in two years they'll finish their season with more losses than victories. For two years in a row, the Cowboys will rest among the losers, an ignominy they haven't suffered within the lifetime of many of their fans.

Defeat always has been hard for Schramm, a kind of grief, says his wife, Marty, who in twenty-eight years has never sat with her husband at a Cowboys game. Schramm prefers the press box, where he can react to what's happening on the field without fear of offending anyone.

"Years and years ago when he was still with the Rams, I said to him, 'Well, you can't win them all,' his wife says. "And he looked at me like I had lost my mind and said, 'Why the hell not?' I've never said that again. No matter what you try to say to make him feel better, it just doesn't work. So I just leave him alone, and he suffers by himself until he gets around to thinking about the next week's game."

But on this gloomy Monday morning after his most miserable Sunday, Schramm already is thinking of the next game. "As an example of how low this period is," he says, "we're going to Washington to play the Redskins Sunday, and I just received a note informing me that Eugene Lockhart broke his right leg yesterday. He's out for the rest of the year. And his replacement, Steve DeOssie, is out with a sprained ankle."

While the lowly Falcons were humiliating the Cowboys last Sunday, the Washington Redskins — the vilest and most tireless Cowboy-haters in the league — were wrapping up their fourth NFC East title in seven years. And with three games still left in the regular season. Very like the Dallas Cowboys used to do it.

"So I just said, 'Damn it, what's the first thing people think of when they think of Texas? Cowboys!' So I called them the Cowboys. But for a lot of people — particularly old-timers and ranch folks — a cowboy wasn't a glamorous person. It was like calling the team the Laborers or the Farmhands. A lot of people in Dallas didn't like the name either. Dallas was where the East ended. It was cosmopolitan for God's sake! Fort Worth was the West. And they were saying, 'Cowboys? Jesus! That's not Neiman-Marcus!'"

Listening to Schramm talk about how the Cowboys got their name is like listening to Adam talk about how the beasts in Eden got their names. He was there in the beginning, was in charge, so he named them.

"Very few people ever have the opportunity to start something completely from scratch and build it into something great," he says. "I had always wanted to do that."

For almost three decades, the Dallas Cowboys have been Schramm's life. He became their boss in the fall of 1959, before they even existed, when they were just a gleam in the eye of Dallas oilman Clint Murchison, Jr., who was badgering the owners of the NFL to let him start up the first new team in thirty years.

When the league finally gave its OK, it was Schramm who hired a baby photographer named Gil Brandt to scout for players and the thirty-five-year-old defensive coach of the New York Giants, Tom Landry, to build them into a team. It was Schramm who devised the fancy paperwork that kept Southern Methodist University's All-America quarterback Don Meredith and New Mexico's star running back Don Perkins out of the clutches of the established teams and made them the stars

among the has-beens, misfits, and rejects who were the early
Cowboys.

"Our practice field was a minor-league baseball park in Oak
Cliff," Schramm says. "It was an old, dirty place. The rats ate
the players' shoestrings at night."

As everybody expected, the Cowboys didn't win a game during that 1960 season, and they remained losers for four more
long and dreary years. But in 1966, with a team that included
thirteen free agents, they made it to the NFL championship
game, and it took Vince Lombardi's mighty Green Bay Packers
more than fifty-nine minutes to beat them.

The 1967 championship game was a rematch of the two
teams. On the northern Wisconsin tundra in subzero weather,
the Cowboys lost by four points in the final seconds. The game
would go into NFL legend as the "Ice Bowl," one of the most
exciting games ever played.

"We were so proud to be playing the legendary Packers for
the championship, and so proud that we played them so well
that those losses weren't all that disappointing emotionally,"
Schramm says. "The Packers were the Establishment and we
were the underdogs. Everybody in the United States was pulling
for us. Those games were the beginning of our popularity."

They also were the beginning of a new Establishment. While
the once-awesome Packers faded into mediocrity, the Cowboys
gradually took their place as the class of the NFL. After they
broke into the ranks of the winners, it began to seem they
would stay there forever. Children were born and grew to
adulthood without seeing the Cowboys have a bad year. They
played twenty consecutive winning seasons — a record
unmatched by any other team.

During those years, they made the playoffs every year but
one. They played in five Super Bowls in ten years. They won
two. Schramm marketed them tirelessly. The radio network that
aired their games grew into the largest in the NFL — almost
two hundred stations in seventeen states and Mexico. The
team's newspaper, the *Dallas Cowboys Official Weekly*, was second in circulation only to the venerable *Sporting News* among

sports newspapers. The crews from NFL Films, who traveled about the league filming all the games, noticed that in whatever city the Cowboys were playing, there was a large claque of Dallas fans, so the filmmakers titled the Cowboys 1978 high-lights film: *America's Team.*

Writers and broadcasters, always in search of grist for the insatiable sports media mill, grabbed the phrase and turned it into a big deal. Yelps of protest rose from front offices, locker rooms, and sports bars across the country. Players on other NFL teams swore oaths to wreak destruction upon the arrogant shining knights in the blue-starred helmets, while the Cowboy players modestly disavowed any part in the "America's Team" hoopla. The last thing they needed or wanted was for their rivals to have another reason to want to whip them.

"But it was a fact," Schramm says. "At one point, almost 30 percent of all sales of NFL Properties — things with NFL logos on them — were the Cowboys. The closest team to us was less than 10 percent, and that was usually a Super Bowl team. It was a strange phenomenon. On one hand, you had the Dallas Cowboys Cheerleaders, who were young and pretty and sexy and something new to football. And on the other hand you had Tom Landry and Roger Staubach. I think most people out there still want their sports hero to be an all-American, Jack Armstrong kind of guy. Roger fulfilled that. He was popular with every group — the young people, the old people, the men, the women. And Landry personified something very solid and steady. There would always be that strong face, that strong person on the sidelines, always under control, always taking care of things.

"And we had our characters — colorful guys like Duane Thomas and Thomas Henderson. And before that we had characters like Don Meredith and Walt Garrison. And Bob Hayes, the World's Fastest Human. And Bob Lilly, our first superstar. And Drew Pearson. And Tony Dorsett. People write about us as a cold, computerized organization, but we've always been a mixture of solid people and wild people. We've been different from everybody else. That's how we became America's Team.

"The first thing, though, is you have to win. And if you're going to be accepted in all parts of the country by all kinds of people, you've got to have a certain class about you. An air. A style."

The *Dallas Cowboys Official Weekly* last month quoted Boston Celtics president Red Auerbach: "There are only three teams in sports that have achieved true national status. The old Yankees, the Dallas Cowboys and us. That's not ego, that's just fact."

"He's right," Schramm says. "it *is* a fact. We've reached a level that's above others in professional football. But if you don't win, it won't work. You lose a little of your mystique every year that you're away from the playoffs and the Super Bowl."

Professional football began with the establishment of the American Football Association, forerunner of the NFL, in 1920. Schramm was born the same year. Although Texas is his real name — Texas Ernest Schramm, Jr. — he's a California native. His parents — Texas, Sr., and Elsa — had moved to San Gabriel, then a bucolic orange grove town outside Los Angeles, from San Antonio. Tex, Sr., was a stockbroker who made it through the crash of '29 without going broke, and the family remained economically well off and socially prominent throughout the Great Depression.

But Tex, Jr., was a problem. He flunked the first three grades of school. His father hired tutors for him in the summer so he could pass to the next grade.

"I was a hyperactive child," Schramm says. "Today I probably would be taking some kind of special education. In the fourth grade, they sent me to military school. I didn't get along well there. I stayed a year and a half and came down with the measles and damn near died. I went home. They sent me back to public school in the sixth grade, and I failed the first semester."

When he was a junior in Alhambra High School, he started dating Martha Anne Snowden, a freshman. He called her

Marty. She called him Tec, to distinguish him from his father, who was called Tex.

"Tec was a football player, a track star," she says. "All we did when we were dating was go out dancing and to sporting events. He was a nice-looking young man, and I liked him. But it wasn't easy. He was hard to get along with. We broke up probably every other week, but we always got back together. Tec is very, very opinionated. Everything is either black or white to him. There's no in-between, no middle ground. He's always right. At least he likes to *think* he's always right."

It took Schramm an extra semester to graduate from high school, and he had to spend a year at Pasadena Junior College before he could qualify for college, but he finally was accepted by the University of Texas, his father's alma mater. "I just wasn't interested in studying," he says. "I did whatever I had to to get by, and no more."

On December 21, 1941 — midway through his third year at UT and two weeks after Pearl Harbor — he enlisted in the Army Air Force at Randolph Field in San Antonio. "It wasn't that I was overly patriotic," he says. "My draft number was up, and I had been deferred because I was in college. As soon as the war came, everybody knew all the deferments would be taken away. But I wasn't a good enlisted man, either. So when they had tryouts for officers candidate school over at Kelly Field, I tried out. To the surprise of everyone, they accepted me."

Four months after his enlistment, he married Marty. He was stationed in Hawaii as a ground officer during much of the war and was discharged as a captain. He returned to Austin with Marty and a new baby, enrolled at UT again as a full-time journalism student, and got a full-time job as a sportswriter at the *Austin American-Statesman.*

"We lived in a tiny apartment over a one-car garage," Marty says. "I had to crawl across our bed to get to our daughter's crib. That's how small it was. And we had another child while Tec was in school. He was exhausted, going to school in the daytime and working at night. He would start reading a book and would fall asleep. So I would read the books and tell him what they were about. He made great grades."

Schramm claims to have read only two books in his life — a biography of Wyatt Earp when his car broke down in a small Arizona town and he had to wait for a new engine to arrive from California, and Mario Puzo's *The Godfather*, while waiting for some fishing chairs to be installed on a boat in Florida. "It's not that I can't read," he says. "I just can't sit still long enough to do it. I don't play cards, either, for the same reason."

In 1947, not long after Schramm had graduated from UT, his father learned that the Los Angeles Rams, who had just been moved to California from Cleveland, were looking for a publicity director. He phoned Tex, Jr., and urged him to contact the Rams' principal owner, Dan Reeves. Schramm did, and got the job. In 1954 he was named general manager and assistant to the president. To replace himself as publicity director, he hired a young man named Pete Rozelle, who later would become commissioner of the NFL.

Unhappy with a power struggle that was developing between Reeves and the Rams' other owners, Schramm left the team in 1957 to become assistant sports director of CBS. As Squaw Valley, California, was preparing to host the 1960 Winter Olympics, he came up with a novel idea: Why not put the games on television? The response from network executives was tepid. Would American sports fans watch skiers and skaters? Could sponsors be found? But they gave Schramm the go-ahead, and he devised the method of covering the Olympics that's still used today — live coverage of diverse contests in a number of locations, coordinated by a central anchorman. The Squaw Valley games, anchored by Walter Cronkite, were a huge success. The Winter Olympics have been among the more popular sporting events on television ever since.

"I liked the CBS job," Schramm says, "but I wanted to get back into the NFL if the right job came along. Then I heard about Clint Murchison wanting to start a team from scratch in a new city, and the idea totally intrigued me. I called an old college friend of mine named Bill Sansing, and he contacted some of Clint's partners and told them I was interested. Clint invited me to come down to Dallas. I had one talk with him one afternoon, and that was it."

Murchison had offered a salary of $36,600 a year and a stock option in which, as long as he remained with the club, Schramm could buy as much as 20 percent of the stock at 1960 prices. He also promised to let Schramm run the Cowboys.

Twenty-five years later, in failing health and with his financial empire collapsing, Murchison had to sell his team. He asked Schramm to find the right buyer. Just before turning over the Cowboys to H.R. "Bum" Bright and his nine partners, he raised Schramm's salary to $400,000 a year and gave him a $2.6 million bonus.

The Dallas Cowboys Cheerleaders were Tex Schramm's idea. So was using the computer as a tool to scout out new players. So was hiring his friend Pete Rozelle as the NFL commissioner. So was the design of the modern playing field, with the goal posts at the back of the end zone and the hash marks closer to the center of the field. So are many of the rules under which modern NFL games are played — the stadium clock as the official time, the sudden-death overtime, and many other revisions over the past two decades that were designed to make the game more exciting for the television age. Checking decisions of game officials against a video replay was his idea, too.

Along with Lamar Hunt — owner of the Dallas Texans, who are now the Kansas City Chiefs — Schramm initiated the merger of the NFL and the American Football League in 1966 and was the principal architect of professional football's current structure, with its playoffs and Super Bowl. He was the most outspoken opponent of the NFL's would-be rivals — the World Football League in the 1970s and the United States Football League of the '80s — and rejoiced more loudly than anyone over their collapse.

Although he now owns only 3 percent of the Cowboys, he's the chairman of the NFL's Competition Committee, which makes the rules of the game, and is one of six men on the Management Council's executive committee, which manages the league for the teams' owners. He's the only person who serves on both committees. He's so powerful in NFL affairs that some owners have referred to him jokingly as "Mr. Vice Commissioner."

He's called other things, too. In 1971, the Cowhoys' ineffably colorful running back Duane Thomas described Schramm as "sick, demented, and totally dishonest," and then fell into a silence that lasted the entire season. Schramm responded: "Well, that's pretty good. He got two out of three."

Anywhere in the land, whenever a voice is raised in complaint or anger against the Dallas Cowboys or the NFL or the owners, it's likely to be Schramm's name that's cursed. Many still blame him for the Management Council's decision in 1987 to continue the season with replacement teams while the regular players were on strike. Still, the executive committee of the council voted 6-0 to do so. They blame him for the owners' decision to play one more "scab" game after the regulars ended their strike, although the owners' vote to do so was 23-6.

Several Cowboys have complained that Schramm's visible and vocal opposition to the players' union cause has made their lives on the playing field more dangerous in a league that already hates them. New York Giants center Bart Oates declared Schramm to be a "moral-less person" and promised that the Giants would beat the Cowboys without mercy in the first regular game after the strike — a promise he was unable to fulfill. And after Atlanta accomplished what New york couldn't, Falcons' kicker Mick Luckhurst — the team's player representative in the union — sneeringly dedicated the game ball to Schramm.

The heat doesn't bother him, Schramm says, and he makes no apology for his conduct during the strike. "I was outspoken because it was important that everybody understand the rules of the game we were playing," he says. "The players called me a hardliner because I was a strong supporter of the replacement games, but there was nothing original about that idea. When the players went on strike in '76 during the preseason, we kept playing. And I thought we made a bad mistake when they went on strike in '82 and we locked them out and went dark for fifty-eight days.

"This time, I thought they should have an option. So did the other members of the executive committee But somebody had to say, 'We are going to play the games; the games are going to count; we're not going to pay the players for games they don't play.' Somebody had to say those things with conviction, so everybody would know what the ground rules were and the players could make their decisions accordingly.

"And while the strike was going on, everybody in management was saying, 'Boy, hang in there. Be tough.' But when it was over, everybody wanted to be a good guy and pat everybody on the back. So I was branded the hardliner. I don't mind. That doesn't hurt me."

What hurts is what he's seeing happening more and more often to the team he built from scratch and gave a name.

"I have a lot of regard for history," he says. "And, yes, I want to be remembered. I want to leave something special. Everybody who was a member of the Cowboys during that great period when we were out of the playoffs only one year in twenty and went to five Super Bowls in ten years, they carry that with them forever. A lot of people contributed to that string of winning seasons. Being a Cowboy meant a lot to them. And as long as the string continued, all those who had contributed to it continued to be part of an ongoing thing. But when that string was broken, that achievement ended for all the people who had contributed to it, clear back to 1966.

"It disturbs me when you have an opportunity to create history and you let it slip by," he says, "because that particular opportunity will never come again."

So, on the most miserable day of a long and glorious career, when you are 67 years old and the next opportunity to make history is so far down the road that it can't be seen, does the thought of retiring cross your mind?

"Oh, sure," he says. "You think about that when you're down. But then you have these two tremendous desires: One, to get back up. And two, to remember that you ain't ever going to let it happen again."

[December 1987]

In the Old West, probably more people were killed over water than anything else. Since the closing of the frontier and the creation of law and order, legislation and litigation have replaced gunplay and range warfare in most (but not all) quarrels over water rights. Emotions still run high in water fights, however, and when the fight is between Texans and New Mexicans, neither side is loathe to wave the bloody shirt.

For years it has amazed me that Western and Southwestern journalists haven't written more about water, the most important story in those regions, and one that will continue to grow in importance as population keeps growing and water resources keep shrinking.

This story about the water-rights fight between El Paso and New Mexico barely scratches the surface of what journalists ought to be doing, but at least it does scratch.

WATER FOR THE DESERT

Poor New Mexico! So far from heaven; so close to Texas.
— Manuel Armijo, governor of the Department of New Mexico,
1827-29, 1837-44, 1845-46

There's an old saying in New Mexico: "The two things a New Mexican values most are his wife's honor and his water rights, not necessarily in that order." And in the minds of many, the gravest threats to both come from Texas.

This time the trouble is about water. El Paso is trying to get it. New Mexico is trying to keep it. Both sides claim their survival is at stake. The legal and political issues of their fight are as complex and prickly as a den of rattlesnakes intertwined with a tangle of barbed wire in a catclaw thicket. And, after nearly a decade of bitter litigation, no end of the struggle is in sight.

The fight is shaped by geography, climate, and history. El Paso, tucked into the western corner of Texas between Mexico and New Mexico, far from other Texas population centers, is the fourth largest city in the state and keeps growing. Its population — well over 500,000 — has tripled in the last thirty years. Just across the Rio Grande is Cuidad Juarez, the fourth largest city in Mexico and one of the fastest-growing cities in the world. In 1980 there were 726,000 people in Juarez. In 1988 there are 1.3 million. The Mexican government thinks there will be 2.2 million by the end of the 1990s.

El Paso and Juarez are in the Chihuahuan Desert. Even in the old days, before so many people lived there, water was scarce. El Paso City Ordinance No. 1, passed at the first meeting of the town's first City Council in 1873, made it a crime to bathe in the town's drinking water supply, an irrigation ditch. Today, El Paso and Juarez get most of their water from the same underground water source, which they're sucking dry.

"El Paso is running out of water," says Pete Schenkkan, the Austin lawyer who represents El Paso in its fight with New Mexico. "Two-thirds of their supply comes from a mined source of ground water in Texas — 'mined' meaning that it's being pumped out of the ground faster — a *lot* faster — than nature can replace it. Other people are pumping this same water, including a lot of people in Mexico. How fast it's depleted is not under El Paso's sole control. And the only available new source of fresh ground water in Texas is 120 miles east of El Paso. All these facts are undisputed."

Schenkkan, who says El Paso's present water supply will last another forty years "if we're lucky," ticks off more undisputed facts: "Only a few miles north of El Paso, just across the New Mexico line, in the Hueco and Mesilla bolsons, is a whole lot of ground water that isn't being used, and there are no existing plans for anybody on the New Mexico side of the line to use it. It is undisputed that that water is the best quality water available to El Paso. And it is undisputed that that water is the cheapest new supply source for El Paso."

New Mexico, however, had a law, which it passed in the 1950s when the developers of oilfields in Kermit and Wink, Texas, were transporting large quantities of water from neighboring Lea County, New Mexico.

"The statute said, 'Thou shalt not export ground water from New Mexico,'" Schenkkan says. "There were a lot of existing cases that indicated the law was unconstitutional." So in 1980 the El Paso Public Service Board, which is responsible for the city's water supply, filed suit in federal district court in New Mexico. "We weren't asking for anything shocking," Schenkkan says. "We were asking very politely that the judge decide whether or not the law was constitutional."

New Mexicans failed to appreciate El Paso's good manners. "The lawsuit came as a complete surprise," says Dr. Ira Clark, emeritus professor of history at New Mexico State University and author of *Water In New Mexico*, an 839-page history. "El Paso hadn't even asked us for water. They didn't approach us in any way. It looked wholly conspiratorial. It looked like they were trying to steal our water."

(Some scholars, including Clark, believe New Mexico's fear of Texans began in 1841, when Texas President Mirabeau Buonaparte Lamar sent 321 soldiers and merchants to Santa Fe with a letter in which he outlined the benefits that would accrue to the New Mexicans when they became citizens of the Republic of Texas. The Texans expected to be welcomed to Santa Fe, but Governor Manuel Armijo sent his army out to challenge them. Betrayed by one of their own, the Texans were tricked into surrendering and were marched to prison in Mexico City. Another scholar, Dale Walker of The University of Texas at El Paso, says the New Mexicans' Texaphobia may date back to 1680, when the Pueblo tribes of Northern New Mexico rebelled against their Spanish oppressors and drove them out. The retreating Spaniards settled in the El Paso area, but returned to New Mexico in 1693 and reconquered the pueblos.)

Reaction to El Paso's suit was swift and strong. "The Elephant Butte Irrigation District issued public statements comparing us to the Nazis and the Russians and accusing us of a sneak-thief attack on the soul of New Mexico," Schenkkan says. "They tried to make it into a holy war. They tried to organize a boycott of El Paso businesses. They issued bumper stickers. They took out paid ads and just did a tremendous amount of demagoguing. It had its predictable effect on New Mexico politicians statewide."

Passions have cooled somewhat since 1980, but New Mexico's determination to keep its water out of Texas hasn't. In a hearing in August 1988, Schenkkan told the New Mexico Supreme Court that El Paso is being treated "like an enemy nation." He said his opponents, "scorched-earth policy has so poisoned the political atmosphere in New Mexico that no New Mexico elected officials, including judges or high-ranking appointed officials" can treat El Paso fairly.

Not long after the suit was filed, New Mexico State Engineer Steve Reynolds declared the Hueco bolson and the Lower Rio Grande area near Mesilla to be underground water basins. Under New Mexico law, anyone who wants to drill a well in an officially declared water basin must file an application with the state engineer.

El Paso immediately filed applications for 266 wells along the Lower Rio Grande and sixty in the Hueco area, almost all of them on public land administered by the federal Bureau of Land Management. From these wells, El Paso intended to transport about three hundred thousand acre feet of water per year across the state line.

Since then, the flurry of legal motion has been dizzying:

On January 17, 1983, Federal District Judge Howard Bratton declared New Mexico's ban on the export of ground water to be unconstitutional. New Mexico could not discriminate against El Paso simply because it's in another state, he said.

As soon as it became legal to transport water across the state line, the New Mexico attorney general drafted a bill repealing the embargo statute, but stating that anyone wishing to take water out of the state must get a permit from the state engineer, and that he can't grant the request "if it impairs existing water rights, is contrary to the conservation of water within

New Mexico, or is otherwise detrimental to the public welfare
of the citizens of the state."

The bill was introduced in the legislature on February 16.
Within six days it was passed unanimously in both houses and
signed by the governor.

In December 1987, after fifty-eight days of hearings, Reynolds
denied all 326 of El Paso's applications for well-drilling permits,
on grounds that there is sufficient water in Texas to supply El
Paso's needs.

When El Paso filed an appeal of Reynolds' decision in the
district court of Dona Ana County, several judges quickly dis-
qualified themselves from the case. The state Supreme Court
then appointed District Judge Manuel Saucedo of Deming to
hear the appeal.

But the Elephant Butte Irrigation District — which represents
farmers who use the waters of the Rio Grande impounded in
Elephant Butte Reservoir to water their fields and orchards —
filed a motion to dismiss El Paso's appeal. Saucedo scheduled a
hearing of the district's motion on August 15, 1988.

But on August 8, El Paso filed a motion that Saucedo dis-
qualify himself and grant a change of venue. So Saucedo canceled the August 15 hearing of the irrigation district's motion
and set November 7, 1988, as the date to hear El Paso's
motions.

But the irrigation district, the state engineer and New Mexico
State University filed a writ of superintending control with the
state Supreme Court, asking the court to hear the merits of the
Elephant Butte Irrigation District's motion to deny El Paso's
appeal of Reynolds' denial of the well-drilling permits.

But the Supreme Court denied the writ and knocked the ball
back into Saucedo's court.

Meanwhile, Schenkkan is trying to get the case out of the
New Mexico state courts and back into federal court, where he
thinks it belongs.

"There's a serious problem of an appearance of partiality in
the case," he says. "Members of the New Mexico government,
including the governor, have made statements to the legislature,

calling this case a fight for survival and urging the passage of
new statutes to block El Paso and appropriate millions of dollars to finance the fight against us. When you have statements
like that from the governor and the attorney general and the
state engineer and the land commissioner and New Mexico
State University, it creates a problem for the judicial branch —
particularly the elected judicial branch — to be as fair as they
can. The basic position of many people in the New Mexico
government is: Not one drop for El Paso, no matter what it
takes in the way of messing up New Mexico law, no matter
how much money it costs."

El Paso's opponents deny that their fight is inspired by anti-
Texan bias. They say they're simply trying to maintain the deli-
cate balance between man and nature in a fragile — and threatened — environment.

Bill Stahmann, owner of Stahmann Farms, is the largest
pecan producer in the beautiful, fertile Mesilla Valley. Like the
cotton-growers and corn-growers and the other pecan-growers
in the valley, he irrigates his thirty-six hundred acres with water
from the Rio Grande. He filed the original protest against El
Paso's applications for its wells.

"There's a lot less water here than El Paso thinks," he says.
"Basically, what's available is what runs down the river. We get
about ten inches of rain here a year. A big portion of that
evaporates. So rainfall is not a big addition to our water supply. What supplies us with water is the river. It's the river that
replenishes the aquifer, not the rainfall. So if they take a lot of
water out of the aquifer, it will lower the river. And if the river
goes, everything else goes."

Ira Clark, who spent twenty-five years writing his giant book
about water, agrees. "The reason I'm opposed to El Paso getting
that water isn't the state line," he says. "Whether we like it or
not, water is a factor that should limit the growth of cities in
the West. I believe what's good for El Paso is good for southwestern New Mexico, too. But I think El Paso isn't sure what's
good for itself. It's a little too ambitious to be an industrial city.
They want to attract water-consuming industries and the jobs

that come with them. That's faulty reasoning. They want to draw the water down so fast that it's eventually going to wreck El Paso and the Lower Rio Grande Valley of New Mexico. They're not looking to the future at all.

"And El Paso is only the tip of the iceberg," he says. "If El Paso succeeds, people all around us — Denver, Phoenix, Tucson, Amarillo — are waiting to take water out of New Mexico, too. We're very worried about that. Water is one of the few resources we've got. We're one of the poorest states in the union. Without water, we have nothing."

[September 1988]

Sometimes a great institution is simply an extension of the soul of the person who is running it. Sam Rayburn's House of Representatives was such an institution. So was Stanley Marcus' Neiman-Marcus. So was Joe Miller's Bar.

A Few years after this piece was written, Joe Miller died of cancer. Before he died, he gave instructions that his body was to be cremated and his ashes were to be scattered over the Gulf of Mexico off South Padre Island, so that when his children came to visit their dad, they also could get a tan and have a good time.

His bar is still in business, but, like Sam Rayburn's House and Stanley Marcus's store, it ain't the same.

JOE MILLER'S

A saloon is a place where people go when they don't want to be anywhere else.

—Louie Canelakes

It's 5:30 P.M. on the Friday after Thanksgiving. The regulars are motoring into Joe Miller's parking lot. There's a bearded radio raconteur in a Datsun pickup, a bearded journalist in an arthritic red Volkswagen, and a bearded author of historical romances in an ancient sedan of unidentifiable brand or vintage. They are thirsty, but the barroom door is locked. "My God!" the raconteur booms. "What do we do now?"

"I don't know," the author moans. "This is the only place I know of in Dallas that sells beer."

They huddle like lost sheep in a wind. They stare toward the laundromat, the gas station, the storefronts of the little strip shopping center at Lemmon and McKinney that's anchored on the western end by Joe Miller's. The journalist tries the door again. It's still locked.

They've heard that there are other bars along McKinney. They climb into their vehicles and caravan to the nearest one. The host bars the door. "No denim allowed," he says. The author and the journalist are wearing jeans. They try another bar nearby. Normally denim isn't allowed there either, the bartender says. But it's a slow day, so what the hell.

They sit in a corner, staring dejectedly into a yellow mum in a glass vase in the center of the table. A spotlight shines down from the ceiling. It illuminates the flower to a glare. It's a fancy place. The music is loud. The other customers are dressed to the nines. They don't seem to be having a good time.

"Why would Joe do this to us?" the radio guy says. "I can understand being closed on Thanksgiving, but hell, this is *Friday.*"

"Why would you rather be at Joe's than here?" the journalist asks.

The radio guy points at the booming stereo speaker. "Joe doesn't have that," he says. "He also doesn't have video games. Or pool. Or darts. Or shuffleboard. There aren't a lot of air-heads looking to get picked up. Joe pours a good drink. You can talk in there. Just about anybody you'd want to talk to is there."

"You can have serious conversations in there," the author says.

"I met Don Coburn at Joe's," the radio guy says. "How many places in Dallas can you go and meet a Pulitzer-Prize-winning playwright? I met Preston Jones — God rest his soul — at Joe's. I met Blackie Sherrod at Joe's, or one of the other bars where Joe used to work. I been following Joe from bar to bar for over twenty years now, ever since he landed in Dallas. The main thing Joe Miller's has in Joe Miller."

The three have another drink, but their hearts aren't in it. They pay the tab and split.

On Monday the door is unlocked and things get normal. The clock with Joe Miller's face on it — the halves of his mustache are the hands — says 5:30. There's a fire in the fireplace. The couches around it are full. The tropical fish swim lazily in their murky aquarium. The tables are full. Customers are three deep

at the bar where Joe Miller and Louie Canelakes are pouring
drinks. "Monday Night Football" is on TV, but the sound is off.
The noise of the place is voices — not shouting, not singing,
just talking. It's the usual Joe Miller's crowd — journalists, lawyers, judges, politicians, advertising people. Not many
strangers. A stranger would say nothing is going on. But when
an out-of-town journalist or trial lawyer comes to town, he
never asks to see Southfork or the School Book Depository. He
wants to go to Joe Miller's.

"Yeah, that's neat," Miller says. "Guys from both papers bring
their buddies in here, and word gets around, you know? They
hear about the place from somebody down the way. A lawyer
comes in, he decides he likes the place, the next time he comes
he brings a couple other lawyers with him. That's really all
there is to it."

Miller was one of the first Canadians to discover Dallas. He
found it sort of by accident. He was just wandering through
town in 1958 and stopped. "Hey, I needed a job," he says. "I got
one here."

The road that brought him to Texas was a long and winding
one. Sometimes in the wee hours he will discuss his past with a
night-owl regular, but not often. Other times, during earlier
hours, he fends off questions. "Hey, man, I don't like to talk
about personal things, know what I mean?" On this particular
Monday, he will talk about himself, but not much.

"I was a one-parent child," he says. "An only child. My
mother put me in a Catholic home. I was raised by the nuns in
Toronto. They seemed terrible when I was there. But looking
back, considering what my options were then, they were OK.
All nuns go see *Patton* twice a year, but they're OK. Went
home when I was thirteen, went to high school, split when I
was seventeen, sold magazines around Ontario. Worked in a
gold mine. Hung around bars when I was nineteen, started
working in them, been in them ever since. Had a lot of different jobs. Once I got a pocketful of dough, off I'd go. When the
money would run out, I'd be looking for a job again. Went out
to California, tried to get a job there. They always wanted to

see my ID and whatnot. Went to Immigration, they told me to go back to Canada and get my shit straight. Which I did. Hitchhiked down here. I was about twenty-three years old then. When I hit Dallas, I was out of money, and I thought, 'Hey, I'd better keep my mouth shut and my nose clean.' Went down to the Chauteaubriand, got a job tending bar there, worked awhile. Got called a goddamn Yankee a lot. Had a place of my own on Lover's Lane for about a year, but it burned down. Then there was about a nine-month period at Sloan's Steak House. Then — approximately '74, '75 — went to The Den at the Stoneleigh Hotel for about three years. Opened up here July of '77. Be seven years next summer."

Sometime in there, he married his wife, Linda — who says Joe's main appeal for her is that "he's never boring" — and she bore him two beautiful daughters — Amy, now thirteen, and Ali, now ten. "You got to be strong to be the father of a thirteen-year-old," Joe says. "Real strong."

His soliloquy is delivered in a tough, streetwise voice reminiscent of Rodney Dangerfield. He looks a little like Dangerfield — a sort of cross between Dangerfield and the Ayatollah Khomeini — and, when he's in a crazy mood, he does the best Dangerfield impression in town. (The second-best is done by Louie Canelakes, Joe's bartender and alter ego. Louie looks like a Greek Orthodox monk in civvies, but his spirit is a prematurely reincarnated Joe.)

Joe says people like his place because it's a good bar. "It's a place with no hassles," he says. "You don't hear people in here bitching about the drinks or the service. We have our problems sometimes, but, you know, we try. You walk in here, you don't feel like you're going to get ripped off. Hey, you're comfortable, and there's a couple of guys or ladies that you know in here. The decor's not much, but nobody's bitching. Music, video games, pool, darts, stuff like that — they work for other people. But I just think, over the long haul, I don't want them. I like a place where I can sit around and talk. Everybody here likes to talk. Some lawyers and politicians like to talk to the press, knowing it ain't going any further unless they want it to.

The press and the lawyers and the politicians all want to know what's going on, right? And they can find out here."

Attorney John Collins, one of the regulars, says one of the joint's attractions for him is the Joe Miller Rule. "That's the real reason we come in here," he says. "The Joe Miller Rule states that anything that's said in Joe Miller's cannot be spoken, printed, broadcast, or otherwise publicized unless it has been confirmed by eleven o'clock the next morning. And that contributes to free speech. I also come here because I like to get down with the folks. I like to find out what potential jurors are thinking. You can come into Joe Miller's and find out what the facts are. That way, you don't have to ask them so many questions when you start a lawsuit. You can get a real feel for America in here. You can economize on your drinking, too. Like a judge friend of mine in East Texas said, "Joe Miller's drinks are a little like a woman's busts. One's not enough, and three's too many.'"

Sometimes, however, a customer will exercise the right of free speech a little too vigorously and some of Joe Miller's unwritten — even unspoken — rules are invoked. "Yeah, I've thrown people out," he says. "It's sort of a judgment call. Usually it's somebody who's had too much to drink, he gets too loud, and maybe he's hassling somebody. Maybe somebody starts singing, and I say, 'Hey, we don't like singing in here,' and they'll say, 'Well, who the hell are you?' And I'll chase him out. There have been a few times when I threw a guy out for *no* reason except that *I* had had too much to drink. Had a few push-and-shoves in here. Had one just the other night. He was an actor. He was drunk, and he took a sucker shot at me. I didn't hit him. I just tripped him and said, 'All right, goddamn it, this is no way to go.' You know, if some guy gets obnoxious, the regulars are going to think, 'Hey, how long is Joe going to let this shit go on?' Nobody's going to *say* anything, but they're *thinking* it.

"But the only thing that *really* pisses me off is some guy who gets drunk somewhere down the road and then comes in here and raises hell because I won't serve him. I don't get too many of them. You eliminate a lot of trouble by not having those games and stuff. And if people come in here wanting to get picked up, they're in trouble. Nobody's on the prowl here. But, contrary to some people, I ain't running no men's bar. Ladies come in. They're professional people themselves. They come to enjoy the conversation. And people here don't ask, 'What's your sign?' Know what I mean? Here, if somebody gets out of line, his friends will take care of it most of the time. Somebody will break it up before I get there. It's that kind of room. It's like a living room, know what I mean?"

Sometimes, however, Miller's wrath falls even upon the regulars. Collins and journalist Sam Attlesey — another devout member of the Miller faithful — remember a certain St. Patrick's Day.

"All ten of us had been in this place for three years almost every night," Attlesey says. "We were as regular as we could be. And we came in doing the bunny hop and singing. Well, you would have thought we were strangers. Miller said, 'What is this? Cut that shit out! Sit down and order something!' Hell, when I first met Joe, I didn't like him. I thought he was one of the biggest and gruffest assholes in the world. It took me a couple of months to like him. But I noticed potential in that Canadian. I could feel it."

Maybe it was potential that Alex Burton — the previously mentioned radio raconteur — noticed so many years ago at the Chateaubriand, when Joe was young. Or that attracted Frank Schaeffer (a.k.a. Christina Savage, author of *Love's Wildest Fires*). Or the late playwright Preston Jones, whose long evenings at Joe Miller's ran the gamut of emotions from mellowness to rage. ("Preston was Brendan Behan and everybody else wrapped up in one," Joe says. "And this was his Algonquin.") But potential for *What?*

Not to be the classic bartender. Miller hates crying drunks, and he won't talk politics. "A lot of customers will volunteer stuff about themselves," he says. "They'll lean over the bar and say, 'You know, Mary and I are divorced.' And I just say, 'Hey, geez, I'm, you know, sorry about that,' and then I change the subject. I don't like to get into people's business, and I don't let them get into *my* business. You can talk about the football game, the party you went to, there's a whole lot of things to talk about. But, no, not politics. Sanity makes me stay away from politics. We got both sides coming in here, right? If I'm in somebody *else's* bar, it's a different movie. I got opinions. I'll talk politics there. But here, I stay out of it. Oh, every now and then I find myself jumping in. But the older I get, the less I do it."

Miller's potential simply was for being himself and allowing other people to be themselves — as long as they don't get obnoxious. "I've worked for a lot of different people," Louie says, "and Miller has given me more latitude to be myself than anybody. And this is the best place I've ever worked. Some nights, Joe and I are like moderators of a panel discussion. Sometimes we're missionaries in darkest Africa. It's different every night. A good bar is whatever you need it to be at the time. And more than half the people who come in here are more than customers. They're friends — hell, *family*. If this was *my* bar, I'd put *my* pictures on the napkins and the signs and the clock instead of Joe's. That's the only thing I would change.

"But Joe's the cornerstone of this place, and Joe's unique. He probably makes less money than anybody I ever worked for. Joe just follows his heart. He seldom follows his wallet. And he lets me do the same. Business is a very mercenary thing, but if a guy's broke, Joe will help him out. Hell, Joe's the Clara Barton of the newspaper war, isn't he? If a guy has been good by us, we'll be good by him. It's not a one-way deal. Nothing is indispensable to this place except Joe. I'm sure a lot of other people would like to start a Joe Miller's. But, hey! Where are they going to get a Joe Miller?"

(December 1983]

When I was assigned to write a profile of Clint Murchison, Jr., the disease that eventually would kill him already had deprived him of the power of speech, so an interview with him was impossible. At first, his friends and acquaintances, wanting to protect him, refused to talk about him, too.

Then Gordon McLendon, another Dallas multimillionaire, who had known Murchison nearly all his life, agreed to an interview. I had written about McLendon — many remember him as the "Old Scotchman," whose golden voice recreated major-league baseball on the radio for the American hinterlands during the 1950s — a couple of times before, and I guess he liked me. We had a great conversation one sunny morning at his ranch on the shore of Lake Dallas.

After I told them that McLendon had given me an interview, others of Murchison's friends agreed to answer my questions, too, although some still insisted on anonymity.

So the story got written, and several people who knew Murchison told me it was the best piece they had ever read about him.

I hope that's true. And I wish I had known the man.

THE FALL OF THE HOUSE OF MURCHISON

About once a week, some of his friends drive up to 6200 Forest Lane and load Clint Murchison, Jr., and his wheelchair into the car. The nerve disease that's wrecking his body has made him physically helpless. Only with great difficulty can he speak a few coherent words. But he can listen and think, and he likes to go out with his buddies for lunch and a few laughs.

Not long ago, the group went to one of a chain of restaurants that belongs to Murchison's children. The special of the day was turkey and dressing, and one of the men ordered it. After a few bites, he began to regret his choice. "Goddamn it, Clint," he said, "the turkey's cold and the dressing tastes funny. This is terrible!"

Murchison, struggling to form the words, replied, "S-s-sue me. E-e-everybody else is."

The men at the table laughed, but the joke was barely an exaggeration. The Continental Illinois National Bank and Trust Company is suing Murchison for $75 million, Citicorp Real Estate is suing him for $10 million, First Federal Savings of Arkansas for $15 million, Merrill Lynch Private Capital for $13.5 million, Marriott Corporation for $6 million, California First Bank for $14 million, Wells Fargo National Bank for $11 million, Midwest Federal Savings and Loan of Minneapolis for $20 million, Arab Banking Corporation for $18 million, and European American Bank for $18 million. In February a deputy sheriff stood on the steps of the Dallas County Courthouse, ready to auction off the twenty-five-acre grounds surrounding Murchison's home. The sale was stopped by a federal court order, but three creditors — the Toronto-Dominion Bank, the Mona-Post Corporation, and Citicorp — then forced Murchison to file for voluntary bankruptcy. Estimates of his debts range as high as $225 million, and an army of lawyers and accountants is trying to sort out the tangle of business holdings that Murchison's attorney has described as "obscure, fantastic, and phantasmagorical."

The bankruptcy signifies more than the collapse of a great American fortune. It brings to a bitter finale one of the more fascinating of the Texas "wheeler-dealer" sagas. And it compounds the burdens on a man who often is described as "gutsy" and "decent" and at age sixty-one is suffering a devastating and incurable disease. Murchison probably is the most likable multimillionaire in Texas. He's known for his willingness to help others, for his unwillingness to "act rich," for his loyalty to his friends, for his shyness and his sense of humor. He's the man who created the city's first great professional sports franchise and, through it, gave Dallas its image as a "city of winners."

In 1984 — less than a year before the disasters hit — Murchison was installed in the Texas Business Hall of Fame, the sportscasts still called him "the only owner the Dallas Cowboys ever had," and *Forbes* magazine still placed him high on its annual list of the richest people in America. He was said to be worth $250 million.

The accuracy of such lists always is dubious, because they are based more on reputation and guesswork than on hard financial information. "Clint would never confirm that figure," a business associate says. "He knew it wasn't right." But the Murchisons had appeared on such lists for almost half a century, since Clint Murchison, Sr., had taken his gambling instincts and his "nose for oil" into the West Texas boomtowns and emerged from the Depression a multimillionaire.

By 1953, when *Fortune* magazine published a two-part profile of the elder Murchison, he controlled or owned 103 companies, ranging from such traditional Texas interests as oil, gas, cattle, and banks to a fishing tackle company, drive-in movie theaters, tourist courts, a silverware factory, Martha Washington Candy, and *Field and Stream* magazine. "Even those who know a little," *Fortune* said, "don't pretend to understand how Clint got mixed up in so much outlandish stuff, or how he keeps track of it all without going batty or broke." His wealth was estimated at $300 million and growing.

Even after his death in 1969, the Murchison interests and fortune continued to expand under a holding company called Murchison Brothers, the partnership of the founder's sons, Clint, Jr., and John. John was two years older than Clint, Jr., and was the conservative member of the team. He collected art as an investment and liked such three-piece-suit enterprises as banking and insurance. "He would have been content to run a portfolio of stocks and clip coupons," a friend says. "Clint, Jr., is like his father. He's a gambler."

Gordon McLendon, a longtime friend of the Murchisons and a multimillionaire himself, believes it was Clint, Jr.'s similarities to Clint, Sr., that led to his financial downfall. "He's as remarkably like his father as he was remarkably *unlike* his brother," he says. "His father — we all referred to Clint, Sr., as 'The Boss' — loved to go into businesses of every description. Clint, Jr., did, too. His father loved to stay borrowed up to the hilt. Clint, Jr., did, too. They depended on inflation to take care of things. They believed the people who borrowed money and invested it in land and other things that appreciate with inflation would win. And those who saved their cash were going to be losers.

"Well, for a long time it was true," McLendon says. "We had a steady increase in inflation for many, many years, and oil prices kept rising. So Clint, Sr., wasn't beset with the same difficulties that now beset his son. He never got caught in a credit squeeze. And everything indicated, through the 1970s, that that would continue to be the case. Then — all of a sudden — along comes the recession. And with the near-demise of OPEC, the price of oil dropped, the energy business has remained in a long slump, and Clint's revenues have been affected seriously. He liked to use his credit. It's what he learned from his father. Clint, Sr., told me himself, years ago, when he was in his wheelchair: 'If you've got credit at the bank, Gordon, you use it. That's the way you get to the top.' Well, that can be good advice when the interest rate is five percent. But when the interest rate is twenty percent, it can lead to disaster."

The Boss — Clinton Williams Murchison, Sr., — had a name for his way of doing business. He called it "financin' by finaglin'." Other people called it "wheelin' and dealin'." By whatever name, it requires a shrewd mind, a gambler's instinct and nerve, a finely tuned sense of timing and more than a little luck. Murchison had all those, and — along with Sid Richardson, H.L. Hunt, Hugh Roy Cullen, and a few other men who would become the folk heroes of their generation — he was young and energetic in a time and place that were made to order for the likes of him.

He was born in 1895 in Athens, a small town in the piney woods of East Texas. His grandfather had founded the First National Bank there and his father was its president. He grew

up in the comfort of small-town prosperity, and his father sent
him to Trinity University in San Antonio. A few months after
he enrolled, however, he was expelled for shooting craps. The
university offered to reinstate him if he would sign a pledge not
to gamble, but he refused. Instead, he returned to Athens,
worked listlessly in the bank until the United States entered
World War I, and joined the Army. In 1919 he wandered to
Fort Worth with nothing in his pocket but his honorable dis-
charge and teamed up with his boyhood friend, Sid Richardson, who was trading in oil leases.

Boomtowns were springing up almost overnight in the oil
patches of North, West, and East Texas, gushers were roaring in
almost daily, and speculators were winning and losing fortunes
just as regularly. Murchison and Richardson won more often
than they lost, and tales of their wheeling and dealing soon
entered the folklore of the oil business.

One night in Wichita Falls, for instance, Murchison heard a
rumor that a wildcat well was about to come in near the Oklahoma border. He dragged Richardson out of a poker game,
whispered his news, and the pair drove to the well site, bluffed
the guards, and got close enough to the rig to smell the oil.
Early the next morning, they were in Oklahoma, where they
spent $50,000 buying oil leases. By noon the day after, they
were back in Wichita Falls, and they had sold their leases for
$200,000.

By the early 1920s, Murchison had become a wildcatter, too,
drilling on some of the leases he owned. He would sell shares
in a lease to finance a well, trade more shares for a rig, put
aside a few shares for himself, and go to work. Soon he was
drilling fifty to sixty wildcats a year, and was uncommonly
lucky. "Murchison," Richardson said, "is the kind of man that
tells you, 'Here, hold this horse while I run and catch another
one.' First thing you know, you've got your hands full of Murchison horses."

By 1927, when he was thirty-two years old, he had won
between $5 million and $6 miilion in the oil fields. But his wife
died that year, too, leaving him to rear three small sons —

John, Clint, Jr., and Burt, who would die when he was eleven years old. Murchison moved his headquarters to Dallas, and in the late 1930s he began to diversify his business interests. "At that time he was well on his way to success and wealth in gas and oil," *Fortune* wrote, "and if he had been alone in the world he might never have wandered. But since he had two sons in their teens, whose business talents were unpredictable, it seemed unwise to keep all their legacy in one immensely risky petroleum basket."

The Boss sent his boys east to prep school. John went on to Yale, but quit to join the Army Air Corps when World War II broke out. Clint, Jr., fell in love with football and took more kindly to education. Although only five-foot-seven and 120 pounds, he played halfback for Lawrenceville, his prep school in New Jersey, made Phi Beta Kappa in electrical engineering at Duke University in North Carolina, earned a master's degree in mathematics at the Massachusetts Institute of Technology, the country's toughest school of science and engineering, and was commissioned as a second lieutenant in the Marine Corps Reserve. After the war, the boys returned to Dallas. At their father's knee, they learned how to wheel and deal.

"Money is like manure," The Boss told them. "If you spread it around it does a lot of good, but if you pile it up in one place it stinks like hell." And he told them, "Cash makes a man careless."

Because of that philosophy, The Boss was nearly always short of cash, and most of his deals included very little of his money. "Murchison . . . declares one of his best assets is a full knowledge of the use of credit," *Fortune* wrote. "His borrowing, which has been an immensely profitable business practice, has become an addiction."

His favorite method of financing his schemes was what the bankers call "leverage" — using a small amount of capital and a large loan to gain control of a company with large assets. The assets of the company being acquired — or some existing asset — are used as collateral for the loan. The Boss and his sons got into the construction business, for instance, with only $20,000 of their money and an $80,000 promissory note. The company they acquired was Tecon, which over the years would remove the overhanging shale that threatened to close the Panama Canal and would build the tunnel under Havana Harbor, the St. Lawrence Seaway, and other multibillion-dollar projects around the world.

Once The Boss established or acquired a company, however, he left its operation to others. His executives had the authority to make important decisions without consulting him, and he never coached them from the corner or second-guessed them. His role was to watch the world, figure out what it wanted or needed, and dream up new ways to make money out of it. "Clint just dreams things up," an associate said. "Then he sits back and lets other people sweat doing the dirty work."

This way of doing business required enormous trust and confidence in his associates. And one Sunday afternoon in the 1950s, when CBS moved its television cameras into Murchison's living room to feature him and his family on Edward R. Murrow's popular "Person to Person" program, Murrow asked him how he went about hiring the right man for the right job. "I do it by playing poker with him," Murchison replied. "I can tell more about a man by the way he plays poker than by any other way."

The only sign on the modest two-story building in downtown Dallas read, "1201 Main." But it was the headquarters of The Boss's growing empire in those days, and the birthplace of a second empire, which was called simply "Murchison Brothers."

"John and Clint, Jr., weren't interested in the same kinds of business," says one of their longtime business associates. "John had his interests and Clint had his. John looked after their banks, their insurance companies, and steady things like that, and Clint would be going gung-ho on some crazy deal somewhere. Business has always been kind of a game for him, just as it was for his father. Clint, Jr., would rather take a deal that had a lot of daring to it than a deal that was a cinch. Cinch deals bored him. He wanted to blaze a lot of new trails and do something different. He wanted something that stimulated him, something they said couldn't be done. But he and John were equal partners in the partnership. They each owned half of everything the other was doing, and each had the right to commit the other to the deal."

Although the team was a Murchison Brothers operation in which John owned an equal interest, it was Clint, Jr., who became known as "the only owner the Dallas Cowboys ever had." His love of football was passionate, and it was he who wanted to bring a National Football League franchise to the city. He got it, literally, for a song.

Clint, Jr., had campaigned for several years to persuade the owners of the NFL teams that they should expand their league to Dallas. Such a move required the approval of three-fourths of the owners, and George Preston Marshall, then owner of the Washington Redskins, strongly opposed it. Sometime during the fight, Marshall had a falling-out with the Redskins' bandleader, Barney Briskin, and fired him. Briskin happened to be the composer of "Hail to the Redskins," the team's fight song, and still owned the rights to it. In his pique, he sold the song to Murchison. Then Murchison offered Marshall a deal: He would sign over the rights to "Hail to the Redskins" to Marshall if Marshall would vote in favor of an NFL team for Dallas. Marshall capitulated.

Murchison Brothers paid $50,000 for the franchise and $650,000 for players selected from the other teams in the expansion draft. Clint hired Tex Schramm to run the front office and Tom Landry to run the team. Then, following his father's management philosophy, he left them alone. In 1960, the Cowboys' first season, they lost eleven games, tied one, and won none. During iheir first five years, they lost $3 million of Murchison Brothers money and never won more than five games a season. "I followed the Cowboys real close during those early years," says Frank Crossen, a friend and business associate of the Murchisons. "There were so few people in the stands that Clint could tell who was there and who wasn't, and I was afraid he might call the roll."

Impatient fans began screaming for Landry's hide, and Murchison responded in 1964 by offering him a ten-year contract — an offer that was unprecedented in professional sports. "We were impressing everyone, including Tom, that we did have confidence in him," he said later. "He had as long as he needed to do what he wanted to do. We were building for long-range success."

In 1970, when the Cowboys finally won their first Super Bowl, Murchison made a rare appearance before a microphone. "Well," he said, "I know that people have wondered when the Cowboys would get here. I just want to say that this marks the successful completion of my ten-year plan."

"The way Clint handled the Cowboys was pretty typical," says Crossen, who heads Centex, a construction corporation that the Murchisons used to control. "He was the same way with us. He never told us what we ought to do or what we ought not to do. He had faith that we would run it right."

And the more complex the game of business became, the more he enjoyed it. "He has a brain that's awesome in its ability," Gordon McLendon says. "Sometimes his mental ability led to what I've always thought of as a business failure in him. He didn't like a business deal unless it was *extremely* complicated. If you put a perfectly good deal to him, and if it was simple, he would sit there and listen very patiently until he could introduce enough elements to complicate it and give him a real problem to solve. I attribute it to his MIT education.

"For instance, one time he bought an apartment in New York and was remodeling it," McLendon says. "He must have changed architects five times. He must have revised the plans twenty times. Because of his own technical abilities in mathematics and engineering, he would get the wiring and the circuits so complicated that even the best of the architects would get lost. And he took years building his house on Forest Lane and designing the most incredibly complex precomputer electronic system imaginable to control the lights, the music, the drapes, the front doors, everything. It was the most elaborate, maybe ingenious, bewildering thing that I had ever seen."

In the mid-1960s, The Boss was struck with a degenerative nerve disease similar or identical to the disease now afflicting Clint, Jr. He retired to his ranch near Athens, where he died in 1969. But the Murchison name remained golden. The brothers' empire included more than a hundred corporations, ranging in their interests from home building to insurance to oil and gas to banks, hotels, country clubs, data processing, publishing houses, and television stations. Although their assets were worth billions, most of them were highly leveraged. It didn't seem to matter. Clint, Jr., and John had credit at the banks, so they used it, just as The Boss had taught them. They borrowed tens of millions of dollars from banks across the land simply by signing promissory notes.

Then, sometime around 1977, John and Clint, Jr., began dissolving their partnership. "They were extremely fond of each other, and to my knowledge they never had any really serious disagreements," a friend says. "Theirs was an unusual relationship. But John's children were getting older, and a lot of their trusts were maturing, and he decided it would be wise to begin to liquidate Murchison Brothers, which was their principal holding company. There was no great urgency about it. John and Clint, Jr., were both young men and in pretty good health. But Murchison Brothers wasn't a viable operating vehicle anymore because they had their own families. John had three girls and a boy, and Clint had three boys and a girl. So they started a kind of casual disengagement, dividing things up. But in 1979, John died in an automobile accident and the whole ballgame changed. Half of everything that belonged to Murchison Brothers was in John's estate. The liquidation wasn't casual anymore."

"John's death was the beginning of the end for Clint," one of his friends says. "Suddenly everything they had owned in partnership *had* to be liquidated, and they always had a highly leveraged operation. Interest rates started going sky high, the bottom fell out of the energy market, and everything started sliding downhill. If you have to make a payment on a note or pay a note off and you don't have the cash to do it, then you have to sell something to raise the money. The good stuff goes first, the middle stuff hangs around while you talk to a lot of people, and the sorry stuff — you don't know what the hell you're going to do with it. So Clint started selling off his good stuff so that he could liquidate and give John's estate its half. And he had to keep breathing life into what was left, hoping things would turn around. Clint's the victim of a set of bad circumstances. His ventures aren't that bad. We're not talking about a dummy here. He just got in a bind and, unfortunately, he isn't a Continental Illinois Bank or a Chrysler Corporation or a Lockheed Aircraft. He's in a hell of a better shape than any of *them* were, but since he isn't a public entity, neither the government nor anybody else is going to bail him out or give him more time. If his creditors could give Clint time, I think he *could* pay them all off. He has some exciting projects in the works. But the market has changed, and the economic situation has changed, and it will take a long time for them to pay off. And when the banks call your notes, you have to pay them *now.*"

Simultaneously with his efforts to liquidate Murchison Brothers, Clint, Jr., became heavily involved between 1979 and 1983 in about a dozen huge, highly leveraged real estate ventures, ranging from a luxurious residential development in suburban Washington, D.C., to elaborate resorts in Florida, California, and Hawaii to a mammoth subdivision project in New Orleans. Loans on the ventures have been estimated at $300 million to $400 million, and most of them have been guaranteed by Murchison. This makes him personally responsible for their repayment. In 1983 and '84, some of the deals began to smell sour, and the bankers started calling their notes.

Murchison sold the Dallas Cowboys in 1984 for $60 million and the Texas Stadium Corporation for $20 million to Dallas businessman H.R. "Bum" Bright and a group of associates. "Not many people realize that John owned as much of the team as Clint did," a friend says. "So $30 million of that money went to John's estate. John's kids were kind of unhappy when they learned that their father didn't own half of the stadium corporation, too, but he didn't. In the beginning, the stadium corporation was more of a headache than an asset. But it has turned out to be a real cash cow. Bum Bright is going to make a fortune out of it. Of course, the $50 million that Clint got from the sale went directly to some of his creditors."

While Murchison was trying to juggle his financial crises, the worst thing that could happen to him did. "Several years ago, Clint started having trouble with his balance," McLendon says. "He would stagger and bump into things, as if he were drunk. He thought it was an inner-ear problem. But not long afterward, the thing started moving *rapidly*. His balance became more and more unsteady. His speech became halting and difficult to understand. A couple of years ago, he said to me, 'Gordon, the doctors are telling me I'm going to be in a wheelchair in six months. You saw Dad in all the latter stages of his illness. Does this look like what Dad had?' And I said, 'Well, Clint, I hate to say it, but yeah, it looks a lot like what he had.'"

Murchison's illness is an incurable, degenerative nerve disease that a friend says is closely akin to multiple sclerosis and Lou Gehrig's disease. "It's the deterioration of the myelin," he says, "which is the stuff that coats the nerve endings, like the rubber that goes over an extension cord. When it starts deteriorating, it short-circuits things, like an old PBX board. It's genetic. It's the same thing his father had, but his father had a stroke to go along with it. I guess you could philosophize and say that if you have a blessing like great wealth, you get a great curse to go with it. Maybe it goes back to the ancient pharaohs."

In 1978 Clint, Jr.'s, second wife, Anne, was giving her "testimony" before a group of fellow born-again Christians. She described her life as a "fairy tale dream come true." John Murchison was still alive. Clint was in good health. The troubles hadn't yet begun.

"We have our own private island in the Bahamas," she said, "a beautiful penthouse in New York, and an absolutely gorgeous home right here in Dallas in the middle of twenty-five acres of perfectly manicured grounds, all staffed with lots and lots of servants. There is even someone who washes my windshield every morning and makes sure I have enough gasoline in my tank. There are a number of airplanes to jump on to take me anywhere I might wish to go, exotic trips with VIP treatment wherever we go. I have a closet full of the finest clothes. If I chose to, I would never have to lift a finger."

Now the island, the penthouse, and even the huge Dallas house — forty-three thousand square feet of luxury, all on one floor, covering an acre at Preston Road and Forest Lane — are for sale. The perfectly manicured grounds are for sale, too, and probably will be subdivided. By the time the Murchison Brothers liquidation is complete and Clint, Jr's, assets are sold off to satisfy his creditors, the proceeds from the sale of his North Dallas estate may be all that he owns. That money would be protected under the Texas Homestead Act and the creditors couldn't touch it. If the mansion is sold for what it's worth, Murchison — on a drastically reduced scale — still might be a millionaire.

But as surely as the star on the Dallas Cowboys helmet symbolizes the kind of team they became, the fact that they no longer belong to Clint Murchison symbolizes the devastation he has suffered. "The Cowboys were his dream and his pride and his joy," says Robert Foley, a longtime friend. "Before John died, I think Clint believed he could arrange his assets in such a way that he could buy out John's interest in the Cowboys and keep them. And when it finally became apparent to him that he couldn't do that, the ballgame was really over. He *never* would have sold the Cowboys unless there was absolutely and irrevocably no alternative. He knew the jig was up. What we're looking at now is just a prolonged clean-up operation."

Foley is one of the men who go to lunch with Murchison every week. "If what has happened to him had happened to me," he says, "I would have blown my brains out two years ago. But Clint feels no bitterness whatsoever about it. With his financial empire collapsing and a dread disease debilitating his body, he can still sit there in that wheelchair and laugh and joke. It's kind of pathetic and not pathetic at the same time. I guess life is pathetic. Maybe Clint knows that. Anyway, he just keeps rolling along. He's incredible. I've never met anyone else like him. He's one of a kind."

[April 1985]

From when I was in the third grade, or whenever it was that I became a serious student of Texas history, I knew that the Texas Declaration of Independence was signed on March 2, 1836, at Washington-on-the-Brazos. And I knew that Washington-on-the-Brazos had served as capital of the Republic for a brief time. Then the town disappeared from Texas history, or at least from my reading of it.

I had wondered why its importance as the birthplace of Texas independence hadn't been drilled into young Texan minds. I had wondered why nobody was making pilgrimages to it, as to the Alamo and San Jacinto.

So just before Texas Independence Day, 1983, I went to find out.

THE DYING BIRTHPLACE OF TEXAS

On February 27, 1836, Col. William Fairfax Gray of Virginia rode into Washington-on-the-Brazos in the Mexican province of Coahuila y Texas. "Disgusting place," he wrote in his diary. "About a dozen cabins or shanties constitute the city; not one decent house in it, and only one well-defined street, which consists of an opening cut out of the woods. The stumps still standing."

A hundred years later, an anonymous traveler touring Texas for the CPA Texas Writers Project, a Depression-era program to give writers a little work, passed through the town. Washington, he wrote, was "a down-at-the-heels country village largely populated with Negroes of the old plantation type; the women, clad in formless 'Mother Hubbards' and wearing sunbonnets, gossip over rickety fences or sit quietly on sagging porches, smoking their pipes." He estimated the population at a hundred.

But Washington-on-the-Brazos has declined since the old days. H.A. "Bubba" Stolz, who has lived in the community all his life and operates its crossroads store, says the population is about fifty now.

"That's if you count the dogs," he says. "It may have been about a hundred when I was a kid, but we had more dogs then." And he doesn't expect a tide of visiting humanity Sunday when the public gathers at the nearby Washington-on-the-Brazos State Historical park for the 147th Birthday of Texas celebration.

"Last time I went to one of them things was in 1936," he says. "Had a good crowd that year. Cars all up and down the road out there. Governor Allred made a speech. But they ain't had a good crowd since. They ain't even having it on the right day. March 2 is on a Wednesday, and they're holding it on a Sunday, hoping to catch a few drifters, I guess."

Every Texas school child has heard about Washington-on-the-Brazos, or will before he gets through his compulsory Texas history course. It was at Washington, on March 2, 1836, while Colonel Gray was visiting, that fifty-six rebellious Anglo colonists and three angry Mexicans signed the Texas Declaration of Independence. It was there that Sam Houston was appointed commander-in-chief of the Armies of the Republic. It was there that the delegates got the news of the fall of the Alamo and scattered like a covey of quail before General Santa Anna's advancing army. It was there, ten years later, that the Treaty of Annexation was ratified and the Republic of Texas became part of the United States. It was there that the Lone Star flag was lowered as a national banner for the last time.

Yet, in comparison to the millions of Texans and tourists who during the years have visited such shrines of Texas liberty as the Alamo and the San Jacinto monument, almost no one comes to Washington-on-the-Brazos. The village stands as proof that, even in Texas, a real estate development can flop.

The town's principal founder, Capt. John W. Hall, had high hopes for the place. He acquired the tract of land on the west bank of the Brazos River, on a bluff overlooking the important

La Bahia ferry crossing. He had the site surveyed and platted in 1833, and in 1835 formed the Washington Townsite Company with four other partners. One of them, Dr. Asa Hoxley, named the place Washington, after his home town in Georgia.

Then the company advertised in Texas newspapers that town lots would be sold at public auction on January 8, 1836. The partners persuaded the delegates to Texas' revolutionary provisional government to move from San Felipe — where they had been airing their grievances against Mexico since November — to Washington. They advertised to prospective land buyers "the strong possibility, if not certainty, that Washington will be the future capital of Texas."

A group of Washington businessmen rented an unfinished gunsmith's shop from Noah T. Byars and Peter M. Mercer to serve as the convention hall. They agreed to pay $170 rent for the three months that the business of the revolutionaries was expected to take, stipulating that Byars and Mercer "have the house in complete order and repair for use of the members of the convention. . ." Obviously, they hoped to stage an impressive meeting and maybe persuade some of the delegates to invest in their enterprise.

But this colonial Washington-on-the-Brazos Convention Bureau fouled up. When Gray arrived on February 27, he found the delegates sleeping under trees and eating cornbread and fat pork, the only food in town. On February 29 it rained. On March 1 a norther blew in. The gunsmith shop hadn't been finished. There was no fire in the building and no glass in the windows. Cotton cloth had been hung over the openings to cut the wind.

The delegates weren't about to spend three months there. The convention convened March 1 and the delegates were awake all night, writing the Declaration of Independence with fingers that were turning blue, dodging the wind, and stealing a lot of their material from the Declaration signed in Philadelphia in 1776. They adopted it without a dissenting vote the next day, which was Sam Houston's forty-third birthday. (Houston, incidentally, was one of the older delegates. Their average age was thirty-eight.)

On March 4 they elected Houston commander-in-chief. On March 6 a courier brought Col. William B. Travis's last letter from the besieged Alamo in San Antonio de Bexar. "The spirits of my men are still high," it read, "although they have had much to depress them . . . I hope your honorable body will hasten on reinforcements . . . Our supply of ammunition is limited." One of the delegates, Robert Potter, moved that the convention adjourn and march to the rescue. But Houston dismissed the idea as "madness," told the delegates to stay in Washington and create a government for the new republic, then he mounted his horse and dashed off to take command of whatever army he could find.

On the day Travis's letter was received in Washington, Santa Anna's army stormed the Alamo and slaughtered all its defenders. When the delegates were informed of the disaster, some of them fled. Most of the others got drunk. But the convention held together long enough to write and adopt the Constitution — again, closely modeled after the U.S. document — on March 17. Then the delegates, sure that Santa Anna was on their heels, joined the terrified Washington residents in their flight to safety east of the Brazos. Their panicked flight became known in Texas history as the Runaway Scrape.

The Washington promoters, apparently disappointed that their big convention lasted only seventeen days instead of the three months they had planned, never paid Byars and Mercer the $170 rent for their hall.

After Houston defeated Santa Anna at San Jacinto on April 21, the government moved from Harrisburg to Galveston to Velasco to Columbia. Finally, Congress decided it would locate the capital in whatever town made the best offer. Again, the Washington Townsite Company made its bid for importance, but its town came in second to Houston in the balloting. However, Congress didn't like swampy, pestilent Houston, either. In 1839, it voted to move the government to the western town of Waterloo, which it renamed Austin.

Two years later Sam Houston, who was serving his second term as president of Texas, declared that Austin was too suscep- tible to Indian attack and that the capital should be moved east again — preferably back to his own namesake, Houston. A quarrel broke out between the Houston backers and the Austin backers, and Washington-on-the-Brazos was settled upon as a compromise capital. With the House of Representatives meeting in the gambling hall above Hatfield's saloon and the Senate in a grocery store loft, Washington was the capital of the Republic from October 1842 until February 1846, when Texas joined the Union and the government was moved back to Austin.

Despite the loss of the capital, steamboats kept coming up the Brazos to haul the cotton away from the plantations sur- rounding Washington, and it was a fairly prosperous little town for a while. In 1852 nearly a thousand people lived there. Then in 1866 the town fathers goofed again. They refused to pay the $11,000 bonus that the Houston & Texas Central Railroad demanded to put Washington on its line, so the rails went to Hempstead, Navasota, and Brenham instead, leaving Washing- ton with its useless river port. Economic decline and the Civil War brought the town's doom, and a big fire in 1912 destroyed what was left.

Today Washington-on-the-Brazos is two or three houses, Bubba Stolz's store, Wilbur Thane's Garage, Reba's Country Cupboard — a restaurant that Reba Dickschat operates in her house, since the restaurant building burned down awhile back — a stone cube of a building housing United Telephone Serv- ice's switching equipment, a post office housed in one of those little brick boxes that the Feds build in small towns, and a place called the Washington-on-the-Brazos Emporium. "That damn thing is never open," Stolz says. "The owner teaches school."

Stolz could throw a rock underhanded out the back window of his store and hit the weathered frame replica of the gun- smith's shop where the Declaration of Independence was signed. The small, barn-like building is part of the state park, which also includes the restored home of Dr. Anson Jones, last president of the Texas Republic, some picnic tables down by the river, and the Star of the Republic Museum, operated by Blinn College. The museum contains exhibits portraying the history of Texas under its six flags, and an exhibit on the commerce of frontier Texas — views of planters, slaves, muleskinners, bull-whackers, keelboatmen, steamboat pilots, merchants, craftsmen, and such.

Museum director Ryan Smith says about a hundred thousand visitors a year come to the park, many of them groups of schoolchildren from as far away as Dallas and Marshall. He's expecting a good turnout Sunday, if the weather is clear.

But absent, as usual, will be Bubba Stolz, who hates the park and holds a grudge against the Washington-on-the-Brazos State Park Association, which was the moving force behind its crea-tion. The land on which old Washington sat was owned by the Stolz family.

"The state condemned part of it in 1914 and stole it from my granddaddy," he says. "Then they came back in 1938 and con-demned some more and stole it from my daddy. In 1975 they tried to get the rest from me. Tried to take the store and every-thing. But I told the son of a bitch that if he didn't get out of here, I'd kill him. They've left me alone since."

Bubba, fifty-seven years old, is the third generation of Stolzes to keep a store on the same site during almost a century. Although the store building has been replaced twice during that time, it's doubtful that the interior appearance of the place has changed much.

Stolz will sell you dog food, wine, beer, cigarettes, candy, chewing gum, combs, razor blades, flashlight batteries, lighter fluid, aspirin, flyswatters, rubber bands, or Exxon gas. He'll slice some baloney and make a sandwich for you and open you a beer, and you can sit in one of his straight-back chairs in front of the gas heater in the center of the floor and eat and talk.

Or at the bar, which is prominently posted with the usual warnings against buying beer for minors and carrying weapons in establishments that sell alcoholic beverages and a sign advising the customer of Bubba's qualifications: "Bartender fully licensed to dispense advice." Outside, two signs, one in each window, warn: "No Shirt, No Service."

Leaning back in his chair, his eyes hidden behind the dark green glasses he apparently wears all the time, Stolz says his son will take over the store after him, and maybe his grandson after that. He thinks they'll probably have to fight off the Brazos State Park Association, too. "I sure wish we owned that park again," he says. "Damn. They ain't doing anything useful with it. Used to, you could camp overnight down there and fish in the river, but they cut out all the good stuff. You can't do nothing there. It's a one-time park. You just drive in and drive out, and you've seen it all."

To see the rest of Washington-on-the-Brazos, the birthplace and erstwhile capital of Texas, you don't even have to drive. Just look through Bubba Stole's screen door. If Col. William Fairfax Gray should happen through again, he still wouldn't be impressed.

[February 1983]

For many years, the weekend in October when the Longhorns of the University of Texas at Austin and the Sooners of the University of Oklahoma met in Dallas to play a football game in the Cotton Bowl was sort of a Southwestern Mardi Gras. For many who trekked to the city from north and south, the game was mainly an excuse for a weekend of debauchery and mayhem. Some years, in preparation for the festivities, downtown Dallas stores would board up their display windows and hotels would remove the furniture from their lobbies to preserve it from destruction by the revelers. Hundreds would be arrested.

The event is more sedate now — so sedate, in fact, that there's talk of ending Dallas's annual Texas-OU Weekend and playing the football game in Austin and Norman in alternate years. Dallas residents wouldn't care much if they did, but its hotel, restaurant, and bar owners would.

One year, I decided to make the trip from Norman to Dallas along the route the Sooners took in the old days, when the journey was a real adventure and put the travelers in the mood to howl.

THE TRAIL OF BEERS

I was standing on the northbound Interstate 35 bridge across the Red River, leaning over the rail, looking down at the water. It had been a dry summer, so there wasn't much to see. Just a few muddy rivulets meandering lazily among dry, orangish sand bars, a tangle of brush that a long-ago flood had washed against one of the bridge pylons, a few empty bottles, and a hat. A cowboy hat. Straw. A Resistol, probably. Partly in the water and partly out, lying at a jaunty angle on the slope of a sand bar. It was muddy and waterlogged. It had been in the Red River a long time.

This, I knew, was the Hat of the Unknown Okie, the University of Oklahoma football fan who drove to Dallas many years ago for Texas-OU Weekend, saw the game, got drunk, climbed into his pickup in the Cotton Bowl parking lot, and was last seen heading north on Harry Hines Boulevard at a high speed with a beer cup in one hand and a Fletcher's Corny Dog in the other.

Legend has it that the Unknown Okie haunts the Trail of Beers, the road from Norman to Dallas, the route followed during the annual October migration of red-and-white-clad Sooners, who cross the Red River in swarms and descend southward toward Fair Park screaming, "Texas sucks!" Legend has it that the Hat of the Unknown Okie is an omen. It rises to the surface of the Red River only once each year, just before the Texas-OU Weekend, and if a southward-motoring Oklahoman happens to spot it as he's crossing the bridge, he will know how to bet wisely on the football game that he's gunning toward Dallas to see. If the hat is nearer the Oklahoma bank, the Sooners will win; if it's nearer the Texas bank, the Longhorns will win. I've not personally heard this legend, but I believe it.

Nowadays, however, the traffic zips so quickly and smoothly along Interstate 35 that few OU fans are inclined to pull over to the side of the bridge, get out of the car, and look. They aren't in the mood for ghosts. Dallas and the OU campus are only three hours apart by modern air-conditioned car, and since the Oklahoma Legislature has passed about four anti-drinking- and-driving laws, many Sooners never pop a top until they cross the Red River into more lenient Texas. They arrive in the city noticeably sober. Their school-colored T-shirts and gimme caps are neither wrinkled nor sweat-stained as they check into their North Dallas hotel rooms, strike up the first choruses of "Boomer Sooner," settle into the calm-eyed life of international-city sophisticates, and chat quietly of the bit of sport that's scheduled for Saturday afternoon.

But before the Norman-to-Dallas stretch of Interstate 35 was completed in the mid-1960s, it was not thus. The Trail of Beers

was winding, two-lane U.S. 77 then. Traveling it was an adventure. It required sitting for seven or eight hours in bumper-to-
bumper carbon monoxide, suffering the cries of ammonia-
scented babies, sweltering in unair-conditioned cars under summer's last burst of solar fury, braking for the red lights and stop
signs of a dozen tiny towns, and sipping tepid 3.2 beverages to
gird the psyche for the jeers of the Texans awaiting the caravan
in the towns below the river. Texas-OU Weekend wasn't for the
faint of heart in those days. It required strength, courage, and
the kind of pluck that made Oklahoma OK.

Ah, to relive those days. . . .

It was a hot September day on the OU campus. Students
moved in pairs and groups across the steamy green lawns
toward their red brick class buildings, talking of professors and
courses and books. The school year was still new. The Sooners
— ranked No. 1 in the country by the preseason experts — had
yet to play a game. But the big sign on Owen Stadium is a permanent reminder of their heritage and mission — "National
Champions 1950 1955 1956 1974 1975" — and the first small
symptoms of football fever were appearing. A car in the
stadium parking lot had a sticker on the back window. It was
the silhouette of a longhorn with a red circle around it and a
red diagonal slash across it, like one of those international
traffic signs prohibiting this or that. In the stadium shop where
almost anything you want in red-and-white is for sale, a couple
of anti-Texas pins were on display. "Time for a Bevo burger,"
suggested one, depicting a hamburger with horns. "We're still
on top," informed the other, depicting a map of Texas and
Oklahoma. Sure enough, Oklahoma was on top.

The student clerk, Lonnie Warner, said the anti-Texas T-shirts
wouldn't be in stock for a couple of weeks yet. "Everybody
buys them like crazy," he said. "We can't keep enough in the
store. Norman dies — I mean, literally — on Texas-OU Weekend. Everybody leaves. It's like school has ended. It's a mad-
house around here on that Friday. Everybody is trying to get

down to Dallas. A lot of people just blow off their Friday classes and go Thursday."

In the nosebleed heights at the top of Owen Stadium, a vivacious senior named Be-Be Elliott was modeling Sooner garb for a photographer. "Oh, yeah, I'm going to Dallas," she said. "I'm going to get crazy on Commerce Street. Get wasted, have a good time, meet people, and just yell, 'OU is No. 1!' and 'Texas sucks!' Yes! It's too much fun!"

A gust of wind grabbed the big OU flag she was holding, almost knocking her down the steep steps. "You know why it's always windy in Oklahoma?" she asked. "Because Nebraska blows and Texas sucks. But the Texans say they don't fall into the Gulf because Oklahoma sucks, so. . . ."

Far below her, the Sooners themselves were trotting onto the practice field just outside the stadium. Some were wearing red jerseys, some white. Some jogged in place, some did a few calisthenics, loosening up. "During practice the day before they go down to Dallas," Be-Be Elliott said, "they play 'The Eyes of Texas' over the loudspeakers, and everybody comes out and watches. Even in the training rooms and the weight rooms, they play 'The Eyes of Texas' all the time, just to get them mad."

"Does it work?" I asked.

"Well, I don't guess it worked last year," she said. "We've got to get the referees listening to it, too, I guess."

Last year's game ended in a tie. I vaguely remembered some squabble about referees, but the reason for it escaped me. Texas-OU games don't stick long in my mind. "I've heard that Oklahoma is going to have an easy time of it this year," I said.

"I hope so," Be-Be Elliott said, "but I don't know. I don't think you can ever have an easy time at an OU-Texas game. Whatever their rankings are, they're out for blood."

Wilson's Country Volkswagen Store on the outskirts of Lexington is famous in South Central Oklahoma for two reasons: the fact that it sells nothing but VW parts, and the big sign on the wall facing the highway:

OKLA. 15
TEXAS 12
REFS 3

Referees again. Oklahoma seemed obsessed with them. I stopped to inquire why. Leroy Wilson, the proprietor of Wilson's Country Volkswagen Store, wasn't in. He was in Dallas, buying more Volkswagen parts. "Oh, he's a staunch Okie, all right," said Marvin Wood, an employee. "He come back from last year's game, and he was smoking. Boy! Was he smoking! He got back on Monday, and the first thing he did, he had that sign made, and by Thursday he had it up on the side of the building. He takes that OU-Texas game very, very seriously."

Wood gave me a tour of Wilson's Country Volkswagen Store. On the desk in Wilson's office was a 45 RPM record of "Boomer Sooner." Out in the display area, behind ropes to keep admirers from touching it, was a souped-up VW Beetle, painted white with red flames on the sides. The engine — which must have been taken from a Mack truck — filled the part of the car where the backseat used to be. Two chrome diesel exhaust pipes stuck through the roof. Another sign near the front of the store portrayed a little guy in an OU football helmet relieving himself on a map of Texas. Wood reached under the counter and pulled out an ancient red-and-white stadium seat. "Go Gomer" was printed on it.

"Who's Gomer?" I asked.

"He used to be the OU coach," Wood said. "That was a while ago." High on a wall above a collection of beautifully restored vintage automobiles, another huge sign urged, "BEAT TEXAS." Added to it, on a smaller, newer panel was "AND REFS."

"What does Leroy have against referees?" I asked.

"Don't tell that Texan nothing," boomed a voice from the front of the store.

It belonged to Ed Forrest, a truck driver who was waiting for Wilson's employees to unload some freight from his rig. "Are you a *real* Texan?" he asked.

I replied that I am.

"Well, Texas has so many foreigners in it now that you never know," Forrest said. "The *real* Texans have to put signs on their pickups that say, 'I'm a native Texan.' That's the only way you can tell the Texans from the foreigners now. I was born a Missourian myself, but I'm a born-again Okie."

"It's catching," said Jackie Loller, who was waiting for her VW to be fixed.

"Yeah, don't sit around here too long, or *you'll* be born again," Forrest warned me. "I been here since '46, when I got out of the paratroopers. I left Missouri and went and joined them paratroopers, and I married one of these damn Okies, and I can't get out of Oklahoma now."

"It penetrates the skin," Loller said.

"Do you ever go to the Texas-OU game?" I asked.

"Hell, yes!" Forrest said. "I go down every year! Since '46. Getting to Dallas in the old days was rougher than hell. Damn bumper-to-bumper traffic all day. Man, it could take you six, seven, eight hours to get down there. You had to go through every little town, and wait on this one, and wait on that one. The damn farmers would pull out in front of you, then you had to cuss them. Hell, I can drive it in three hours and fifteen minutes on that I-35. Of course, I-35 cut off all the little towns. They don't do near the tourist trade that they used to. The service stations and all that have had to move on out by I-35 even to survive."

"My son lives in Dallas, and he's an OU graduate," Loller said. "The first year he was down there in his office, they put him right next to a University of Texas graduate, and the Texans put up orange-and-white crepe paper and all that. And it just happened, that first year he was down there, OU won. But he just went to work the next day and didn't say a word. He was about to bust, but he just quietly said, 'Thank you, Lord.' You'll find that all the people in Oklahoma are serious about two things — OU and the Dallas Cowboys."

"I don't like the Cowboys," Forrest said. "I don't like Texas. Period."

"But you're not a native Oklahoman," Loller said.

"Hell," Forrest said, "every time OU goes down there, they play the referees, too."

"What happened last year?" I asked.

"Oh, one of our boys didn't step out of bounds, and the referee said he did," Forrest said. "Those Southwest Conference referees. . . ."

"But don't some of them come from up here?" I asked.

"Well, yeah," Forrest said. "Some of them do, but. . . ."

"What year was it the cops had to escort that old referee out of the Cotton Bowl?" Marvin Wood asked. "They had to bring the Texas Highway Patrol in there to get him out. Some people wanted to kill him."

"I don't like Dallas, I don't like Fort Worth, I don't like Houston," Forrest said. "If you've ever tried to pull an eighteen-wheeler through them, you'll know why. That's the most rudest bunch of drivers down there I've ever seen in my life."

He predicted OU will win this year, 27-23. "You have to figure in at least fourteen points for the referees," he said.

Beyond Lexington, the old Trail of Beers is lined with fields of oil well pump jacks, cotton, and corn as high as an elephant's eye. About a hundred yards to the west, traffic was whizzing by on I-35, but U.S. 77 was empty. So were the villages of Wayne and Paoli. So — at 5:30 P.M. — was the larger town of Pauls Valley, a pleasant, Norman Rockwell kind of settlement near the bank of the Washita River in what the sign at the edge of town says is the "Valley of Promise." Pauls Valley is one of those towns where cars are still parked diagonally, headed into the curb, along the broad main street, and the First National Bank's classic sidewalk clock with the stained-glass faces still tells you the correct time. But nearly all the parking spaces were empty, the stores had closed for the day, and nobody was around to care what time it was. A motel at the edge of town advertised on its sign that it's "American-Owned" — apparently a big selling point among Oklahoma motel operators these days. Many establishments advertise the nationality of their owners, some of them in neon.

In Wynnewood, the only thing happening was the stink of the Kerr-McGee oil refinery, and at Davis, the Sooner Cafe was closed. The sign in the window said it's open from 11 A.M. until 7 P.M., except on Sunday and Monday, but at 6:15 on a Wednesday it was locked.

Painted red and trimmed in white, the Sooner Cafe must have been a popular oasis on the Trail of Beers in the old days. There's even a big highway map on the front, showing the route from Oklahoma City to Dallas and Fort Worth. But it was impossible to tell for sure whether the place was just shut down for the night or forever. Its slate shingle siding was cracked and broken. The white paint along the eaves was peeling. A peek through the window revealed no light or life. But a rick of seasoned oak was stacked neatly at the side of the building and the aroma of wood smoke came from . . . where?

At the B&C Saddle Shop in Ardmore, a dusty, moth-eaten stuffed golden eagle sits on the counter, staring glassily over Bud Stewart's array of saddles, bridles, ropes, and spurs. The huge bird was sitting there when Stewart bought the shop in 1977, he said, and he doesn't know how long before that. The photographs on the wall — fading shots of rodeo feats in the 1920s and a quadruple lynching in an Ada, Oklahoma, barn around the turn of the century — have been there even longer. Stewart said he has no idea how long. "This place has been a saddle shop as long as anybody around here remembers," he said. "I guess they've been here that long."

Stewart, dressed like his cowboy customers and packing a man-sized pinch of snuff between his lower lip and gum, didn't give a hoot about Texas-OU Weekend, he said. Never has, he said. "I'm not going to lie about it," he said. "I'm not much of an OU fan. I like professional football. I watch it on TV. But I've never been to Dallas for that game. I've never even gone up to Norman to see OU up there. I kind of keep track of them. I know they're No. 1 right now. I don't know how they can be No. 1 before they've even started. I can't figure that one out. But I think it's nice that they're No. 1. But, oh, yeah, that game's a big deal around here. A lot of people go down to

Dallas for it. When that happens, the traffic really picks up around here. There's like a caravan. Just a steady stream of cars going to Dallas. Some of them drop off the interstate and come through town on 77, the main drag here, and then get back on the interstate. And sometimes a lot of people come up here from Texas to watch it on TV. They have it blacked out down there, you know."

Not far south of Ardmore, Interstate 35 is as straight as it is anywhere else, threaded through blasted-out gashes in the Arbuckle Mountains, but the old Trail of Beers treats the bored traveler to a roller-coaster ride up and down and around the timbered slopes, which wouldn't be called mountains anywhere but Oklahoma. They're hills, about the same height as the hills in the Texas Hill Country. It's a beautiful little piece of tamed wilderness, and a number of resort communities and parks line the shore of Lake Murray, a small cousin of Lake Texoma farther south.

The next town — and the last in Oklahoma, except for the moribund hamlet of Thackerville — is Marietta, once a major stop on the Trail of Beers, where I-35 is lined with service stations and franchise food spots, but the locals still eat at The Hut. The two old guys in the next booth were conducting a long, detailed seminar for their wives about gas mileage of various American-made automobiles and the virtues of pickups versus cars in terms of comfort. "I'll take a pickup every time," one of them said. "I like the way you can sit up in them and look around. Cars these days, well, you have to lie down in them, and your legs get cramped."

"Yep," the co-moderator agreed.

I asked the waitress if she ever comes down to Dallas for Texas-OU Weekend.

"No, honey, I have to work," she said. "Do you ever come up here on weekends? We have a real good seafood special on weekends. It's six-ninety-five.

"People come all the way from Fort Worth for the seafood special," she said. "Probably from Dallas, too. But I couldn't say that for sure."

For such a legendary watercourse, the Red River is easy to miss if you aren't watching for it. There's a billboard-size "Leaving Oklahoma" sign on the north bank and a small "Texas State Line" sign on the north bank, and a little farther along, a billboard-size "Welcome to Texas" sign and, of course, the sandy riverbed and its murky rivulets. But it's the Fur House that catches the eye.

The Fur House is a small structure built of native stone on the south bank. A big sign advertises it as the "First Stop in Texas." Other signs hawk cold drinks, candy, souvenirs, but a long time has passed since anybody bought or sold anything there. Its windows and doors are missing. Its ceiling sags forlornly. An equally decrepit building next door used to be a service station, back in the days when a station was two gas pumps and a small room where the attendant could get out of the sun.

But it was easy to imagine the generations of weary Oklahomans who had pulled into the Fur House in cars that had running boards for their first taste of Texas hospitality and refreshment. And it was near there that I spotted the Hat of the Unknown Okie. It was smack in the middle of the river, halfway between Texas and Oklahoma. Did this portend another tie? Or had the Unknown Okie not yet decided how many points the referees were likely to score this year?

South of the Red River, the original Trail of Beers has been reduced to pitiful vestiges of its former self. Just "Business Route" exits off I-35 with "U.S. 77" signs still hanging over them for nostalgic reasons. On the road maps, U.S. 77 no longer exists between the river and Dallas. But Don Hockley, who is forty-nine years old, remembers its glory days.

Hockley was minding his father's store, just a block off the Gainesville courthouse square. The store has been there a long time and still sells pretty much what it always has — jeans, work shirts, boots, and hats. It's a dark, inviting place, smelling of new denim and leather, and Hockley was dressed in a wardrobe of the store's merchandise.

"There used to be an old, narrow iron bridge across Red River," he said, "and people would hang dummies from it. They used to hang up dummies here in town, too. You know, like you burn in effigy. Dummies of OU. And big, insulting signs, and all kinds of banners and streamers across the highway. Everybody was waiting for them, in every town from here to the Cotton Bowl. And they would start coming, and cars would be solid on the road. Absolutely solid. But they'd keep coming. It was very seldom that any of them stopped here, because it was big stuff. *Big* stuff. No hurting or anything like that, but a lot of jeers and screams. The VFW hall was on the highway, and the VFW guys would get drunk and go out by the road and yell at the cars when they came through. I wouldn't swear that the Oklahoma people were all drinking, but I'm sure some of them were. A little bit. On the Oklahoma side of Red River, there were nearly twenty nightclubs. Well, let's don't call them nightclubs. Let's call them joints. You could die in there anytime. And this area was dry. The next wet stop was Dallas. So, yeah, probably some of them were drinking. It was awful, awful crowded. And they would come through with their red-and-white streamers flowing from their cars. They would flap in the wind, you know, and you would hear it. Every car was decorated like that. Always. The motels would fill up clear to Denton. You couldn't get a room in Dallas. Dallas was big in those days, but we're talking '50s, and it didn't have all the hotels it's got now. So a lot of them would come through here the evening before and stay in Denton. But the end of the trip was really what they used to call the Harry Hines Circle, at Northwest Highway and Harry Hines. There were a lot of motels and liquor stores and joints around there."

Hockley squinted at the ceiling, recreating that annual scene from his youth. "They don't decorate the cars anymore," he said. "And on the highway now, it's just zip, zip, zip and they're gone."

Dick Claybourne was standing behind the counter of Gene's Liquor Store No. 1, which he manages. The store had just

moved into a new shopping center at Harry Hines and Willow-
brook. In its old building, which has been torn down, it was
called Circle Liquors, but the Circle was destroyed years ago, so
the name didn't make sense anymore, so when the owner, Gene
Murphy, opened the new place, he changed the name.

"The Circle used to be the most dangerous intersection in
Dallas as far as wrecks were concerned," Claybourne said.
"They used to spray-paint an X on the street where someone
was killed in an accident, and there were a lot of X's at the Circle. I hated that damn thing. During OU Weekend, everybody
drove a convertible in those days, it seems, and there would be
eight, nine, ten people in the damn car, and they'd be throwing
bottles and stuff like that. If Oklahoma won, the liquor stores
would be full of red. Once you got north of Walnut Hill, it was
dry all the way to Oklahoma, so this was the last stop, and
they would stop by the busload. The old place had a drive-
through window, and, I tell you, it stayed hopping. They all
had to buy Coors beer. They just had 3.2 beer in Oklahoma
then, and they thought Texas beer had more alcohol — which I
think is a crock — and they would buy Coors by the case and
take it back home with them. I tell you, the Circle and this
part of Harry Hines was a lively place in those days. Twenty or
twenty-five years ago, the Tower Motel over there was a palace.
I mean, they had big-time performers and movie stars and politicians. That's where they stayed when they came to Dallas.
Right there at the Tower. Ward Bond. You know? The movie
star? Ward Bond died in one of the motels on Harry Hines.
Candy Barr made the first two-reel porn movie, *Smart Aleck*,
in one of them. And there were places along here where you
could get eight hamburgers for a dollar."

The southern terminus of the Trail of Beers, like the Trail
itself, is only a remnant of its old self now. Many of the motels
are gone, and the Tower and some of the others that are left
have slid toward seediness. Most of the restaurants where the
Okies used to celebrate their victories and mourn their defeats
have gone out of business or moved to other locations. The
Harry Hines strip is lined with go-go joints, pawn shops, nude

modeling studios, tattoo parlors, and hookers. The Oklahoma crowd is dispersed among a dozen or more new North Dallas hotels. And, like many Dallas neighborhoods, the old strip is falling piece by piece to the bulldozer and redevelopment.

"To be honest with you," said Narendra Patel, manager of the Circle Inn Motel, "OU Weekend doesn't mean anything to me anymore. It's just like a normal weekend. It has lost the mystique it used to have."

"Yeah," said Larue Stone, the motel's telephone operator. "And it's kind of a shame. Those people used to have so much fun."

[October 1985]

The architecture of downtown Dallas is coldly modern. Nearly all its buildings are tall, phallic towers of glass and steel, dedicated to the machismo of big business. There are few small structures, and fewer older ones, and even fewer historic ones. (By "historic" I mean "where something interesting happened before today.") That's why, to me, the Adolphus Hotel is the most valuable building in the city.

THE ADOLPHUS

One of the best things to do in downtown Dallas on a sunny day is sit on the grass near one of the fountains in Bell Plaza and look at the Adolphus Hotel. Bell Plaza is one of the few places downtown where skyscrapers don't block out the sun, and the Adolphus is one of the few buildings downtown that's interesting to look at for more than a few seconds.

The Adolphus doesn't look as if it were built yesterday, and it wasn't. The original hotel — the twenty-one-story, dark-brick tower that you look at when you sit in Bell Plaza — was finished in 1912. Among Dallas buildings, that's truly ancient. The Adolphus is to Dallas what the Parthenon is to Athens, say, or what the Tower is to London. It's one of the oldest things around, and a lot of stuff has happened there.

Gen. John J. Pershing reviewed a parade from one of its Commerce Street balconies. So did Gen. Douglas MacArthur. William Jennings Bryan made a speech there. Franklin D. Roosevelt dined there one day during the Texas Centennial celebration in 1936. Charles Lindbergh stayed there. So did Harry Truman. When he found that the Presidential Suite was furnished with a bottle of bourbon and a bottle of scotch, he asked that the scotch be exchanged for another bottle of bourbon. Boxers seemed to love the place. Jack Dempsey stayed there, and Max Schmeling and Primo Carnero. Carnero was so big that a special bed had to be installed for him in those pre-king-size days. Whenever Joan Crawford was coming to town, she wrote ahead with an eight- or ten-page list of her requirements, including extra towels (she always cleaned the bathroom herself as soon as she arrived), two bottles of vodka daily, a carton of breath mints a week, and twenty pillows. It was in the lobby of the Adolphus that a mob of screaming women from Highland Park and North Dallas spat on Lyndon and Lady Bird Johnson during the 1960 presidential campaign. Many political historians believe public outrage over the incident tipped Texas into the Democratic column and gave John Kennedy the presidency.

Nearly everyone who lived in Dallas during the 1920s, '30s, '40s or early '50s has an Adolphus story or two, many of them based on romantic memories of the Century Room, the hottest nightspot in town, where you could listen to the music of Rudy Vallee, Bing Crosby, Phil Harris, Sophie Tucker, Artie Shaw, Hildegarde, or Glenn Miller, laugh at Joe E. Lewis, or watch the ice show that played for a decade on the Century Room's movable ice stage.

In those days, the Adolphus was one of those hotels you see in the old movies starring William Powell and Myrna Loy, where the men wore tuxedos every night and the women were glamorous in slinky white gowns and feather boas.

It lived up to the enthusiasm it inspired when it opened for business on October 5, 1912. The next day the *Dallas Times Herald's* excited reporter wrote: "Opening to the public the finest hotel in the Southwest and one of the most handsomely appointed hostelries to be found on this Continent, the doors of the Adolphus swung open yesterday and Dallas realized in full fruition an ambition that has been cherished by her citizenship for the last two years."

The hyperbole wasn't confined to Dallas's civic boosters. The American Institute of Architects — which would know something about such things, you would think — called the new hotel "the most beautiful building west of Venice." If the Venice the institute had in mind was the one in Italy, that was pretty heady praise for the prairie town of one hundred thousand souls that Dallas was then.

But the Adolphus isn't a tribute to old-time Dallas's aesthetic taste. It's a tribute to its appetite for beer. When Adolphus Busch decided to expand his Anheuser-Busch beer empire beyond the confines of St. Louis, he chose Dallas as the site of his first out-of-town brewery. Texans developed a real affection for Budweiser and Busch developed a real affection for Dallas. He came down so often in his private railroad car and stayed so long that he began to regard Dallas as his second home.

From the beginning of its history, Dallas has known how to deal with such people. It puts the touch on them. A delegation went to Busch and asked him to underwrite a nice hotel for the city. Busch not only agreed, he agreed enthusiastically and took an intense personal interest in the hotel's design and construction. And surely it was Busch himself who added some of the best touches.

Next time you're sunning yourself in Bell Plaza, take a close look at the lush adornments on the Adolphus's Commerce Street facade. Most of them you'll recognize. The sculptured figures of Night and Morning. The terra-cotta representations of Mercury, Ceres, Terpsichore, and Apollo. The gargoyles and cherubs. The various heraldic devices. All basically Louis XIV in style, you'll notice, with touches of XV and XVI here and there. But look closely at those rounded doodads near the top of the facade. Don't they resemble the ends of beer barrels? And that beautiful turret on the southeast corner of the building. Doesn't it look a lot like a beer stein?

Now cross the street and go inside. See that huge chandelier over the escalator that moves people from the front desk up to the main lobby? That's the only thing in the Adolphus lobby today that was in it the day it opened for business. The chandelier and another just like it hung in the French Pavilion of the St. Louis World's Fair in 1904. Busch bought them and hired somebody to weld some brass eagles on them and hung them in his stables in St. Louis. When he built the Adolphus, he brought one down and installed it in the lobby. The other still hangs in his stables, where the Clydesdales live. Recognize the eagles? They're on every can and bottle of Bud.

Now go on up to the French Room. Isn't that the fanciest dining room you ever saw? The fanciest room west of Versailles, probably. King Louis would feel at home among the clouds and cherubs and the gilt and the beautiful colors there. But do you see those little flowers painted here and there among the plaster curlicues? Those are hops. That you make beer with.

Like most grand hotels, the Adolphus began a slow decline in the 1950s, when the automobile replaced the train as the way to travel, and the motel replaced the hotel as the place to stay, and the restaurants and nightclubs moved from downtown out to the highways, where the people were. Most of the hotels died. The Baker — the Adolphus's rival across Commerce Street — fell victim to the wrecking ball. The Adolphus almost did.

Then Westgroup Inc., a Los Angeles company, and the New England Mutual Life Insurance Company bought the hotel, ripped out the whole shabby interior, rebuilt it with fewer and larger rooms, furnished the public areas with lovely antiques, and restored its former splendor. They also had the good sense to hang on to Busch's whimsical touches. Today the Adolphus is a . . . well, a new old hotel containing hundreds of beautiful objects and oddities and eccentricities. The penthouse, where Adolphus used to stay, still has its own private elevator. The four elevators in the lobby are all different sizes. Nobody seems to know why. There are fifty-nine colors in the French Room carpet. And that beer-stein turret? Know what it is *inside* the Adolphus? A closet. In the bedroom of Suite 1912.

[May 1986]

In 1986, when the Prince of Wales was about to come to Dallas to present the Winston Churchill Award to H. Ross Perot, it was suggested that I arrange an extensive interview with Perot for a magazine piece. At the time, Perot was known among journalists as a man who could be called upon to deliver a quote or two in reaction to some event, but he didn't grant long interviews.

I phoned his office, told his secretary what I wanted, and got the usual secretarial response: "Mr. Perot is in a meeting right now, but I'll give him your message." And nothing would happen. So I would call again. "Mr. Perot is out of the office right now, but I'll tell him you called." I called almost every day for a month, and was getting nowhere.

Meanwhile, I kept reading everything I could find about the man and jotted down questions I would ask him in the unlikely event that I ever got the chance.

Then, about 5:30 one afternoon, my phone rang. It was Perot himself. "Could we do that interview at 10 o'clock tomorrow morning?" he asked. I said we could, silently thanking the gods of journalism that I was ready.

I met him in his office. He was in an expansive mood and we talked for about three hours.

Perot's life has taken a number of twists and turns since that day, but this piece has served as background of the subsequent stories written about him.

THE LIFE AND ADVENTURES OF
H. ROSS PEROT

Asked where he would be today if he had stayed at IBM, H. Ross Perot replied: "Somewhere in middle management, in trouble, and being asked to take early retirement."

But twenty-four years ago he quit his job as an IBM salesman, wrote a personal check made out to cash for one thousand dollars, and opened a tiny computer business called Electronic Data Systems. At the time, his company was nothing but a name in the Dallas phone book. It owned no assets — not even a computer — and employed no staff. Perot was its president and the chairman of a board that consisted of his wife, Margot, and his mother, Lulu May. Since then, however, EDS has grown into the nation's largest computer services company — an international enterprise with more than thirty thousand employees. Last June, on his fifty-fifth birthday, Perot sold the company to General Motors for $2.5 billion. Of that sum, more than $1 billion belongs to him. The sale made Perot GM's largest stockholder and the richest Texan. And he's still the chairman of EDS, for his intensely competitive spirit, inexhaustible energy and incredibly consistent good luck were among the EDS assets that General Motors wanted most.

During the past two decades, Perot also has become America's most interesting billionaire, organizing and financing quixotic missions of mercy (some successful and some not), espousing a faith in the goodness and blessedness of America that seems almost childlike in this cynical time, and almost casually giving away millions of dollars in all sorts of philanthropies, some so unusual as to border on eccentricity.

In 1969 he tried to fly to Hanoi with medical supplies, Christmas dinners, and encouragement for U.S. prisoners of war, but the North Vietnamese wouldn't let him into the country. In 1976 he anonymously gave fifty thousand dollars to financially ailing New York City to buy new horses and saddles for its mounted police. In 1979 he organized, financed, and participated in a paramilitary commando mission to rescue two EDS employees held prisoner by the government of Iran. He sneaked into the Tehran prison himself to promise the men that they would be rescued, and they were. Then he persuaded British spy novelist Ken Follett to write up the adventure. Follett's book, On Wings of Eagles, became a best-seller and soon will be a television movie in which Richard Crenna plays Perot. In 1980, at the request of Texas Gov. William Clements, a Republican, Perot led the state's war on drugs and personally provided bodyguards and safe quarters for undercover narcotics agents. In 1982 he financed his son's successful effort to become the first pilot to fly around the world in a helicopter. The helicopter, called *The Spirit of Texas*, has been enshrined in the Smithsonian Institution's National Air and Space Museum. In 1983, at the request of Gov. Mark White, a Democrat, Perot headed the Select Committee on Public Education, which drafted one of the most sweeping reform programs in Texas public school history. Two of its provisions, which require athletes to study and teachers to be competent, have made Perot's name a cuss word in some households. In 1985 he paid $1.5 million for one of the original copies of the Magna Carta, brought it home from Britain, and installed it in the National Archives, where the Declaration of Independence and the Constitution are displayed. He's one of Dallas's most open-handed philanthropists, quietly giving millions to such diverse causes as schools, hospitals, a new concert hall for the Dallas Symphony Orchestra, and a public arboretum, but he has allowed nothing but a Boy Scout building in Texarkana to be named for him. Last month he bought an extremely rare book collection — eleven hundred volumes of Shakespeare, Chaucer, Milton, and other writers, printed between 1475 and 1700 — and gave it to the University of Texas. And he's still waiting for the trustees of the Museum of the American Indian to accept his offer of $70 million and move the museum from New York to Dallas.

Next week the Prince of Wales will come to Dallas to attend a dinner in Perot's honor and present him with the Winston Churchill Award. The award is given by the Winston Churchill Foundation of the United States, established in 1959 by friends and admirers of Churchill to honor him and encourage the spirit of Anglo-American cooperation he symbolized. In the announcement of the award, foundation president John Loeb, Jr., called Perot "one of the remarkable men of his time." "In public and in private life," Laeb said, "he has demonstrated the imagination, boldness and vigor which characterized Churchill."

Sitting in a rocking chair in his office at EDS headquarters, Perot looks like an ordinary guy, not very tall, with big ears, a

1950s haircut and a busted nose. He sounds like an ordinary East Texan, and he says that's what he is. He grew up in an ordinary Texas town in an ordinary house with ordinary parents and went to an ordinary public school with ordinary students and ordinary teachers. He was lucky to grow up in such a place with such people, he says. "I've been very, very lucky all my life," he says. And as he tells of his growing up, his listener can imagine him as one of the ordinary young men in the four Norman Rockwell paintings that hang in his office.

The painting he especially likes portrays a young American Marine, home from the battlefields of World War II. He's sitting in the neighborhood garage where he used to work, visiting with the older mechanics and a young boy. He's holding a captured Japanese flag, and telling his friends how he captured it. The mechanics and the small boy are gazing at him in awe. A yellowing newspaper page describing the Marine's heroism is tacked to the garage wall.

"That picture is a constant reminder to me that throughout the country's history, ordinary Americans have gone out and done extraordinary things," Perot says.

There's another thing he says sometimes. It's an entire speech by Winston Churchill: "Never give in. Never give in. Never. Never. Never." And he predicts that after he and General Motors revolutionize the automobile business, America will be exporting cars to Japan.

In 1930, when Henry Ross Perot was born, his parents, Lulu May and Gabriel Ross Perot, lived in a small house on the edge of Texarkana. It was beyond the end of the blacktop and there was a big pasture with some horses in it, but it was only a mile and a half from downtown.

"When I saw *Places in the Heart*, it was like looking at my childhood," Perot says. "The Depression was tough on adults. But if you came from a good family, the adults sheltered the children from all the hardship. I never knew my parents were having a hard time. My father's personality was very much like Will Rogers. He was soft spoken. He had a dry wit that people loved. And he was always optimistic. He was a warm, strong, gentle man.

"And my mother. . . . Well, we lived about six blocks from the railroad tracks, and the tramps would jump off the trains and come up to our house, looking for food. They were really dirty and tough-looking, but my mother would feed them. People showed up every day and she never turned anybody away. One day a man came by and said, 'Lady, do a lot of people come through here looking for food?' And she said, 'Yes.' And he said, 'Don't you know why?' And she said, 'No.' And he said, 'You're a mark.' He showed her where the tramps had made a mark on the curb in front of our house. That was a sign to other tramps that they would be fed there. After the man left, I said, 'Mother, do you want me to wipe that off?' And she said, 'No, leave it there. Those people are just like you and me. The difference is, they're down on their luck.'"

On a shelf in Perot's office is a photograph of what used to be an annual tradition in farm communities across Texas and the South. Four men are posing with the first bale of cotton ginned in Texarkana that year. The men are the buyer of the bale, the two farmers who raised the cotton, and the broker who brought the farmers and the buyer together. The broker is Perot's father.

"Some of the brokers would try to take advantage of the farmers," Perot says. "And when the farmers figured out that they had been cheated, they would take their cotton somewhere else next time. Dad always treated the farmers fairly because he wanted them to bring their cotton to him every year. With him, business wasn't just one deal. That was an important lesson for me. I was lucky, getting to see my dad doing business down where the rubber meets the road, dealing with real people on real issues that involved the difference between going broke and making another crop. That and the practical experience I got as a child are the only business training I ever got."

His training was informal, but it started early and lasted for the rest of his years in Texarkana. Since a cotton broker was busy only during picking season — September through

November — Gabriel Ross had a lot of time to spend with his son. They rode horseback together almost every day after school. Young Ross's favorite possession was a saddle that his father gave him, and an old horseshoe — clean and polished and attached to a wooden plaque — is on the shelf beside the picture of the first cotton bale. It was from Perot's first horse. His father had it mounted on the plaque. The boy became an excellent horseman. He performed trick and fancy roping in local rodeos, and when he was seven years old he went into business as a professional wrangler, breaking horses for a dollar a head.

"Normally, you don't get on a horse until he's about eighteen months old," he says, "but I was so small I could ride them when they were only thirteen months old. I got thrown a lot. That's how I broke my nose. And I don't know how many concussions I got. We just called them being 'knocked out.' Nobody thought there was any real danger in being knocked out. We never went to the doctor anyway, because it cost five dollars. After a while, I figured out a way to break a horse without being knocked out. I would tie up one of his legs with a rag and make him stand on three legs. In five minutes he would be exhausted and trembling. Then I could untie his leg and ride him as long as I wanted to. I didn't get bucked off anymore, so I wasn't always recovering from some injury, and I could ride more horses than before. The more horses I rode, the more money I made."

The next fall, he supplemented his bronc-busting income by selling Christmas cards door-to-door, and in the spring he sold garden seeds. "The card business was great until Christmas was over," he says, "but then it was gone. And the seed business was great until everybody had his garden planted, then it was gone. They were seasonal businesses, like my dad's, and I learned that seasonal businesses aren't reliable, so I started selling *The Saturday Evening Post*. It came out every week. About four years ago, Vail was for sale. You know, the ski resort in Colorado? And somebody contacted me to see if I wanted to buy it. I said, 'No, I learned when I was eight years old not to go into a seasonal business.'"

Subscribers paid twenty-five cents a week for the *Texarkana Gazette* in the 1940s. The paperboy kept seven and a half cents of it and paid seventeen and a half cents to the company. A good route would yield the carrier about five dollars a week. When he was twelve, Perot applied for one, but jobs were still so scarce in Texarkana that grown men were competing to become paperboys and the *Gazette* had no route available. So Perot offered to start a route where the newspaper didn't have one.

"Texarkana had two slums," he says. "We didn't call them that, but that's what they were. New Town was the black slum and Avondale was the white slum. They were next to each other. I told the men at the paper that I would start a route in New Town and Avondale if they would let me keep seventeen and a half cents for each subscription and give the paper seven and a half cents. They laughed and said, 'We'll make you that deal, because you're going to fail anyhow. Most of those people can't read.' So I went out and started knocking on doors. Everybody in New Town and Avondale wanted the paper. *Everybody!* My route was so long I couldn't cover it on a bicycle, so I delivered the papers on horseback. If those people couldn't read, what were they doing with the newspaper? They were papering their walls with it. They were putting it under them in their beds. Paper is good insulation. I gave them great service. I put the paper right on the porch. And I was making twenty-five to thirty dollars a week. The newspaper thought that was too much, so they tried to change my rate to what the other carriers were getting. I appealed directly to the publisher, Mr. C.E. Palmer. 'Sir,' I said, 'I made a deal, and these guys are reneging.' Mr. Palmer started laughing. He laughed and laughed. He said, 'Well, son, I'm going to assume you're telling the truth, and we're going to honor our commitment.' Since then, whenever I've got a problem I always go to the top, to the man who can say 'yes' or 'no' and get things done."

Two others of the Norman Rockwell paintings also portray
servicemen just home from war. One shows a sailor lying in a
hammock. He's smiling, happy to be back in his good old
American backyard. The other portrays a soldier standing
before a mirror, trying on his old civilian clothes. They all
were covers on *The Saturday Evening Post* during World War
II. The fourth Rockwell is a much smaller canvas. It portrays a
father sending his just-grown son into the world. The father is
a hunched, worn, Depression-whipped man. The son, dressed
in a red necktie, a white shirt, and an ill-fitting blue suit, is
bright-eyed and eager, still unmarked by hardship. There also is
a Gilbert Stuart portrait of George Washington and, behind
Perot's desk, the most famous painting in America — *The
Spirit of '76.* It used to hang in the White House.

The office, the reception area, and the corridor outside also
contain a flag that flew over the U.S. Capitol on the day Neil
Armstrong took his giant step for mankind; a bust of John Paul
Jones; a bust of Theodore Roosevelt; bronze statues of cowboys
and horses by Harry Jackson and Frederic Remington; a huge
photograph of the late Lt. Col. Arthur "Bull" Simons, the
retired Green Beret who led the EDS rescue mission to Iran; a
wooden eagle clutching a banner that reads, "Eagles Don't
Flock"; a painting of a prisoner that was given to Perot by the
families of the POWs he tried to help; a huge photograph of
Ross, Jr., the helicopter pilot, in his flying garb; a set of
McGuffey Readers, from which generations of Americans
learned their letters and their morals; and many snapshots of
Perot's wife, Margot, and their four daughters, Nancy, Suzanne,
Carolyn, and Katherine. Beside the door to his inner office is a
wooden plaque, lettered in gilt: "Every good and excellent thing
stands moment by moment on the razor's edge of danger and
must be fought for." And on a windowsill, encased in glass, is
the canceled thousand-dollar check with which he started the
company.

"My parents always told me I could be anything I wanted to
be," he says, "because I was fortunate enough to be born in this
country."

Perot had an older boyhood friend named Josh Morriss, Jr., who went to the U.S. Naval Academy at Annapolis. Whenever he would come back to Texarkana for a visit, he would talk to Perot about the school. Perot had never seen an ocean — had never been farther from home than Fort Worth, in fact — but he decided he wanted to go to Annapolis, too. He began writing letters to Texas senators and congressmen, requesting an appointment to the academy, but his family had no political clout. When he finished high school he enrolled at Texarkana Junior College.

But, as he says, he's very, very lucky. And in 1949 W. Lee "Pappy" O'Daniel happened to be retiring from the U.S. Senate and was shutting down his office, preparing to return to Texas. And one of his aides said, "Senator, we have an unfilled appointment to the Naval Academy."

And the senator said, "Does anybody want it?"

And the aide said, "Well, we've got this kid from Texarkana who's been trying for years. . . ."

And the senator said, "Give it to him."

Perot laughs. "The aide called me years later and told me that story," he says. "Senator O'Daniel appointed me to the academy without even knowing my name."

At the end of his first year at Annapolis, Perot was rated at the top of his class in leadership ability and in English. He also ranked first in the eyes of a young woman named Margot Birmingham whom he had met on a blind date. But when he graduated in 1953 he was assigned to a destroyer that was about to begin a yearlong cruise around the world. He kept Margot's picture on his desk and wrote her lots of letters.

"When you go to sea for a year, that's like ten years of short cruises," he says. "There were three hundred of us on board. We were together in cramped quarters twenty-four hours a day, and we were at sea for six and seven weeks at a time. That's the best practical experience in management and leadership that I could have gotten anywhere in the world. And it was a heck of a trip for a kid who had never been anywhere but Fort Worth — seventeen seas and oceans, twenty-four countries."

As the junior officer on the ship, Perot was assigned the
duties that the other officers didn't want. They put him in permanent charge of shore patrol and named him Protestant chap-
lain. "The Korean War was still on and the first couple of
Sundays, I thought I was Billy Graham," he says. "I thought I
had missed my calling. The fantail was filled with people.
Then, about the time we got to Midway Island, they declared
the truce in Korea. The next Sunday, nobody came to church.
My congregation had been just a bunch of foxhole converts."

In 1956 he married Margot. She got a job teaching school in
Rhode Island, and he went to sea again, this time on an aircraft
carrier. One day he was in command of the bridge and a group
of important visitors came up to watch him run the ship. One
of them — an executive with IBM — liked the way the young
officer handled himself. He offered to hire him when he finished
his hitch in the Navy. "I didn't know a thing about IBM except
that they made typewriters," Perot says. "But it was the first
time anybody had ever offered me a job, and that made me feel
good. A year later, I got out of the Navy and came to Dallas to
sell computers. Everything that Margot and I owned was in the
trunk of our 1952 Plymouth."

He turned out to be a better salesman than IBM wanted.
"From their point of view, I was selling too much," he says.
"They told me that they couldn't promote me because I was
making more as a salesman than the next several levels of
executives above me. It was so easy to sell IBM equipment then
that I wasn't having any trouble at all exceeding my quota. I
told them, 'Look, the only thing I'm doing different from the
other salesmen is that I work all day and they don't. And if I
work all day, I'm going to exceed my quota.' I told them it was
OK with me if they promoted me and paid me less money, or
they could just pay me a smaller commission than the other
salesmen. But I had to stay busy. I couldn't stand being idle.
Well, I never dreamed they would accept my suggestion. That
was the biggest mistake of my business career. They actually
did it! They cut my commission by eighty percent! They paid

me only a fifth as much per sale as they did the other guys!
But I had the largest quota in the western region of the United
States, and I still exceeded it, and IBM *still* wouldn't keep me
busy. And that really upset me."

He had noticed that most of the businesses that bought computers from him didn't really know what to do with them, and
in 1962 he came up with what he thought was a good idea.
Instead of just selling computers, why couldn't IBM sell complete data-processing departments, including hardware, software, and staff? The IBM computer experts could run the
computers and the banking experts could get on with their
banking and the insurance experts could get on with their
insuring, and everybody would be doing what he did best.

"I took my idea to IBM," Perot says. "They were very atten-
tive. They heard me out, but then they turned me down. They
said that eighty cents of every computer dollar was in hardware
and only twenty cents was in software, and they didn't think a
twenty-cent return was worth the effort. Since then, that ratio
has reversed. Eighty cents of every computer dollar is in software now. IBM didn't know that was going to happen and I
didn't, either. The twenty cents looked good enough to me."

Several months after his idea was rejected, he was sitting in a
barbershop, waiting for a haircut, reading the *Reader's Digest*.
"There was one of those little one-liners at the bottom of a
page," he says. "It was from Henry David Thoreau: 'The mass
of men lead lives of quiet desperation.' And I said, 'There I am.
That's me.' And I decided, 'By golly, I've got to try it.'"

"It's a horrible disappointment when I tell this story at Harvard Business School," he says. "No five-year plan, no cosmic
nothing. It's nothing like they teach you up there. It's just a
series of events that led from one thing to another."

He quit his job, went home, and wrote a check for the one
thousand dollars minimum capitalization that the state government requires to start a corporation in Texas. "My plan was so
simple it was pathetic," he says. "The Navy had been sending
me letters every month, saying, 'Why don't you come on back

in?' So I figured if EDS didn't work, I could always go back
into the Navy and make a living. But a month after I quit
IBM, the Navy stopped sending me letters. I called them and
asked why. And they said, 'You're thirty-two now. We're not
interested anymore.' So there went my escape hatch."

He was in the computer business, but he owned no computer
and had no employees. He bought the unused time on a 7070
mainframe computer owned by Southwestern Life Insurance
Company and hit the road. "The 7070 was the biggest commercial computer that IBM made, and there were a hundred and
ten of them in the country," he says. "There was a cluster on the
East Coast, a cluster on the West Coast, and a cluster around
Chicago. My plan was to find somebody who was using a 7070
who was out of computer time and try to sell them some of the
time I owned on Southwestern Life's computer. I went through
seventy-eight of the hundred and ten 7070 users and never sold
a moment's time. Then I hit number seventy-nine in Cedar
Rapids, Iowa. It was Collins Radio. They bought some of my
time, and for two months they flew planeloads of tape and
planeloads of people to Dallas. But I didn't have any operators.
I had to go around to other businesses and find 7070 operators
and get them to work for me after they finished their regular
jobs. The thing that Collins Radio just raved about afterward
was the quality of my operations staff. I didn't have an operations staff! But the key guys who helped me get through that
job are still on my payroll. They've never done another day's
work for me, but they get an EDS check every month. And
when EDS stock was issued, they got some. Because if those
guys hadn't done that job for me, there wouldn't be any EDS.
But when that job was over, I paid all my bills and had a hundred thousand dollars in the bank."

He began recruiting his staff and looking for bigger jobs.
Then he encountered a problem that he hadn't anticipated. The
Dallas office of IBM organized a five-man team to try to put
him out of business. "Everywhere we showed up, they showed
up," he says. "They told one horror story after another about
what would happen if this little shirttail outfit was allowed to

do data processing. This wasn't IBM New York. It was a decision by local management in Dallas, and the guy who made it
never got anywhere with IBM. But it was the greatest thing
that could have happened to us. We were David versus Goliath.
And at Frito-Lay, IBM so overreacted that Herman Lay, who
had gotten into his business by cooking potatoes in his kitchen,
started thinking, 'These boys must have something, or IBM
wouldn't react this strongly. I think we ought to do business
with them.'"

Frito-Lay signed a contract with EDS for $5,128 worth of
data processing a month, and EDS was in business to stay. "We
beat that IBM team five times out of five," Perot says. "There
was one guy on it who was really good, so I hired him. And
IBM panicked, because they thought I was getting ready to take
them to court, but I had hired the guy just because he was
good. That was the end of the team."

At the time, the Frito-Lay sale was the biggest in the history
of the computer services industry. "Some of our individual sales
now are $1 billion, so you can see how the industry has
grown," Perot says. "I used odd numbers like $5,128 in those
days to make it look like I knew exactly what I was doing and
had figured everything down to the last penny. And I would go
in to a company and say, 'I want my team to work on your
premises so we'll be right here where the problem is.' In fact, I
didn't *have* any space of my own to put the people. I couldn't
afford it. We *had* to work on their premises. And I would say,
'We want you to pay us in advance.' And they would say,
'Why?' And I would say, 'Well, that's customary in the computer business.' In fact, if they hadn't paid me in advance, I
couldn't have paid my people. That's the blocking and tackling
that started EDS. It was a great adventure and a lot of fun.
And I wouldn't want to do it again."

The Perot home in North Dallas is large and comfortable,
but not nearly as grand as one would expect of the richest man
in Texas. Before he joined the General Motors board and had to
buy the new models, he drove a ten-year-old car. The finest

meal he remembers was a sixty-five-cent all-you-can-eat special in a mom-and-pop restaurant in Pittsburg, Texas, when he was a kid. He sometimes shops for his shirts and socks at Target and Kmart. The millions of dollars he has given to charitable and cultural causes have been given in the name of the men and women who work for EDS because, he says, "whatever wealth is around here, they created, and I want to make sure that my children never lose sight of that fact."

He really is, he says, just an ordinary, lucky man. "Money," he says, "doesn't mean anything to me. I've never wanted a lot of money. I never expected to have a lot of money. Don't get me wrong. I'd rather be rich than poor. I'd like for it to happen to everybody. But I was a lot more excited the day I got to be an Eagle Scout than the day I found out how wealthy I am. A lot of what happened to me was just an accident in timing. I could have had my idea at the wrong time and I wouldn't have pulled it off. Or I could have had the right idea at the right time and not been able to attract the right people to make it work. All I did was react to an opportunity and, luckily, the opportunity worked. Success is like Halley's Comet, you know. Every now and then it just comes around."

[February 1986]

The bubonic plague always has fascinated me, I suppose because it was history's first destroyer of entire populations, as nuclear warfare has become and AIDS someday may be. Over the centuries, many fine writers have written about it (Boccaccio, Defoe, Poe, and Camus come to mind), for death on a grand scale always is fascinating to literary — and journalistic — minds.

Although the plague remains a serious — and sometimes lethal — illness to those who contract it, modern antibiotics have diminished it severely as a threat to humankind generally. Nevertheless, when presented with the opportunity to add my own contribution to the world's writings on the subject, I couldn't resist.

DEATH IN THE DESERT

It was a whir, not a rattle. It was a hot sound, dry as the desert itself. Guy Moore and Sam Crowe stopped digging. They saw the snake then, coiling itself, tongue flicking, tail shaking faster than the eye could follow, whirring amidst the ruins of the rat's nest they had wrecked.

"I don't think we'll find a rat in there," Moore said.

"No," Crowe replied.

They backed away from the rattler and moved to another of the many mounds of twigs and cow manure and dry leaves, the thatched roofs of the burrows that rats had made beneath the little mesquite trees in this pasture southwest of Fort Stockton, Texas.

"This doesn't look good either," Crowe said. "The entrance is covered with cobwebs."

They dug into the nest with shovel and rake, scattering it, sifting its debris, searching for a live rat or a sign that one was living there. Instead, they found a rat jawbone and a few tufts of hair.

It was the way their work had gone during all the hot afternoon. In more than a dozen nests they had uncovered, they had found five live rattlesnakes, a few rat bones, a few wisps of rat hair, but not a single live rat and no evidence of rat activity.

"Three or four months ago, there were hundreds out here," Crowe said. "They were running all over the place."

"This confirms what we suspected, doesn't it?" Moore said.

Crowe, the Fort Stockton district supervisor of the U.S. Department of Agriculture's Animal Damage Control Program, is the boss of the government trappers who protect the area's livestock from predatory animals. But on this day he was helping his friend Moore search for a new enemy that has established itself in the West Texas ranch country.

Moore is the zoonosis control specialist for the El Paso regional office of the Texas Department of Health. A zoonosis is a disease that can be communicated from animals to humans. The disease for which he was searching kills rodents and is carried from rodents to humans by fleas. It can also kill humans. The deaths of many rats are an almost certain sign of its presence.

It's called the plague.

All the rats in the pasture had died.

Moore is careful in his way of talking about it. Still, the people ought to know. "All that most people know about the plague is what we studied in school about the Dark Ages and how millions of people died," he said. "But we don't want to compare this to the great plagues in medieval Europe. Most people in this country don't live with rats and fleas the way people did then. And the drug for treating the plague these days is tetracycline, a common antibiotic that's given by most physicians. So we don't want to give people a scare they don't need. We're not living in the Dark Ages. Still. . . ."

In the fourteenth century, the plague killed twenty-five million people in Europe, about a quarter of the continent's population. The survivors called it the "Black Death." In 1664-66, the Great Plague of London wiped out more than seventy thousand of the city's four hundred sixty thousand inhabitants. It was thought to be caused by the configuration of the stars and planets in the heavens, or by God, punishing people for their sins. The doors of houses that the plague hit were painted with red crosses and the words: "Lord have mercy on us." Carts moved from house to house every night to pick up the hundreds of new corpses and carry them away for burial in deep pits.

There were a number of popular preventives and remedies in those days, but none as effective as tetracycline. Some people thought sniffing vinegar or tobacco would ward off the sickness. Some thought three or four peeled onions, left on the ground for a few days, would absorb all the plague in a neighborhood. Some thought burning old shoes would cleanse the air of a plague-infested room. Or one could put a few sheep into an infected room three or four days before a full moon, leave them there for a month, then wash them with warm water and give the water to pigs to drink. If the pigs died, it was believed, the infection was gone from the house.

In 1894 a plague outbreak in China and Hong Kong killed about ten thousand people, and ships carried the disease from the Asian ports throughout the world. During the next twenty years, it killed an estimated ten million people. In 1900 it arrived in San Francisco and infected one hundred twenty-one people. They were the first known plague victims in North America. Because medical treatment of the plague hadn't improved much since the Dark Ages, one hundred thirteen of the victims — 93 percent — died.

Since then, the plague has been spreading slowly eastward. A few cases have been diagnosed in recent years in Idaho, Colorado, and Arizona. New Mexico has been home to two-thirds of all plague cases in the United States. Since 1949, when New Mexico's first case was diagnosed, one hundred eighty-one people have caught it, most of them in the northern half of the state. Twenty-eight have died.

"The most frequent cause of death has been delay in getting medical attention," said Ted Brown, an environmental specialist

for the New Mexico Department of Health. "And many of
those who died were very heavily infected. They had been bitten by a large number of plague-infested fleas and got a huge
inoculation of plague bacteria. When that happens, the body
can't handle it and the patient tends to die about two days after
the symptoms appear. But most times when the patient dies, he
has been sick for a week, maybe ten days."

The plague symptoms — fever, nausea, aching head and
joints — are also the symptoms of so many ordinary ailments
that some victims, especially in rural areas many miles from
medical facilities, don't take them seriously enough.

Bill Huey, who lives on the edge of the wilderness at
Tesuque, New Mexico, thought he had the flu when he caught
the plague in 1983. "I started out with achy joints and a fever,"
he said. "The fever just went higher and higher, so after I had
been sick for three days, I went to the hospital and they started
diagnostic procedures. Fortunately, they started treating me
with massive doses of tetracycline before they found out what I
had, or I would have died. My temperature rose to one hundred six degrees. I had heavy sweats, chills, hallucinations. I
felt terrible. I had been through a heart attack, and the plague
was worse than that. I hurt all over."

When his illness was diagnosed as the plague, Huey guessed
that he had been bitten by a flea from his dog. State health
officials wanted to know where the dog picked up the flea.

"There was a large population of rock squirrels near my
house," Huey said. "The Health Department people went out to
check their hurrows. They were all empty. The rock squirrels
had died off."

It's spread in this fashion: Infected fleas jump on an animal
— a rat, say — and bite it to drink its blood. Plague bacteria
are introduced into the rat's body. The rat gets sick and dies.
The fleas must find a new host or they will starve. They leap
onto the first warm-blooded animal that happens along. Some
animals — cattle, horses, sheep, goats, pigs, dogs — aren't
affected by the disease when the fleas bite them, but they can

carry the fleas to other animals that are. Some animals — cats, rabbits and other rodents, humans — are highly susceptible.

There are three varieties of the disease. Bubonic plague, its most famous and least deadly form, is distinguished by the swelling and discoloration of the lymph nodes in the armpits and groin. These swellings — called buboes — give the disease its name. Septicemic plague — the type that Huey had — occurs when the bacteria are introduced directly into the blood-stream without going through the lymph system. It's more dangerous than the bubonic variety because no buboes form, which makes it more difficult to diagnose.

Both bubonic and septicemic plague are transmitted only by the bites of infected fleas and can't be passed from one victim to another. But pneumonic plague can. When plague affects the lungs, it causes a kind of pneumonia and the disease can be passed from the victim to other people by sneezing and coughing. This is the rarest form of the disease, but also the most deadly. Victims of pneumonic plague rarely recover.

"The odds against a person catching the plague are terrific," Huey said. "You *aren't* going to catch it. Period. But then, some people do." The only human plague death in Texas was in Odessa in 1982. The other known victims in the state — at Wink in 1984 and Fort Stockton in 1988 — survived. But the odds against catching the plague in Texas are no longer as terrific as they used to be.

Since 1977, Moore has monitored the wildlife of thirty-six-county Public Health Region 3 — sixty-four thousand miles stretching from El Paso County in the west to Mason County in the east, and from Gaines and Dawson counties in the north to the Rio Grande — for animal diseases that can affect the health of humans. From time to time, he would find an animal that tested positive for plague, but it was always an isolated case. Then, in January 1988, a Midland County rancher called the Department of Health office in El Paso. He had found a large number of dead rats in one of his pastures. Moore investigated.

"It was a major die-off," he said. "Two species of rat — the hispid cotton rat and the white-throated wood rat — had been wiped out in the area. So had the cottontail rabbits and a prairie dog town in the middle of the die-off area. We had only one prairie dog bark at us the whole two days I worked there. I had never seen anything like it. I started going out to each county in the region and actually digging up rat nests. When you find dead ones in the nest, that's the number-one sign that it's probably the plague."

During 1988, plague-infested rodents were found in twelve counties of his region — Dawson, Borden, Martin, Howard, Ector, Midland, Glasscock, Sterling, Crane, Upton, Pecos, and Brewster — and in Mitchell County, adjacent to Region 3.

"In West Texas, most of our communities are small," Moore said, "and they're all surrounded by the country. The towns and the wilderness intermingle abruptly. So it's important to find out where the plague is and how close it is to our populations. If the plague gets into a town, we'll have to take some kind of control measures, such as dusting animal hurrows with insecticide. But we can't kill every flea in West Texas. And rat eradication isn't a control measure. If you kill off a bunch of rats, then you have a whole bunch of hungry fleas looking for something to get on. When you get right down to it, there's not a lot we can do, except warn the public that the plague is here."

Next day, Moore and Crowe drove to another pasture, about twenty miles north of Fort Stockton, to check a prairie dog town that Moore has been monitoring. It was a gorgeous, sunny morning, and nature's mood was happier. Prairie dogs were dashing hither and yon, disappearing into one hole and reappearing from another, sitting up and barking, warning each other of the strange creatures in the pickup. The rats were alive in their burrows, resting for their nocturnal feeding time. Life in their part of the desert was continuing as it had during all the long centuries before the plague was in Texas.

"This is good," Moore said. "If the plague had gotten here, the prairie dogs would be dead."

And he hopes they may be safe for a while. Although the summer is the worst plague time of the year in the cool mountains of northern New Mexico, the onset of the hot Texas summer may be making life safer here. "We have more fleas in the summer, but heat seems to retard the reproduction of the plague bacteria," Moore said. "There may be a few isolated cases, but I think the die-off is over.

"But the plague is here to stay. Things will get quiet for a while. Then, when conditions are right again, it'll be back. And it will continue to move east."

[June 1988]

This simple story was suggested to me by my friend Thom Marshall, who had known B. Rufus Jordan for many years. I felt sad, sitting in Sheriff Jordan's office, listening to him talk about long-dead sheriffs, deputies, and Texas Rangers he had known in his youth. I found myself wishing that he had retired.

Well, he did retire not long after the story was published. One of the write-in candidates beat him.

EVERY INCH A SHERIFF

B. Rufus Jordan was born October 8, 1912, in Gray County, Texas, twenty-three miles south of the courthouse. "I never left," he says. "I never went anywhere, except on business." He remembers when the grama grass was two feet tall and filled the flat earth all the way to the horizon. "When the wind blew, it was like water," he says. "It was like waves on an ocean." He remembers when sheriffs tracked fugitives across the Texas Panhandle with bloodhounds and bank robbers fled the scene in Franklin touring cars.

"Most of the people I used to know when I was young are gone," he says. "Nearly all of our old sheriffs and Texas Rangers that I worked with for years are gone. There's just a very few left. By gollies, I'm seventy-five years old. But I've been blessed with tremendous health for an old, big man. Surely I have."

He's about the size of a small buffalo. In cowboy boots, Western-cut suit, and gray, wide-brimmed hat, he still looks every inch the Texas sheriff. He sits behind his beat-up desk in his hard-used office, chewing tobacco, taking aim at a spittoon on a spread-out newspaper that protects the floor from his misses. His late wife's white poodle, Honey, sleeps on a pillow on the floor. A visitor's chair and two saddles on racks are the other furniture. Spurs and horseshoes hold down piles of papers on his desk. Photographs of grandchildren and bygone sheriffs and deputies and Rangers cover his walls.

"Rufe" Jordan, as everybody calls him — except for those who call him "Mr. Rufe" — was sworn in as sheriff of Gray County on New Year's Day, 1951. He has been sheriff ever since. According to the Texas Sheriffs Association, he has been sheriff longer than any of Texas's 253 other sheriffs. His grandfather was a U.S. marshal in the Indian Territory. His father served Gray County as a deputy and a constable for more than twenty years. Jordan grew up in and around the Gray County Courthouse. He has lived in it for half his lifetime.

When he was nineteen years and seven months old, he became the daytime jailer for a while and pursued the bank robbers with the Franklin getaway car and got shot at. He quit the jail job to work on the oil rigs. Thirteen years later, he hired on as a deputy with Sheriff G.H. "Skinner" Kyle. After working for Kyle almost four years, he quit and went back to the oilfields.

"I'd never wanted to be a law officer," he says. "I was determined to have a degree in law. But due to circumstances beyond my control — my little mother was an invalid for many years, and I had two younger brothers — I had to give up on that and go to work on the rigs. When I quit as Kyle's deputy, I had no thought to run against him. Then some men came to me and asked me if I would run. I said, 'Gentlemen, I'm not interested.' My little mother had always worried about my father being in this business, and I had always told her, 'No, ma'am, you don't have to worry about me. I'm not going into law enforcement.' But the gentlemen met with me a second time. They told me they had confidence I could improve law enforcement in this county. I went to my little mother again and explained to her what was going on. She said, 'Well, son, this isn't new to me. I knew when the time came and you were old enough, you would be in the field of law enforcement one way or the other. Whatever you elect to do, you have my blessings.'"

Jordan ran and won. Ever since, he has lived on the fourth floor of the courthouse, the way Texas sheriffs used to. He spent most of his long married life there and reared his daughter Ann — who's now a grandmother — in the apartment just down the hall from the jail.

He has no plans to move. He's running for reelection. Although he's opposed by two write-in candidates who claim he's too old and old-fashioned to be an effective law enforcement officer in these complicated times, he expects still to be sheriff when swearing-in time rolls around again.

Jordan acknowledges that many things have changed during his thirty-eight years in office. "The penal code has changed three or four times in the last seventeen or eighteen years," he says. "It keeps you kind of busy, keeping up with what's going on, knowing what to do with a fellow after you make an apprehension. You need to carry your book with you sometimes to know what's going on. I'm of the old school. I remember the men who served as sheriffs and Texas Rangers back in the days of my father, when I was just a button, and I evaluate their procedure, and it seems to me it was very good then and would even be good now. But there's been great progress. Surely there has. It's wonderful that we have the forensic sciences, the technicians, the ballistics and everything that we have to help us in the enforcement of the statute law. I'm of the old school, but I'm very strong for the operation of what we've got going at this time."

Jordan's opponents — Dan Taylor and Jim Free — say it's because Jordan is "of the old school" that they're running against him.

"In July of 1987, Sheriff Jordan was invited to join the Panhandle Regional Drug Task Force to help rid the Panhandle of drug dealers," says Taylor, a newspaper distributor and part-time police officer. "He declined to join it. We're the only county in the Panhandle that didn't join. He didn't talk to anybody about it. He didn't even talk to the county commissioners about it. He believes he runs the county, the way sheriffs did in the old days. Rufe Jordan became sheriff the year I was born.

I'm thirty-seven years old. I'm not saying that in the past he hasn't done a good job. But I believe in updated law enforcement, and I think he's still living back in the '50s."

Jim Free — a forty-three-year-old former Pampa policeman now employed as building superintendent of the First Baptist Church, where Jordan is a member — says the task force is his reason for running, too. "I've been fighting with the county commissioners and the sheriff for a good while on this," he says. "We took them a petition with more than a thousand names on it, trying to get the task force in, but we couldn't get anything done. So I decided to go ahead and run. Rufe is seventy-five years old. I think it's time he retired and we got some new ideas in. There are a lot of things that he's just not up-to-date on."

Neither candidate ran against Jordan in the 1988 Democratic Primary. Neither filed as a Republican candidate. It was after the primaries were over, they say, that it became clear that Jordan wasn't going to join the task force.

"I just don't hold with federal loans and grants and things like that kind," Jordan says, "but I never have said I wouldn't join. I just don't get in a hurry to do anything like that. I have to watch, observe, and see what it's like. I've observed some things in years gone by that it seemed like wasn't up to par and up to snuff and could have been eliminated. I just want to see how it operates. I surely do."

As for his opponents, Jordan seems barely aware of them. "I think there's two," he says. "Yes. Two old boys are running. One of them I used to know. The other one I've never seen. This write-in business is very new to me. I've never had any of it before. I don't know much about it."

During the five years since his wife lost her battle with cancer, Jordan's only companion in the courthouse apartment has been the little poodle, Honey. "Where I go, that poodle goes," Jordan says. "I take a lot of kidding about that dog, but that's the way it is." And there have been times when he thought of retiring.

"Mrs. Jordan and I married the fifth day of February, 19 and 34, and we had a tremendous life together," he says. "We surely did. We lacked fifty-six days celebrating our golden wedding anniversary. It was all set up and everything. But we had an enjoyable life. After she passed on, I talked to my daughter about retiring, and she said, 'Well, Daddy, can you sit around and mow the lawn and chew your tobacco?' And I said, 'No, ma'am, I couldn't.' And she said, 'I've wondered about that, too.' And that's all she said.

"And then I was sitting at my desk here one day, and the county clerk — Wanda Carter, whom I've known all her life — came in the door. It was the fourth day of last December. And she sat down and said, 'Sheriff, I want you to read this, raise your right hand and be sworn. I'll notarize it, and you give me a check for six hundred dollars.' I said, 'And what are we doing, Wanda?' And she said, 'We're filing for sheriff.' So that's the way I filed this time."

Jordan has a staff of sixteen deputies, jailers, and secretaries to help him now, but there still are jobs that only the sheriff can do.

On this particular day, a woman comes into his office. She's crying. She's thanking him for something he has done. He pats her shoulder, calls her 'Honey,' and escorts her into the hallway, where they talk. He accepts her thanks, comforts her, sends her away. Later, he explains:

"A very dear friend of mine and a very dear friend of hers and a very prominent member of the First Christian Church here has a boy that's in the Texas Department of Corrections. The boy's mother is a lovely lady, and her husband just died here three or four weeks ago. It was very untimely, I believe. He just died. And they was trying to get this kid back for the funeral. They're very fine people. The grandparents and all of them are fine peopie. It's just one of those things that shouldn't have happened. To anyone. But the TDC commission denied the kid coming back, and the mother was so disturbed. Along in the shank of the evening, around four o'clock, one of the members of the commission called me and said, 'Now, Rufe, if you'll come get this fellow yourself, we'll let him go up there for the memorial services.' So I went and got him. I'm very strong for anything like that if I can do it."

He clasps his hands behind his head. He switches the wad of tobacco to the other cheek and takes a shot at the spittoon. "Sometimes I wonder if it's the big things that are important," he says. "Aside from the enforcement of the statute law, I've come to realize over the years that this kind of thing is important, too."

On Monday mornings, the sheriff's outer office is crowded with people. They fill the benches and line up against the wall, waiting to talk to Jordan.

"Sometimes I wonder why," he says. "But they come in and we talk and we visit. I was raised here. I been here a long time. The elderly people, they want to talk to someone. And I listen, and I visit with them. Maybe their wants are minor, but it's major to them. They're welcome here. We have some great visitations. Surely we do. I'm concerned about all those people. Sometimes you feel like you could maybe sit down and cry, knowing that you can't but you probably should and could if you tried. But it's all in a day's run. As I repeated prior, I never intended to get into this business, but I am in it, and all has gone very well. I have no regrets."

In 1956 "Skinner" Kyle, the man Jordan ousted, tried to recapture the sheriff's office. "The first time I defeated him, he got 1,981 votes," Jordan says. "When he run again, he got 1,980 votes. I guess one of them had passed on. But Kyle was a great old boy. I helped bury him about eight years ago. There was another fellow running that year, named Johnson. I can't think of his first name."

In 1960 he had three opponents. "And in '64," he says, "some old boy run, but I can't even remember his name. That's probably one of the things that makes America great. People can run when they want to."

No one else has wanted to, until now.

"Have you ever come close to losing?" he's asked.

He smiles slightly. "No, sir. I say that as humbly as I know how to say it. I haven't."

[October 1988]

When Roy Orbison was a senior at Wink High School, I was a junior at Fort Davis High School about a hundred miles away. I'm not sure, but I would be willing to bet that I attended some of the dances where he and the Wink Westerners provided the music, for all of us in the Trans-Pecos attended all the dances everywhere in those days.

When Roy died, I was as shocked as the people in Wink were. And when I went to Wink to try to find people who remembered him, I was surprised at how many were still there.

I hope that someday a memorial to Roy and his music will be built.

REMEMBERING ROY

There was none of Elvis Presley's swivel-hipped gyration, none of Chuck Berry's duck-walking across the stage, none of the pyrotechnical frenzy of Little Richard or Jerry Lee Lewis. He just stood at the mike, his knees slightly bent, his shoulders slightly hunched, and sang. It was a country kind of posture. Hank Williams had stood at the mike that way. So had Lefty Frizzell and Hank Snow and Webb Pierce and all the other pickers and singers that the kids in Wink, Texas, had danced to when he was growing up.

There were the clothes and the hair and the glasses — all black, as if designed to hide his body, his face, his eyes. He rarely spoke to the audience, except an occasional terse "Thank you" for its applause. He barely opened his mouth at all, defying his high school music teacher's admonition: "Roy, if you don't open your mouth, how do you ever expect to be a singer?" It was as if he wanted to be invisible, and just leave his voice there on the stage for the people to cheer.

It was said to span three whole octaves. It was called "operatic." Elvis Presley said Roy Orbison was the greatest singer who ever lived. Bruce Springsteen, when he inducted Roy into the Rock 'n' Roll Hall of Fame in 1987, said nobody else could sing like Roy did. His voice seemed to come from some other world, a place of infinite sadness and loneliness, of fear and weariness and lost love, but a world in which there was beauty, too, and hope. All his best songs — "Only the Lonely," "Oh, Pretty Woman," "Crying," "Running Scared," "Falling," "In Dreams" — moved through the three octaves with the ease of light, revealing pain or ecstasy or desire that was almost too pure to bear. Bruce Springsteen said the best way to listen to Roy's voice was alone in the dark.

Such a voice wasn't the kind of thing anybody would expect to come out of tiny Wink, far from the bright lights, in the flat, barren West Texas oil patch, where the only sights for the eyes are mesquite and cactuses and the nodding pump jacks on the well heads, and the main preoccupations of the mind are and always have been oil and gas and getting work and keeping it and football. But it did.

"Yeah, I remember Roy," says Charlie Ogle, an old man now, eating his fried chicken at Wink's only remaining restaurant, the Wildcat Den Cafe. "I used to pitch him quarters over there at Day Drug." He waves his fork toward the street, but Day Drug and most of the businesses that stood along Main Street in those days are gone.

"He used to play the guitar there when he was a little-bitty twerp," Ogle says. "The roughnecks would come in after they got off work, and Roy would sit up on a stool and sing. Every day after school. And them roughnecks and us, we'd pitch quarters at him. Everybody was working in them days. There was plenty of money floating around here. Roy started out with nothing, but I understand he did all right."

Roy was born April 23, 1936, in Vernon, Texas, up near the Red River. His father, Orbie Lee Orbison, was a roughneck. His mother, Nadine, was a practical nurse. The Orbisons moved to Fort Worth and worked in a defense plant for a while during World War II. On Roy's sixth birthday, his father gave him his first guitar and taught him the chords to "You Are My Sunshine." Two years later the family moved back to Vernon and the oil fields, then, when Roy was 10 years old, they followed the boom on out to Wink, in the Permian Basin.

Vernon's representative, Charles Finnell, got House Resolution 49 passed in the legislature last January, making today, April 23, 1989, Roy Orbison Day in Texas.

WHEREAS, the City of Vernon, Texas is justifiably proud to be the birthplace of Roy Kelton Orbison . . . and all Texans are honored to claim him as a native son. . .

WHEREAS, Roy Orbison's brilliant and revitalized career was cut tragically short by his death from a heart attack on December 6, 1988 at age 52. . .

WHEREAS, his death is mourned by music lovers everywhere. . .

Wink observed its own Roy Orbison Memorial Day, proclaimed by Mayor Maxi Watts, three days after Roy died.

WHEREAS, Roy Orbison spent his childhood and school boy years as a resident of Wink, Texas. . .

WHEREAS, Roy Orbison was a 1954 graduate of Wink High School and one of its most successful favorite sons.

WHEREAS, Roy Oribison commenced and launched his musical career while still a resident of Wink. . .

WHEREAS, the residents of the City of Wink are greatly shocked and remorseful over their loss of this famous and renowned friend. . .

The town flew its three or four flags at half-staff. It had named a street after Roy just a few months before he died. "It's the street he used to live on," says Mayor Watts. "We were hoping we could get him to come to Wink for that, but he couldn't get his schedule ironed out."

The house where Roy grew up was torn down during the urban renewal in the 1960s, but everybody in Wink knows which vacant lot on Roy Orbison Drive it used to stand on. And since his death, the Chamber of Commerce has been trying to raise money to build a memorial. "It's going to cost us in the neighborhood of $30,000 to $40,000 for a bronze statue of

Roy that we could display down on the highway so people going through town could see it," says Mayor Watts. "I'd like to see it set up so a person looking at the statue could push a button and hear some of Roy's music at the same time. That would be a neat deal.

"But when Roy had his heart attack was right before Christmas, and people don't have very much money to turn loose of right before Christmas. And these are hard times in the oil patch. I've been real disappointed at the way the fundraising has gone. Right now, we have close to $600.

"Here's a guy who came out of little old Wink, and everybody in the world knows who he is. I feel like we owe him something."

Helen Voyles remembers him on the school playground not long after he arrived in Wink. "He didn't play like other kids," she says. "During recess, the rest of us would be roller-skating, playing jacks, jumping rope and stuff, but not Roy. He played his guitar. He was a quiet type. He had those thick glasses. Kids picked on him. It took a lot to push him. He wasn't scared, though. When he had had enough, he would fight. I remember one time him having a fight up in front of the school. He asked somebody to hold his glasses and said, 'Point me at him.' He couldn't see a thing."

Ron Slaughter, sitting at his kitchen table at his ranch seven miles outside Wink on the Pyote highway, remembers the same fight and laughs. "Gosh dang, if you got him mad, he was pretty high-tempered," he says. "He pulled his glasses off and handed them to somebody, and he just went to windmilling at sound. Neither of them old boys was very tough, thank goodness, and they had them a pretty good match out there in front of the school. They fought the whole lunch hour."

Roy was a small, weak boy in a town where most of the men earned their bread with their muscles and where the only heroes were football players. He was homely, too, and knew it. "He didn't have a muscle on him," Slaughter says. "My gosh, he was a scrawny thing. And he was so white. He looked anemic half the time. And he couldn't see more than a couple of inches without his glasses. But he tried to be one of the boys. He went out for football and they nearly killed him, knocking him around, so he finally gave it up. The guys kidded him unmercifully, but they liked him. That's the way we were back then. If you liked somebody, you needled him. I don't know of anybody who didn't like Roy. I thought the world of him.

"But you know, a genius is never appreciated in his own community. I think a lot about that — the hurt and the ridicule — and I think it helped make Roy. Deep down inside, I think he was always a little bitter about all that."

Slaughter, a year ahead of Roy in school, was an unusual boy himself, for Wink. He played guard on the 1952 Wink Wildcats state championship football team, and he liked to sing. "My teammates thought it was kind of sissy to be in the school choir," he says. "I was very shy about singing, because I knew I was going to take it on the chin. I was going to get a lot of kidding from my teammates. Boy, some of those guys were unmerciful. We'd be in the shower after practice and they'd say, 'Oh, Ronnie, won't you please sing something for us?'"

He became one of Roy's best buddies. "The choir teacher, Mrs. Violet Claiborn, started this quartet," he says. "Would you believe it? Roy sang second tenor in it. I sang the lead. Joe Ray Hammer sang bass and Richard West sang baritone. Mrs. Claiborn let us get away with murder. We'd tell her we had to go practice, and we'd slip off to the bathroom to smoke cigarettes.

"We'd get to singing in the bathroom. It was kind of closed in, and it had good sound effects in there. Finally we started practicing in the bathroom all the time, so we could smoke. We'd imitate the Ink Spots, the Hilltoppers, the Platters. We sang that Johnny Ray song, 'The Little White Cloud that Cried.'

"You know, Roy didn't always have that voice. He used to have to strain for the high notes, and he would flatten out. Mrs. Claiborn was always trying to get him to open his mouth, but he never did.

"Every Saturday night, we would go to the midnight preview at the Oasis Theater over in Kermit. One time the show wasn't too hot, so we slipped out to the bathroom for a cigarette. I had to be real careful about smoking because I was on the football team. While we were smoking, we got to singing. We didn't dream that anybody could hear. Shoot, when we walked out, there was about twenty-five or thirty people standing around the door. Everybody went to clapping. God, it embarrassed me, but Roy loved it."

Roy played the baritone horn in the high school band and marched at all the games. "Just about everybody who wasn't on the football team was in the band," Helen Voyles says. "We were such a small school, we needed everybody. And being in the band was the only way we got to make all the trips."

Roy's hero was Lefty Frizzell, a popular country singer in the '50s, and during his junior year he started his own band and called it the Wink Westerners.

"When Roy sang country, he sang through his nose, like Lefty," Ron Slaughter says. "Nothing like what you hear on his records. He sang hard, hard country. 'Mountain Dew' and songs like that. The little devil could always play that guitar. He could always eat that thing up.

"The first dance Roy contracted to play for, he didn't have any Western clothes to wear. I loaned him a pair of sky-blue Western pants and a black-and-gray-striped shirt, and he wore them things every dance he played until they wore out."

Helen Voyles's parents, A.C. and Genee Morton, owned one of the few pianos in Wink, and Roy and his band held most of their practice sessions at their home. "Mother and Daddy liked music, and they'd let them play all night," Mrs. Voyles says. "Billy Pat Ellis played the drums, Richard West played the piano, James Morrow played the mandolin, and Charles Evans played the bass. And of course, Roy played the guitar. Many a night, Mother or Daddy would get up about three o'clock and peek around the door, and we'd still be just jitterbugging and playing.

"I think the Wink Westerners were making about a hundred dollars a dance. That seemed like a fortune to us, but by the time they got through dividing it, it wasn't much. And then they started playing on TV over in Odessa. I don't know if they got paid for that or not. We would muster up all the money we could to buy a tank of gas and get over there to see them, because none of us had TVs. We thought we had gone to the end of the world, getting that far away from home."

At the time, Troy Parker was office manager for the Cabot Corporation, Carbon Black Division, and living in a company house about five miles from Kermit, on the way to Jal, New Mexico. At night, he was playing guitar in the Kingsmen Dance Orchestra, an eleven-member big-band-sound outfit that had started up just after World War II and was playing dances all over West Texas and Southeastern New Mexico.

"One day we were broadcasting at KERB in Kermit, and Roy was standing there watching us," Parker says. "I was making some chords that he didn't know, and later he asked me if I would show them to him. I didn't know his parents, and I had never seen him before. But then he started coming out to the house whenever he felt like it, and he would just make hlmself at home.

"One time my wife and I wanted to go see a movie downtown. It was *From Here to Eternity*, I think. About eleven o'clock that morning, here comes Roy. He had lunch with us and we told him we were planning to go to the movie. He said, 'Well, don't bother about me. Just go on to the movie.' So we did. And when we got home about five o'clock that afternoon, he was still sitting there.

"He was kind of a pest at times. He rode his bicycle all the way out there once, five miles beyond Kermit. I taught him whatever it was he wanted to know, then loaded him and his bike in my car and took him back to Kermit, but not all the way to Wink.

"He would come to our dances. I don't think he ever had a date. He would just stand around the bandstand and watch us play. Sometimes he would get in and sing with us. One time, I remember, he came to a dance we played up in Jal. I got home about four o'clock in the morning, and there was Roy, sitting on my front porch with his guitar. He had seen me make some chord or some run that he wanted to know, and he just couldn't wait to learn it. I showed it to him and he learned it in about twenty minutes and was on his way.

"That went on for two or three years. There weren't any set-up lessons. He would just show up every couple of weeks. He was a good guitarist. The last time I saw him, he drove up here in a nice, big car, and he showed me some stuff I had never heard of. He had been around some guys who really knew what they were doing."

Parker is retired from the carbon black plant now and lives in Monahans. The Kingsmen Dance Orchestra disbanded in 1978. "We got too old and lost interest in it," he says. "Only three of us are still living. I hardly ever say anything about teaching Roy, because people would say, 'Aw, he's lying.' But he was a real fine young man. Always was. I never heard anything bad about Roy. He was very determined. If he wanted something, he really worked at it. Roy's voice could reach from the basement to the sky, and just as true as a bird, always.

"Funny thing, though. When I first met Roy, his hair was kind of sandy-colored. But he showed up at my house one day, and it was jet black. I've always wondered why."

Susie Gray had dyed it for him. "He just got this idea that he wanted his hair dyed," she says, "so we bought some dye and just dyed it in our kitchen. Roy had been cotton-headed when he was small, and in high school his hair was kind of a sandy blond. I never dyed it again, but it stayed black after that. I don't know who did it for him. At first, everybody giggled and laughed at him. But he liked being black-headed, I guess, and after a while everybody got used to it. I never would've dreamed he would've kept it black all this time."

Mrs. Gray — her maiden name was Newbert — was a year behind Roy in school, and was one of a gang of fifteen or twenty kids who hung out together. "Roy never went steady with anybody," she says. "He was kind of the kid next door. He was a very decent kid. He always sang at different functions around town, even when he was in the fifth or sixth grade. Everybody liked him. We'd ride around. You got your driver's license when you were fourteen in those days, so you started riding around pretty young.

"We had a little old drive-in where you could go and honk and they'd bring you a Coke out. Wink was bigger then. At one time we had three drugstores, and now we have none. We had a couple of department stores and a hardware. Mama and Daddy had an insurance business. We had a movie theater. They're all gone.

"Saturday night, everybody went dancing. The Wink Westerners would play at the Archway and the West End Club in Monahans. You were supposed to be twenty-one to get in. I don't know how we got in when we were still in high school, but we did. I guess they didn't really care, as long as we paid. I've often wondered how come Mama and Daddy let me go. One time at the West End Club there was a knifing in the parking lot while we were there. We didn't know it was happening, but Daddy found out about it, and the next morning he let me know he wasn't exactly thrilled. I don't know why everybody wasn't thrown in jail. Even Roy wasn't old enough to go in those clubs legally, and he was furnishing the music.

"I've been asked if I knew he was destined for greatness in those days. But he was just an average kid. You really don't think of somebody in your small-town high-school band as being destined for greatness. I don't know really how to explain it. We were just here in this little oil-field town."

Roy inscribed his picture in Susie's copy of their high school yearbook to "one of the sweetest girls I know." But it was Helen Morton, whose parents owned a piano, that he took to his senior prom at the school cafeteria.

She wore a pink-and-silver strapless dress, and Roy gave her a corsage of pink carnations. She gave him a white carnation boutonniere. "He really wasn't a very good dancer," she says. "He was like most musicians. He played, he didn't dance."

In the fall, Roy left for North Texas State College (now the University of North Texas) in Denton. He was glad to leave Wink. For him, he would tell *Rolling Stone* years later, Wink was "macho guys working in the oil field, and football, and oil and grease and sand and being a stud and being cool. I got out of there as quick as I could, and I resented having to be there, but it was a great education. It was tough as could be, but no illusions, you know? No mysteries in Wink."

He came home for the holidays, though, and on New Year's Eve he and the Wink Westerners played a dance. "Ten minutes to midnight, somebody requested 'Shake, Rattle and Roll,' he would remember. "At the time, I didn't even know the song, but we started playing it, and after ten minutes, by the time the New Year rolled around, I was converted."

Lefty Frizzell had lost a disciple. Rock 'n' Roll had gained a Hall of Famer.

But things didn't work out in Denton. Roy later described his year there as lonely. He returned to the Permian Basin, enrolled in Odessa Junior College, started a new band called the Teen Kings, and started dating a girl named Claudette Frady. "When Roy went to North Texas and came back, he was a different singer," Ron Slaughter says. "I think that's when he learned to hit those high notes."

Within a year, he had given up on college and had made a record called "Ooby Dooby" for Sun Records in Memphis — a young outfit that also had signed up Elvis Presley, Carl Perkins, and Johnny Cash. It sold three hundred thousand copies and still shows up on collections of Orbison hits. He married Claudette, wrote a song about her, sold it to the Everly Brothers for $10,000, and made the down payment on a white 1967 Cadillac convertible.

"I remember him and Claudette pulling into the filling station there on Main Street," says Bill Beckham, publisher of *The Wink Bulletin* — "The Only Newspaper in the World That

Cares Anything About Wink," according to the masthead.
"Claudette was really a good-looking girl, and that car . . .
well, it was quite a sensation. But he was still the same old
Roy. He spent thirty or forty minutes there, just laughing about
the old days."

The flush times didn't last long. "His Teen Kings band, they
would make about thirty-five dollars apiece a night," says Susie
Gray. "Then they would have to get in a car and drive from
Houston to Fort Worth and rest awhile and play another date,
then drive another six hundred miles. That's a rough, hard way
to live, and the boys were getting tired. Roy had a lot more
determination than the others. Of course, he had the real talent, and he really wanted music to be his life. The others
weakened."

Things hadn't worked out well for Ron Slaughter, either. He
had won a football scholarship at Eastern New Mexico State,
but lost it when he got injured. "I was roughnecking for Roy's
daddy, trying to make some money so I could go back to college," he says. "Roy and Claudette had a child, and they just
weren't making a go of it. His daddy was helping him. I
remember Mr. Orbison saying, 'Hell, I've got to go down and
make a payment on that damn Cadillac.'

"I was living in Andrews then, and Roy came by one night
and we talked, and he said, 'Ronnie, I'm going to make it. I'm
going to Nashville. Why don't you come on and go with me?' I
said, 'Roy, I don't have any talent, and that's not my thing. I
don't want to spend my life singing to a bunch of drunks.'

"I was never sure he was going to make it. Nobody here
thought Roy had that kind of talent. But when he came out
with 'Only the Lonely,' I thought, 'Well, that old boy's got it
made.' And then he came out with 'Blue Bayou' and 'Pretty
Woman,' and I thought, 'Oh, my gosh!'"

Wink didn't see much of Roy after that. Between 1960, when
"Only the Lonely" came out, and 1964, when "Oh, Pretty
Woman" was produced, Roy had become the most popular rock
singer and songwriter in America. He bought his parents a
house near Nashville. He played a few concerts in Odessa and

Midland but he didn't drive the extra miles to Wink. His old classmates learned of his triumphs — twenty-two singles on the *Billboard* charts, eight in the Top Ten, between 1960 and 1966 — and his tragedies and troubles — the death of Claudette in a motorcycle accident in 1966, the deaths of two of their three sons in a house fire two years later — from the TV and the newspapers.

Only one person — Dennis Wolf, who used to shoot pool with Roy and now runs the Chevron station — remembers seeing Roy in Wink again. "It was after his kids got burnt in that fire," he says. "I talked to him over by the park. I was driving around, and he hollered at me. We talked about the fire. Nobody knew he was in town. I guess I was the only one that seen him."

But Bill Beckham and Troy Parker have collected his records. Helen Voyles has saved newspaper clippings about him, intending to paste them in a scrapbook someday. Ron Slaughter and Susie Gray and all his old friends were delighted that, after years in the shadows, Roy was becoming a star again, with Bob Dylan and George Harrison and the other Traveling Wilburys, and on his own with his new album, *Mystery Girl*, which was about to be released. Roy and his second wife, Barbara, held high hopes for it.

Then on December 7, 1988, Wink got the news.

"My husband, Buddy, turned on the TV first thing in the morning," Susie Gray says, "and he hollered, 'Come here! Roy's dead!' I didn't want to believe it. You know how it is when you hear something from a distance. You say, 'I didn't hear that right. That can't be right.'"

Bill Beckham has a photograph of Roy posing with a crowd of Winkites after the Oil Aid concert in Midland in 1987, the last time Roy performed in the oil patch.

"We went backstage, and a guy's standing there guarding the door," Beckham says. "I went up to him and said, 'We'd like to visit old Roy. We went to school with him.' And the guy said, 'Yeah, you and ten thousand more.' And I said, 'Well, you go back there and tell him my name and see what he says.' So he did, and here come old Roy, saying, 'Well, hello. It's good to see you.'"

Susie Gray has some color snapshots of Buddy and herself and others of the old high-school gang, drinking beer with Roy at a party after a concert in Odessa. Roy's smiling, happy to be with them again.

"I think for a while Roy wasn't thrilled with Wink," Mrs. Gray says. "You want to get away from Wink when you're young. You have to get a little older before you want to come back and look at it again. As you get older, you look back with a little more pleasure to the place you grew up.

"Some of us weren't as lucky as Roy. We never got out. And yet, there's not any place else, I guess, where I really want to be. This is a peaceful place, not a bad place to raise kids. And I can't stand trees for very long. They get in the way of the sky."

[April 1989]

Ah, if only we could go home again. . . . And, of course, we can't, not to the hallowed places that we remember, for they've changed and we've changed, and our minds don't remember them as they really were, anyway.

At Homecoming 1988, thirty years after I had graduated from Texas Western College, I went home to my old campus for the first time. Of course, the old school had changed. The student body was four times as large. Even the name had been changed, to The University of Texas at El Paso. El Paso, the city where I had begun my writing career, had changed, too. And so had I.

But the love I felt for the school and the city and the magnificent mountains and desert in which they lie was almost overwhelming and, to me, somehow reassuring. When you truly love a place, I came to realize, you don't have to worry about going home again, for a part of you has remained there all the while.

THE WAY WE WERE

There are no guys sitting on the dorm steps, swapping jokes and lies and laughing. There are no guys dropping water-filled condoms on them from the third-floor windows. There are no firecrackers exploding in the hall, no pay phone ringing in the lounge, no Four Lads crooning "Moments to Remember" on the radio.

Worrell Hall has changed. They've knocked out the wall between my room and Bob Hughes's room next door and made a small classroom out of them. The whole building is classrooms and professors' offices now. On this first day of Homecoming 1988 it's empty and quiet. Too quiet.

Bell Hall is worse. This is where I used to pick up my dates. On late Saturday nights, the big porch would be crowded with couples wrapped in kissy-face, dreading the stroke of midnight, when the dorm mother would flick on the lights, gather in her lovelies and tick-a-lock all the way around. I once participated in a timid but almost successful panty raid here.

Now Bell Hall is full of cold-eyed scientists and mathematicians, and the old dining hall next door, where we once marched and demonstrated in vain protest against the execrable food, is full of computers.

Thirty years have passed since I graduated from Texas Western College, a cozy body of four thousand students in a cluster of small buildings perched on a hill in the Chihuahuan Desert, a stone's throw from Mexico. This is the first time I've come back. There are fifteen thousand students now, and the school is called The University of Texas at El Paso.

On this first day of Homecoming, before the festivities have begun, I wander about the campus, looking for some remnant of my younger self, some sign that I once inhabited this place. Of all the buildings I knew, not one still serves the same purpose it did in my day. They seem small and secondary in the shadows of the huge palaces of learning that have been built beside them.

We've gathered to honor Robert Heasley, UTEP's outstanding ex-student of 1988. He's a local insurance executive who has done a lot for the school. He graduated before I entered Texas Western, so I didn't know him.

This is a relief — to know there's someone at this banquet whom I know that I don't know. I'm not sure about the others. I must know some of them, but I don't recognize anybody. Where's Don Maynard, star of Joe Namath's Super Bowl Jets and the only Miner in the Professional Football Hall of Fame? I would know him. Where's Sue Dickerson, the sex symbol of the Class of '58, who used to prance at the head of the Marching Miners and hurl flaming batons high into the air and catch them? I would recognize her. But Maynard and Dickerson aren't here.

Throughout the cocktail hour we mill, hundreds of us, peering through bifocals at name tags, then glancing at the faces, trying to remember. Do I know him? Should I?

The Class of '58 is one of seven classes being honored this Homecoming. Jim Peak, a big man on campus in '58 and now UTEP's director of development, has reserved a table at the banquet for us and our spouses. Peak and I and four other '58ers show up.

Neil Weinbrenner majored in business and went on to UT-Austin for a law degree. He practices in Las Cruces, New Mexico. The other three — Sonja Spencer Marchard of Los Angeles, Chuck Cragin of Golden, Colorado, and Herb Holland of Tulsa — all majored in geology, but none ever worked as a geologist. Geologists, they say, were a glut on the job market in 1958, much as they are now. Cragin is a financial consultant. Holland is an executive with an electronics firm. I don't find out what Marchard does.

I'm nearly sure I've never before laid eyes on Marchard or Weinbrenner. Cragin looks familiar, though. "Didn't we have some classes together?" I ask him.

"It's possible," he replies. He doesn't know me from Adam's off ox.

I don't recognize Holland, either. Then, out of the blue, he says, "Remember the time the cherry bombs exploded in the toilets at Hudspeth Hall?"

Yes! Hudspeth, the dorm next door to Worrell, was run by a granite-faced dorm mother called Ma Ramsey, an irresistible target for pranksters.

"Remember the guy who got mad and drilled the dorm pay phone six times with a .38?" Holland says.

Yes! Yes! Long-unused memory cells begin to warm up and glow, like tubes in an antique radio. "Remember the time we sneaked a goat upstairs and hid it in the Hudspeth tower?" I ask. "And smuggled food to it from the cafeteria? And it would go, 'Baaaaaah' in the middle of the night, and Ma Ramsey would dash about the halls, looking for it?"

Holland nods, grinning.

"And the time some old boys stole an alligator from San Jacinto Plaza and put it in the college swimming pool?"

Holland and I giggle like fiends. He begins to look familiar. Whether or not we knew each other, we lived in the same territory.

In the Alumni Lodge, some of the Golden Grads are harmonizing on "My Wild Irish Rose." On the patio, Mary Ella and Mary Etta Banks are posing for photographers.

The Banks sisters taught in the El Paso public school system for thirty-four years. For twenty-nine of those years, they both taught fourth grade at the same school. They're twins. They're dressed in identical green polyester pants suits. "We're seventy-eight going on twenty-one," they say in unison.

Golden Grads are alumni who graduated fifty years or more ago. The Banks sisters had planned to graduate together in 1938, but Mary Ella didn't finish the Texas College of Mines and Metallurgy — as the school was called before it evolved into Texas Western and UTEP — until 1939. So Mary Etta is a Golden Grad this year. Mary Ella isn't.

Fifty Golden Grads have returned for Homecoming this year — a record number. They're a lively lot. Leonard Chant of Los Angeles is wearing an orange T-shirt with a big white M on it, white knickers, orange stockings, white shoes, and an orange-and-white Miners cap. He was a cheerleader in 1935, '36 and '37, he says.

"My wife Cathy and I are retired," he says. "We travel about six months every year. We drive all over the country in our van. We try to time our trip back to L.A. so we'll hit El Paso at Homecoming time. We've made it for nine straight years now."

Chick Walker, Class of '38, was one of the football players Chant used to cheer for. "I played every position but center and guard." he says. "We got the heck beat out of us."

In 1937 Johnell Crimen was elected the school's first football queen — a title that later was changed to homecoming queen. She doesn't remember the team's record that year, but she hasn't forgotten the dances after the games. "We dressed to the nines," she says.

Mingling with the Golden Grads is C.L. "Doc" Sonnichsen, who taught nearly all of them. He was chairman of the English Department in my day, my favorite professor and my mentor. He was a favorite of almost everyone who sat in his classes. Now in his eighties, he's still writing and publishing.

Sonnichsen arrived at the school on June 3, 1931, a freshly minted Harvard Ph.D. "Four odd-looking buildings out in the rocky landscape, a mile and a half north of downtown El Paso, were grouped casually around a tall, discouraged-looking hill as if someone had tossed them there," he wrote in *UTEP: A Pictorial History of The University of Texas at El Paso.* "A power house and a small stuccoed residence were in the area (it could hardly be called a campus). That was all. No paving. No landscaping. No people. It was Sunday and the place was deserted, as quiet as a graveyard. I had a hollow feeling in the pit of my stomach as I looked around. I was a tenderfoot from the East and did not yet realize that Southwestern deserts are magnificent."

Sitting quietly at one of the tables on the patio is Fred Bailey, one of the few Golden Grads Sonnichsen didn't teach. The school's enrollment was only 135 when he graduated. He's the lone survivor of the five-member Class of 1920.

Inside, the singers are singing, "There's a Long, Long Trail A-Winding."

Yeah. I'm more than halfway to Golden Gradship.

All over El Paso, on TV, in newspapers, on billboards, on bus placards, UTEP is advertising "Serious Football." That is, football unlike the football that UTEP has played for the last few decades.

In 1956, my sophomore year, the Texas Western Miners won nine games and the Border Conference football championship. In the seventy-five-year history of Texas Mines-Texas Western-UTEP, it's the only football championship that the Miners have ever won. They don't often even come close. From 1914, when they first took up the sport, until the opening of this season, the Miners had played 648 games. They had won 266, lost 354, tied twenty-eight. Last year they won seven and lost four. It was their first winning season since 1973.

This year, on the eve of Homecoming, they're 5-1, having lost only to Brigham Young. El Paso is ecstatic. Although the season is only half done, fans are talking of giddy possibilities. The Miners could win the Western Athletic Conference championship. They could be invited to a bowl.

The Miners' Homecoming opponents are the Colorado State University Rams, who are 0-6 for the year so far. They're the doormat of the conference. A crowd of 45,187 — near capacity — has paid to see the Miners beat up on them. The fans are in a good mood. Not many football nights in their lives have they been privileged to cheer so confidently.

I've never watched a game in the Sun Bowl, a beautiful stadium fitted neatly into the side of a rocky hill. It was built since my time. Compared to the Sun Bowl, Kidd Field, where I watched Don Maynard streak down the sideline like a greyhound and Sue Dickerson hurl her flaming batons into the air, looked like a high school stadium.

The Miners rack up a quick 10-0 lead, but in the second quarter, the Rams score. The Miners lead only 10-7 at halftime.

"I don't like this," says Bill Mischen, a '58 grad who stayed in El Paso and has suffered through many a miserable football season. "I don't like it at all. They look like zombies."

The Marching Miners and the short-skirted Golddiggers drill team take the field, but there are no fire-hurling twirlers. No twirlers at all. I ask Mischen when UTEP stopped having twirlers. He doesn't remember.

The fight song that the band is playing over and over is driving me crazy. It isn't the fight song that I remember, but I know I know it. Oh, yeah. *Out in the West Texas town of El Paso, I fell in love with a Mexican girl. . .* It's Marty Robbins, a little jazzed up. With pom-pons and sousaphones. Wild. Lovely.

In the second half, the Miners wake up. They beat the Rams, 34-14, but Mischen isn't satisfied. "Good grief," he says. "What if they had been playing a good team?"

You play serious football, you get serious fans.

ᏮᏮᏮ

Homecoming is over, but there's one more building I must visit before I leave — one not on campus, but as dear to my collegiate memories as any dorm or classroom.

La Hacienda Cafe is as close to the Rio Grande as you can go without getting your feet wet. In the 1850s, when it was built, it was Simeon Hart's mill, but it was a restaurant and bar when I first saw it, and had been for many years. I recall it as a big, shady, comfortable place, perfect to spend a hot afternoon with a sweating beer bottle. All we had to do was walk down the hill from the campus, and we were there, in La Hacienda's different, lazy world, and the waiter never asked for ID.

Interstate 10 has been built between the campus and La Hacienda since then, so students can no longer walk there. Many probably don't even know about it.

The parking lot is paved now, but the old Alamo-shaped facade is reassuringly unimproved. I step through the door into the cool shade. Ah, yes. I take a seat at a table by the window. Ah, yes. The four antique rifles are still hanging above the bar. The same musty old deer heads stare down from the fireplace chimney. Someone has put sunglasses on the stuffed javelina and a cigar in his mouth, but I recognize him. The menu offers the same lunch — soup, salad, Mexican plate and dessert — for $3.15. It used to be eighty-five cents, but $3.15 is close enough.

I order a beer. The waiter is an old man. Ah, yes. I remember him. I know him. I'm sure he recognizes me, but I don't ask.

[October 1988]

Texas journalist and novelist Bryan Woolley is author of seven previous books including the novels *Some Sweet Day, November 22* and *Sam Bass.* He is a feature writer for the *Dallas Morning News.*

Molly Ivins, who writes a no-holds-barred column on Texas politics for the *Dallas Times Herald,* is a veteran journalist who has worked for the Houston Chronicle, Minneapolis Tribune, New York Times and as co-editor of The Texas Observer.